Global Public Policy

We are in a critical period where civil society organizations actively influence business political behavior, while corporations and business associations are adopting new and flexible strategies aimed at closer contact with civil society. These processes are accompanied by a strong interest of intergovernmental organizations to regulate these relations.

Against the backdrop of such broad reorientations, this book analyzes the new and changing roles business and civil society actors to offer an accurate portrayal of the formation of global public policy. The volume investigates the potential for, and emergence of, new policy arrangements along with their patterns of conflict and cooperation. Building upon theoretical inspirations from various traditions studying international affairs this book develops and applies the concepts of policy arrangements and countervailing power to the field of global business – civil society relations. The authors examine a range of key issues including labor, consumers, global finance, the mining industry, climate policy and the World Economic and Social Forums.

Global Public Policy will be of strong interest to students and researchers of international political economy, international relations and international business.

Karsten Ronit is Associate Professor at the Department of Political Science, University of Copenhagen, Denmark.

RIPE Series in Global Political Economy

Series Editors: Louise Amoore (*University of Newcastle, UK*), Randall Germain (*Carleton University, Canada*) and Rorden Wilkinson (*University of Manchester, UK*)

Formerly edited by Otto Holman (*University of Amsterdam*), Marianne Marchand (*Universidad de las Américas-Puebla*), Henk Overbeek (*Free University, Amsterdam*) and Marianne Frunklin (*University of Amsterdam*)

The RIPE series editorial board are:

Mathias Albert (*Bielefeld University, Germany*), Mark Beeson (*University of Queensland, Australia*), A. Claire Cutler (*University of Victoria, Canada*), Marianne Franklin (*University of Amsterdam, the Netherlands*), Stephen Gill (*York University, Canada*), Jeffrey Hart (*Indiana University, USA*), Eric Helleiner (*Trent University, Canada*), Otto Holman (*University of Amsterdam, the Netherlands*), Marianne H. Marchand (*Universidad de las Américas-Puebla, Mexico*), Craig N. Murphy (*Wellesley College, USA*), Robert O'Brien (*McMaster University, Canada*), Henk Overbeek (*Vrije Universiteit, the Netherlands*), Anthony Payne (*University of Sheffield, UK*) and V. Spike Peterson (*University of Arizona, USA*).

This series, published in association with the *Review of International Political Economy*, provides a forum for current debates in international political economy. The series aims to cover all the central topics in IPE and to present innovative analyses of emerging topics. The titles in the series seek to transcend a state-centered discourse and focus on three broad themes:

- the nature of the forces driving globalization forward
- resistance to globalization
- the transformation of the world order.

The series comprises two strands:

The *RIPE Series in Global Political Economy* aims to address the needs of students and teachers, and the titles will be published in hardback and paperback. Titles include

Transnational Classes and International Relations
Kees van der Pijl

Gender and Global Restructuring
Sightings, sites and resistances
Edited by Marianne H. Marchand and Anne Sisson Runyan

Global Political Economy
Contemporary theories
Edited by Ronen Plan

Ideologies of Globalization
Contending visions of a new world order
Mark Rupert

The Clash within Civilisations
Coming to terms with cultural conflicts
Dieter Senghaas

Global Unions?
Theory and strategies of organized labour in the global political economy
Edited by Jeffrey Harrod and Robert O'Brien

Routledge/RIPE Studies in Global Political Economy is a forum for innovative new research intended for a high-level specialist readership, and the titles will be available in hardback only. Titles include:

Global Public Policy

Business and the countervailing
powers of civil society

Edited by
Karsten Ronit

Routledge
Taylor & Francis Group

LONDON AND NEW YORK

First published 2007
by Routledge
2 Park Square, Milton Park, Abingdon, Oxon OX14 4RN

Simultaneously published in the USA and Canada
by Routledge
270 Madison Ave, New York, NY 10016

*Routledge is an imprint of the Taylor & Francis Group,
an informa business*

©2007 Karsten Ronit for selection and editorial matter; individual
contributors, their contributions

Typeset in Sabon by
Newgen Imaging Systems (P) Ltd, Chennai, India
Printed and bound in Great Britain by
Biddles Ltd, King's Lynn

British Library Cataloguing in Publication Data
A catalogue record for this book is available from the British Library

Library of Congress Cataloging in Publication Data
A catalog record for this book has been requested

ISBN 978–0–415–36511–6 (hbk)
ISBN 978–0–203–01650–1 (ebk)

Contents

Contributors

Michelle Beyeler is a Postdoctoral Research Fellow and Assistant Lecturer at the Institute of Political Science, University of Zurich, Switzerland. Her work addresses the effects of increasing international interdependence on domestic economic and social policies as well as on the organization and articulation of political interests. She has recently published articles in *Global Social Policy* and *Mobilization* and is co-editor of *The OECD and European Welfare States*.

Alex Diceanu holds an MA in Globalization Studies from McMaster University, Canada where he studied at the Institute on Globalization and the Human Condition. He holds a BA in Political Science from Wilfrid Laurier University. His interests include global labor standards, social movement unionism and precarious work. He recently completed a Young Professional International internship at Project Ploughshares, a Canadian peace and disarmament NGO in Waterloo, Ontario.

Aynsley Kellow is Professor of Government, School of Government, University of Tasmania, Hobart, Australia. His research interests include environmental politics and policy, policy-making at the international level, and both business and environment groups at the national and international levels. He has published: *Transforming Power: The Politics of Electricity Planning* (Cambridge University Press, 1995), *International Toxic Risk Management* (Cambridge University Press, 1999) and (with Timothy Doyle) *Environmental Politics and Policy Making in Australia* (Paul & Co Pub. Consortium, 1995). His most recent books are (with David Robertson): *Globalization and the Environment: Risk Assessment and the WTO* (Edward Elgar, 2001), and with Sonja Boehmer-Christiansen: *International Environmental Policy: Interests and the Failure of the Kyoto Process* (Edward Elgar, 2003). He has also published in a number of international journals, such as *Political Studies, International Political Science Review, Policy Studies Journal, Politics, Natural Resources Journal and Environmental Politics*.

Robert O'Brien is LIUNA-Mancinelli Professor of Global Labour Issues and the acting Director of the Institute on Globalization and the Human

Condition at McMaster University, Hamilton, Canada. He teaches international relations and global politcal economy. Recent books include *Global Political Economy: Evoultion and Dynamics* (with Marc Williams) and *Global Unions? Theory and Strategy of Organised Labour in the Global Political Economy* (with Jeffrey Harrod). Robert is also co-editor of the journal *Global Social Policy*.

Shannon K. Orr is Assistant Professor and graduate director at the Department of Political Science, Bowling Green State University, USA, researching the role of interest groups in global climate change policy. She has previously published articles and book chapters on United Nations negotiations relating to both outer-space policy and climate-change policy. Her current research is on the tension between economic and environmental interests in national parks.

Tony Porter is Professor of Political Science, McMaster University, Hamilton, Canada. He is author of *States, Markets and Regimes in Global Finance* (Macmillan, 1993), *Technology, Governance and Political Conflict in International Industries* (Routledge, 2002), *Globalization and Finance* (Polity, 2005), and co-editor, with A. Claire Cutler and Virginia Haufler of *Private Authority in International Affairs* (SUNY Press, 1999). His current research interests include the role of private-sector institutions and technical knowledge in global governance, especially with regard to the global financial and automobile industries.

Karsten Ronit is Associate Professor at the Department of Political Science, University of Copenhagen, Denmark. His field of specialization is the relationship between private organizations in business and civil society and public institutions at different territorial levels. He is author of three monographs on business interest associations and consumer policy, and co-editor (with Justin Greenwood and Jürgen R. Grote) of *Organized Interests and the European Community* (Sage, 1992) (with Ove K. Pedersen and Jerzy Hausner) of *Evolution of Interest Representation and Development of the Labor Market in Post-Socialist Countries* (Friedrich Ebert Foundation, 1995) and (with Volker Schneider) of *Private Organizations in Global Politics* (Routledge, 2000). He has also contributed to various international journals and edited books.

Preface

As is the case with most edited volumes, this book has been on a fairly long journey, a much longer voyage than originally anticipated. The project began to take shape in 2001 when I exchanged initial views with some of the contributors to the book and with others interested in the formats of global public policy and the changing relationship between public and private actors in public policy. Some of these phenomena were already scrutinized in a book entitled *Private Organizations in Global Politics* that I edited with Volker Schneider in 2000, and these I developed further in spring 2003 during my sabbatical at McMaster University, Ontario, Canada.

Thanks to international funding, it was possible for me to make further headway during a stay among the hospitable "Suore Missionarie di Gesù Eterno Sacerdote" in Rapalino, and later I managed to tie together the arguments in the docile and melancholic atmosphere of Arrifes. Each in its own way, these secluded places offered the necessary tranquility and allowed me to develop a coherent framework.

Because of many other commitments, it took too long a time, I feel, to produce my own chapters and get the final manuscripts from the contributors. Each chapter has undergone stages of revision and conscientious work has been devoted to each one, a process that has colored the approach of the book. The book is the final result of a true international endeavor, and the chapters have traveled forth and back across the oceans that separate the contributors to this volume, yet unite us in a joint effort to unravel the elements of global public policy and the part played by business and countervailing powers in public policy. Here I would like to convey my thanks to Robert O'Brien and Tony Porter who have provided useful comments on the general design of the book and the introduction and conclusions.

Finally, I would like to thank the editors of the RIPE book series at Routledge, and especially Randall Germain. And to the good-humored Heidi Bagtazo, Harriet Brinton and Grace McInnes at Routledge I also owe a great deal – first and foremost encouragement and patience, assets highly appreciated by book editors.

Karsten Ronit

Series preface

This book is being published at the confluence of two trajectories. First, it has come to fruition shortly after the death of one of the twentieth century's greatest political economists: John Kenneth Galbraith. This physical and intellectual giant of a man passed away in late April 2006, just as Karsten Ronit's manuscript was being given final approval for publication into the RIPE Series. Galbraith was an important inspiration to the contributors of this book insofar as much of his work was directly concerned with the development of a form of public policy which can address the shortcomings of contemporary capitalist market relations. And even though some of Galbraith's bolder prescriptions have not been widely taken up, his notion of countervailing power, in the form most importantly of public and civic authority, has provided a particularly apt metaphor for the way in which public policy can be understood. For while public policy is rarely determined exclusively through rational debate over its costs and benefits, however defined, neither is it often the direct product of special interests, whether tied to firm, industry, interest group or class. The utility of a "countervailing power" approach lies precisely in the awareness it harbors for contingent, historically rooted contests over the formation of public policy, as the product of a multifaceted and multivariate competition among interested and diverse groups. Understood as such, public policy demands an approach rooted in classical political economy of the kind espoused so eloquently and for so long by scholars and public intellectuals like Galbraith.

The second trajectory concerns the subject of global public policy itself, which is in its infancy. This is so for several reasons, many tied to the strict disciplinary predilections of the academic fields which have tried to make public policy their own special preserve. These include, on the one hand, the tendency of economists to ignore the power of political authority as it has tried to shape the development of public policy across national boundaries. Equally important, political scientists, by tying the actualization of power to the narrow institutional configurations of nation-states, have tended to restrict "global" public policy to the product of international, cross-border cooperation. While this is clearly a part of the picture, it obscures or misconstrues the dynamic and global dimension of policy development today. Again, albeit for different reasons, political economy with its inherently "global" orientation, is a congenial and necessary part of the analyst's toolkit.

Ronit's volume both rectifies the economist's aversion to studying power and attenuates the political scientist's myopia with the nation-state. It recognizes the nuances internal to the development of public policy across different issue areas (finance, the environment, mineral extraction, labor and consumer protection), while acknowledging the structural ties that bind such issue areas with one another. And most importantly, the contributors to this volume share the concern of the editor to explore in concrete empirical detail the contours of the various groups competing for prominence in policy development. It is here where Galbraith's ideas about the utility of countervailing power emerge most strongly, in particular to set up the competitive matrices that push and pull policy at the global level in different and sometimes conflicting directions.

The Routledge/RIPE Series in Global Political Economy seeks to publish innovative and cutting edge scholarship that pushes forward our understanding of how the world is organized, why it is developing in particular directions, and how globalizing tendencies across a range of social relations are reinforcing or undermining these changes. This volume fits in with this mandate because it addresses a core concern of the new global political economy, namely how market relations are being shaped by the competition across public, private and social powers as expressed through new policy arrangements. This volume thus takes its place alongside recent volumes in the Series that examine how governance arrangements in finance and economic regulation more broadly are evolving, as well as those which examine the social and political roots of resistance to prevailing modalities of world order. It can be read profitably among a wide cross-section of social science researchers and their students, and it adds to our growing stock of knowledge concerning the shape of world order in the early years of the twenty-first century. It deserves a place on the bookshelf of every critical political economist interested in these developments.

Louise Amoore
University of Durham, UK

Randall Germain
Carleton University, Canada

Rorden Wilkinson
University of Manchester, UK

Abbreviations

AAI	Agribusiness Accountability Initiative
	Abong Associaçao Brasileira de Organizaçoes Nao Governamentais
AI	Amnesty International
ALP	Australian Labor Party
APEC	Asia Pacific Economic Cooperation
ATTAC	The Association for the Taxation of Financial Transactions for the Aid of Citizens
BCA	Business Council of Australia
BCBS	Basel Committee on Banking Supervision
BEUC	The European Consumers' Organization
BFA	Bread for All
BHP	Broken Hill Proprietary
BIS	Bank for International Settlements
CA	Christian Aid
CADTM	Committee for the Cancellation of Third World
CAN	Climate Action Network
CBJP	Commissao Brasileira Justiça e Paz
CCC	Clean Clothes Campaign
CEI	Centre d'Etudes Industrielles
CFMEU	Construction, Forestry, Mining and Energy Union
CFP Board	Certified Financial Planner Board of Standards
CGFS	Committee on the Global Financial System
CGG	Commission on Global Governance
CI	Consumers International
COP	Conference of the Parties
COPOLCO	Committee on Consumer Policy
COSATU	Congress of South African Trade Unions
CPSS	Committee on Payment and Settlement Systems
CRA	Conzinc Rio Tinto of Australia
CSR	Corporate Social Responsibility
CU	Consumers Union
CUT	Central Única dos Trabalhadores

CWS	Cooperative Wholesale Society
ERT	European Roundtable of Industrialists
ESOSOC	United Nations Economic and Social Council
ETI	Ethical Trade Initiative
EURODAD	European Network on Debt and Development
EWCs	European Works Councils
FEMF	Foundation of the European Management Forum
FF	Fairtrade Foundation
FLA	Fair Labour Association
FLO	Fairtrade Labelling Organizations International
FOE	Friends of the Earth
FONDAD	Forum on Debt and Development
FSC	Forest Stewardship Council
FSF	Financial Stability Forum
GASAG	Global Aviation Security Action Group
GATDD	Global Alliance for Tuberculosis Drug Development
GATT	General Agreement on Tariffs and Trade
GAVI	Global Alliance for Vaccines and Immunization
GBN	Global Business Network
GEN	Global Ecolabelling Network
GFAs	Global Framework Agreements
GIPG	Global Institute for Partnership and Governance Cives Associaçao Brasileira de Empresários pela Cidadenia
GMI	Global Mining Initiative
GRAIN	Genetic Resources Action International
GRI	Global Reporting Initiative
GUFs	Global Union Federations
HAI	Health Action International
HIPC	Highly Indebted Poor Country
IAIS	International Association of Insurance Supervisors
IANGV	International Association for Natural Gas Vehicles
IAPA	International Airline Passengers Association
IASB	International Accounting Standards Board
Ibase	Instituto Brasileiro de Análises Sociais e Economicas
IBC	International Business Council
IBE	Institute of Business Ethics
IBRD	International Bank for Reconstruction and Development (World Bank)
ICA	International Cooperative Alliance
ICC	International Chamber of Commerce
ICEM	International Federation of Chemical, Energy, Mine and General Workers Unions
ICFTU	International Confederation of Free Trade Unions
ICMM	International Council on Mining and Metals
ICPEN	International Consumer Protection and Enforcement Network

IEC	International Electrotechnical Commission
IFAP	International Federation of Agricultural Producers
IGO	Intergovernmental Organization
IIED	International Institute for Environment and Development
IIF	Institute of International Finance
ILO	International Labor Organization
IMF	International Monetary Fund
IMSN	International Marketing Supervision Network
IOCU	International Organization of Consumer Unions
IOE	International Organization of Employers
IOSCO	International Organization of Securities Commissions
IPCC	The Intergovernmental Panel on Climate Change
ISO	International Organization for Standardization
ITWF	International Transport Workers Federation
IUCN	International Union for the Conservation of Nature
MAI	Multilateral Agreement on Investment
MEC	Movimiento de Mujeres Trabajadoras y Desempleadas Maria Elena Cuadra
MMSD	Mining, Minerals and Sustainable Development Project
MMV	Medicines for Malaria Venture
MSC	Marine Stewardship Council
MST	Movimento dosTrabalhadores Rurais Sem Terra
MUA	Maritime Union of Australia
NAALC	North American Agreement on Labour Cooperation
NAFTA	North American Free Trade Agreement
NCPs	National Contact Points
NLC	National Labour Committee
OCO	Organic Consumers Organization
OECD	Organization for Economic Cooperation and Development
PAN	Pesticides Action Network
PC	Public Citizen
PWBLF	Prince of Wales International Business Leaders Forum
SAI	Social Accountability International
TABD	Transatlantic Business Dialogue
TACD	Transatlantic Consumer Dialogue
TDH	Terre des Hommes
TJN	International Tax Justice Network
TNCs	Transnational corporations
UN	United Nations
UNCED	United Nations Conference on Environment and Development
UNCTC	United Nations Center on Transnational Corporations
UNDP	United Nations Development Programme
UNEP	United Nations Environment Programme
UNESCO	United Nations Educational, Scientific and Cultural Organization

UNFCCC	United Nations Framework Convention on Climate Change
UNHCHR	United Nations High Commission on Human Rights
UNICE	Union of Industries of the European Community
UNICEF	United Nations Children's Fund
UNIDO	United Nations Industrial Development Organization
UNODC	United Nations Office on Drugs and Crime
UNTNC	Commission on Transnational Corporations
USAS	United Students Against Sweatshops
WBCSD	World Business Council for Sustainable Development
WCSDG	The World Commission on the Social Dimension of Globalization
WCU	World Conservation Union
WEF	World Economic Forum
WFSGI	World Federation of Sporting Goods Industry
WHO	World Health Organization
WIPO	World Intellectual Property Organization
WMC	WMC Resources
WRAP	Worldwide Responsible Apparel Production
WRC	Worker's Rights Consortium
WSF	World Social Forum
WSSD	World Summit on Sustainable Development
WTO	World Trade Organization
WWF	World Wide Fund for Nature (formerly World Wildlife Fund)
WWW	Women Workers Worldwide

1 Introduction

Global public policy – the new policy arrangements of business and countervailing groups

Karsten Ronit

Introduction

An intrinsic feature of today's globalization is that it embodies the formation of global public policy. Although it is disputed to what extent policy actually catches up with globalized markets, public policy emerges in many economic issue areas to direct or correct the processes of globalization. Public policy is shaped not exclusively by states or through interstate cooperation, but also by a variety of private actors from business and civil society. Indeed, governance reaches beyond the realm of traditional public authority and includes various forms of private rule-making that add to our understanding of public policy-making. Thus, the direct involvement and cooperation of affected parties "offers a number of advantages over traditional public regulation that are particularly relevant for global public policy" (Reinicke 1998: 97). Many of these processes are based upon and give rise to new sets of policy arrangements, and the analysis of this diversity constitutes the subject matter of this book.

In this chapter the various traditions analyzing business political behavior and the countervailing forces seeking to influence public policy within the formal framework of intergovernmental organizations will be scrutinized. This endeavor is, however, no one-way street as many of these organizations have been reforming their institutional infrastructures during the past decade and have adopted new participatory principles to involve conflicting private actors in the formulation and implementation of policy. In addition, studies that examine the myriad of bi-, tri- and multilateral arrangements entered into by business and civil society organizations will be discussed. Although the key players here are private actors, with the major initiative lying consequently in private hands, inputs from public authority are not excluded. Intergovernmental organizations can in numerous ways encourage cooperation between business and civil society.

There is certainly a potential for grasping the evolution of global public policy in these disparate literatures, but there are also significant missing links and an astonishing lack of dialog. Indeed, there is a strong tendency *either* to focus attention exclusively on civil society organizations and their struggle for economic and social change, *or* to treat business political behavior as more or less unchallenged by countervailing groups and to side-step their changing strategies. What is needed to overcome this myopia and mutual disregard is a research agenda that brings together both perspectives in existing research and add new and necessary building blocks.

But what is also needed is a critical assessment of the character of global public policy and the centrality of private forces shaping policy. Although many paths lead to the globalization of public policy, there are also areas where public policy is internationalized and not globalized. In many public and private contexts we find a manifest ambition to create rules and norms that are valid worldwide. In some areas, and for various reasons, however, these rules and norms are not effectively enforced and monitored, whereas in other cases, rules that are adopted in specific territorial contexts tend to gain wider currency and become recognized globally. Many such imbalances and diffusion paths are evident in global policy (Levi-Faur and Jordana 2005).

These patterns are also illustrated through the complex character of both business and countervailing groups. A key ambition of some countervailing groups aims, for instance, to represent weak and under-resourced groups in the developing countries. Many global nongovernmental organizations (although usually with a Northern or Western bias) also focus specifically on economic and social issues in the developing countries – such as child labor, healthcare or education – and assist in the formulation and implementation of global standards. As far as business is concerned, it is common practice for some large corporations and global business associations to develop rules in certain countries and regions and extend these rules to the global level. In this context, civil society organizations, from human rights advocates to consumer groups, can take part in the monitoring process; if codes are violated, business can be held accountable for their mismanagement. In this way, both business and countervailing powers can include the Third-World dimension and contribute to the globalization of public policy.

The rest of the chapter is organized into four sections. In the first conceptual section we extract and combine some key elements in the various traditions that study intergovernmental organizations and business and countervailing forces in a global context. Then we outline some of the basic properties of policy arrangements as a tentative conceptual framework for analyzing public policy. Such an approach accords with traditions for studying different actor categories in domestic politics, where diverse theories are available for examining public policy. Indeed, a critical and cautious transfer of theoretical insights can assist us when studying public policy at the global level. Inspiration can be found in the traditional modes of studying public policy, business political action and countervailing groups.

Second, we discuss the role of countervailing powers and their relations with the business world at the level of policy fields and arenas. The role of labor and consumers as major countervailing forces is important because business must exchange with these two encompassing groups that form part of the immediate environment of corporations. Although we can delineate some general properties of labor and consumers in a global setting, we also need a sectoral take to examine business and countervailing powers across different policy fields. Therefore, it is worthwhile to discuss the potential for new policy arrangements in relation to specific industries and policy fields and identify which factors lead to or impede the creation of such arrangements. Furthermore, steps leading to global public policy are taken in many institutional contexts. However, conferences and summits involving, in one way or another, a host of private organizations can function as a relevant launch pad. Indeed, these forums can be interpreted both as a manifestation of global policy-making and as a potential platform for formulating new cooperative approaches to problem-solving and for designing new arrangements.

Third, we seek to advance our ability to analyze the role of business and countervailing powers in global public policy by distinguishing between those that are driven by public authorities (public driven policy arrangements) and those that are crafted by business and countervailing groups (private driven policy arrangements). The public arrangements harbor various conflicts between those private actors that are invited to participate, although serious attempts are made to accommodate different private interests, but it is also crucial to understand the cleavages of private arrangement. They do not simply constitute a unified pole of a public–private dualism but they also contain an independent and relative autonomous relationship between business and countervailing organizations.

Of course, this general approach to understanding global public policy is not necessarily valid when studying all groups, sectors and arenas empirically. Policy-making in economic issue areas at the global level may take many and unforeseen directions that are difficult to account for in such a general sketch. However, if offers a promising framework for analyzing global public policy, and it is an alternative to market-centric views that argue that a free and unhindered global market economy is unfolding, as well as to state-centric approaches that focus either on states themselves or on their interaction within the context of intergovernmental organizations.

Our fourth section will summarize the key contributions of the individual chapters that follow in the book. These contributions are grouped according to a variety of levels and scenes of exchanges, because policy is produced in different institutional contexts. Some issues relate to broad categories of civil society such as labor and consumers; others are settled at the level of sectors that are relevant to specific industries as well as specific civil society organizations. Furthermore, policy emerges in various public and private conferences of which some major ones are analyzed. Together, the contributions offer a broad account of the emergence of public policy.

Established traditions and missing links

A wide array of public and private rules underpin public policy (Braithwaite and Drahos 2000: 27–33). No single, coherent and mature tradition is engaged in the study of business and countervailing powers and their relation to global public policy and, consequently, a relatively large terrain must be scanned to find those elements that can form part of an emerging, yet relatively fragmented, research agenda. In what follows, inspiration is sought in researching the behavior of intergovernmental organizations, business political action and the patterns of participation and protest of civil society organizations. Here we find both established traditions and missing links, so the task is, consequently, to identify those building blocks that can form part of a coherent research plan.

Intergovernmental organizations – shaping complex environments

Intergovernmental organizations have taken an increasing interest in shaping their organized environments. Far from being the mere sum of their parts, they have embarked on new and flexible strategies that examine the participation of nongovernmental organizations in their decision-making structures, as well as in specific programs, projects and partnerships with a view to enhance the legitimacy and effectiveness of their work. The granting of consultative status to nongovernmental organizations is certainly not a new thing, but in many organizations where this strategy has already been practiced for decades, principles have been reformulated and organizations traditionally more reluctant to the participation of external groups are beginning to recognize their potential.

Current reform strategies of many intergovernmental agencies are encompassing and have many goals – bringing business and countervailing groups together under one umbrella or stimulating cooperation between them beyond the formal framework of these organizations are some out of many issues. It is no surprise that research has reflected upon this development across many intergovernmental organizations and policy fields (Willetts 1996), but in the context of business and countervailing forces it is relevant to scrutinize the efforts being made on shaping new policy arrangements – including these two sets of actors in particular, and how this development can be accounted for.

Only a small number of studies on intergovernmental agencies, however, provide an overview of this general debate or focus attention on the participatory aspects of nongovernmental organizations in specific agencies, including the issuing of guidelines to regulate this relationship (Skjelsbaek 1971; Willetts 1996, 2000; Charnowitz 1997, 2000; Martens 1999; Domask 2003). Furthermore, only a tiny fraction of these accounts deal with attempts to achieve a more balanced representation of business and countervailing groups (e.g. Deslauriers and Kotschwar 2003).

Although the formal and general participation of business is rarely an independent object of study, it is a widespread assumption that the leverage of business – with or without formal representation – is quite significant in many intergovernmental organizations. Civil society organizations have, for their part, historically experienced difficulties in getting access to important policy-making centers. Proceeding from this view, most research orientated toward the examination of the current reform processes discuss the new role attributed to civil society organizations alone, although a key ambition of these institutional reforms – and an ingredient driving global public policy – is to bring together, and mitigate conflicts between, interest groups.

To analyze these reform processes in which a primary objective is to reach a broad and unbiased participation from different groups, an effort is needed to simultaneously study the involvement of business and civil society. Today many civil society groups are struggling to get representation and equal access to meetings, documents, and information; however, it should not be forgotten that business has not always had a carefree relationship with intergovernmental organizations, and vice versa. Some institutional reforms aim to improve this relationship as well, and recent endeavors, for instance the effort within the World Health Organization (WHO) to include the already accredited drug industry more effectively into its policy-making structures, should be read in this light. Organizations involved in various aspects of environmental protection, development issues or trade problems display an ambition to reduce traditional antagonisms by bringing business and civil society organizations closer together under the auspices of inter-governmental agencies, or to foster cooperation on a purely private basis or with some degree of supervision. However, a marked difference is evident across these organizations.

First and foremost, organizations that in the past had a poor or nonexistent record of dialog with nongovernmental organizations, and in particular those representing civil society, have recently received much scholarly attention. Thus, the moves by intergovernmental organizations that manifest a neoliberal orientation and are engaged in macroeconomic or trade issues or in different branches of finance, such as the World Trade Organization (WTO), the World Bank (IBRD) or the International Monetary Fund (IMF), are used as vivid illustrations of elite organizations having a tradition of non-transparent policy-making and a rather weak democratic basis (Fox and Brown 1998; O'Brien *et al.* 2000).

The organizations, however, have not just stubbornly rejected reforms. They have introduced new mechanisms of exchanges without inviting non-governmental organizations into anything resembling core decision-making bodies. At the same time, it is characteristic of some of these organizations that they are strongly averse to letting nongovernmental organizations into policy fields considered a domain for states, and, consequently, do not welcome business participation either. Given the otherwise business-friendly orientation of these organizations, a need to counterbalance this agenda through stronger civic engagement has often been more urgent.

Second, established organizations, or new organizational initiatives and programs keenly experimenting with participation, have been scrutinized. Prime examples come from the UN agencies where the Global Compact has pioneered new forms of engagement. The Compact is an important showcase where civil society organizations are included in concrete projects with business without necessarily being formally accredited by UN organizations. It builds upon inspiration found in the Commission on Global Governance and in some of the special agencies in the family of UN organizations. Key principles promote socially responsible corporate behavior and guide partnerships between business and various stakeholders in civil society. Institution-building and cooperation between interested parties, however, are not between equal partners – power relations are still there (see Barnett and Duvall 2005).

The Global Compact, the Global Reporting Initiative and various follow-up initiatives have relaxed the criteria for participating in certain areas of policy-making and thus encouraged flexibility in problem-solving. This flexibility has consequences for both business and civil society actors. A door is now opened for single corporations to become involved at the lower levels of public policy (Parker 2003). Also, smaller groups of firms find common ground in economic, social and environmental areas without necessarily inviting those larger and more representative organizations that are formally accredited to intergovernmental agencies. The same applies to civil society, where groups with specific agendas or not otherwise routinely involved in the work of these organizations are also welcomed in the context of projects and partnerships. Consequently, the Global Compact program solves a range of collective action problems both in business and among countervailing forces.

Business – opening new avenues of engagement

Although the role of business is reviewed in parts of the literature on intergovernmental organizations and institutional reforms, the basic issue in this context concerns what these public institutions do vis-à-vis business and civil society organizations, rather than the other way round. However, business is also studied as an independent variable and as a particular actor category involved in policy arrangements behind the formation of global public policy.

Prevailing approaches to business power entail some myths, and have deferred research into this highly relevant actor category. Thus, if business structural power dominates the economic and political discourse to which public authority is allegedly tied, intergovernmental organizations are largely bound to follow a business agenda, and, consequently, little or no direct intervention from business is required. An alternative line of argument holds that public authority must be actively leveraged by economic interests, but in this capture-orientated perspective, business does not necessarily act through representative and recognized associations. Instead, large and single transnational corporations become politically influential. Discourse and capture-based thinking present quite different and contradictory arguments, but each, in their way, discourage a dispassionate and empirically based analysis of business actors that exchange with and are recognized by intergovernmental organizations or those civic groups affected by business power.

Turning toward research on business involvement in the formal structures of intergovernmental agencies, we find that very few studies accumulate experiences with the general role of business actors across different industries.[1] In principle, various analytical strategies are available to make a comparative study of business in a global context (see Levi-Faur 2004), but business forms parts of the overall community of nongovernmental organizations, and we must consult this wider body of literature.

We find extensive related research when we focus on particular corporations and industries and their relations with public authority (Hollingsworth *et al.* 1994; Boddewyn and Brewer 1995; Piciotto and Mayne 1999; Grose 2005; Streeck *et al.* 2006). Representative business associations, for instance, are an integral part of policy-making in many industries, and participation in public policy is rarely disputed. Given that business is a globalized interest category with an advanced capacity to organize collective interests, it is somewhat ironic that business–government research is primarily occupied with the role of business in domestic and comparative contexts rather than with business in global politics (Ronit 2006).

Again, the role of business in sectors or industries is not reducible to business interest associations or other outfits that organize interests within a collective framework and that exchange with and become formally recognized by intergovernmental organizations. An established and significant tradition in international political economy analyzes the part played by transnational corporations in both the global marketplace and politics, but tends to sidestep the associational level (Strange and Stopford 1991). Studies anchored at the company level, however, are not particularly relevant in our context because the official policy of intergovernmental organizations is to avoid any accreditation of actors – big and small – that do not properly represent an industry or a segment of business and that therefore are only exceptionally integrated into global policy arrangements.

The study of business political behavior has also moved well beyond the analysis of public policy through intergovernmental organizations and added new dimensions of policy-making (Boddewyn and Brewer 1995). Invigorated by a wave of new business practices, different literatures scrutinize corporate behavior under diverse labels and from perspectives that recognize the strategic importance of stakeholders. The majority of these stakeholders are advanced in various strands of business administration and management studies, whose traditional stronghold lies in the examination of organizational behavior in relation to economic operations rather than in the analysis of politics proper. Without adopting the necessary precaution, corporate behavior that vaguely takes political issues into account is prematurely characterized as political. In cases, however, where corporate action is closely related to the perceptible influence of public agencies, to the bold actions of civil society, and to the monitoring of media or various watchdog institutions, and where corporate activity is directed toward the solution of societal problems, corporate behavior can without hesitation be viewed in a public policy context.

As a result, corporations not only cater to their owners but must also respond to demands and expectations raised by countervailing groups. At present, statements are issued, company codes are voluntarily adopted, partnerships are negotiated and enforcement mechanisms are installed. Although these rule-systems have wide applications, they seem to flourish particularly in the social and environmental domain where they have a public dimension (Glasbergen 1998; Drache 2001; Jenkins et al. 2002).

Nevertheless, the problem remains as to whether a single-firm action or a group of enlightened corporations pioneer problem-solving, serve as an example for other firms, and bring about changes involving a whole sector of business, or whether such initiatives are merely launched preemptively with the goals of avoiding traditional public regulation and of reaching the cutting edge in the eternal battle against other firms. In the latter case, this move may eventually raise standards and have some real consequences for public policy, but usually this outcome is less evident and not always intended. In other words, a crucial issue is whether private rules can become an element of public policy.

These arrangements are categorized as private regimes, self-regulation, private authority, private governance among others, in which norms and rules are adopted and implemented by business – with or without the formal consent of intergovernmental organizations or countervailing forces, but rarely unaffected by these same actors (Cutler et al. 1999; Ronit and Schneider 2000; Josselin and Wallace 2001; Hall and Biersteker 2002; Haufler 2002; Schirm 2004).

In some cases these self-regulatory arrangements operate under the umbrella of public authority as "regulated self-regulation" (Streeck and Schmitter 1985); in some cases outside participation is included because corporations or industries invite these groups into mutually beneficial cooperation. When the role of other actors is duly considered, research is concentrated mainly on the efforts of industries and the linkages with public authority rather than the inclusion of countervailing powers (Boddewyn 1988). At global levels, however, the link-up with civil society actors can in many ways strengthen arrangements (Reinicke 1998: 92). This is a strategy filled with dilemmas inside the business world: Do corporations surrender autonomy to civil society organizations? Is such a strategy to be used only preemptively to forestall public intervention? And can civil society organizations be trusted?

In a number of other cases, schemes are developed by civic groups and do not simply emerge from business. Such cases include, for instance, the garments industry (Ascoly and Zeldenrust 2002), rating and accounting (Noelke 2004) and branches of apparel and forests industries (Bartley 2003). This opportunity creates an important incentive for firms and industries to join such initiatives – assuming they do not launch their own and independent projects (Prakash 2000).

These business strategies, however, must be critically evaluated from a public policy angle. There is little doubt that business has demonstrated a resilient and innovative capability and has in recent years designed many new mechanisms, but there is also much unreliable commentary in the business world itself and in the various literatures on corporate governance, corporate social responsibility, business ethics and other areas. Critical voices occasionally point to a lack of trust in such arrangements (e.g. Arts 2002; Jordana and Levi-Faur 2004: 14), and question whether the balancing of interests is too fragile and will in the long run decouple civil society from private regulation (Haufler 2002: 120).

In research, the profoundness and extent of these endeavors are occasionally overestimated in a rigorous effort to identify novel forms of policy arrangements and compensate for a previous lack of scrutiny, but it is highly questionable whether all these qualify as public policy. Indeed, some can exhibit the same quality as ordinary public policy, whereas other examples have limited validity and demonstrate mainly an enlightened behavior of business without aspiring in any way to become an appropriate alternative to public policy.

Countervailing powers – seeing prospects for exchange

A third strand of research to be exploited in an attempt to understand the changing features of global public policy and policy arrangements is that dealing with civil society organizations. Although in essence, the movement literature is often more comparative than global, the impact of globalization on national social movements, and the transnational patterns of activity, are discussed (della Porta *et al.* 1999).

Civil society organizations form a subgroup of the whole population of nongovernmental organizations with a virtual boom in research. Civil society and its numerous organizational manifestations are not easily circumscribed (O'Brien *et al.* 2000; Ronit and Schneider 2000: Khagram *et al.* 2002). Indeed, this is accompanied by a high degree of fragmentation, and clear and convincing criteria for distinguishing between social movements and more formal organizations are often hard to establish. Civil society organizations are today also studied by different approaches and under different labels by which their potential role in public policy is not always analyzed (Smith *et al*. 1997; Keck and Sikkink 1998; Fiorini 2000; Guidry *et al*. 2000; Colás 2002; Eschle and Maiguascha 2005). The diversity of the organizational landscape should not, however, overshadow organizations' commonality, but we have to search carefully to appreciate their potential as countervailing powers targeting business and shaping public policy.

Indeed, many studies on civil society organizations entail an intra-organizational emphasis. Problems associated with recruiting members to keep the often rather fragile organizations running are highlighted. Consequently, resource mobilization, identity building and survival rank high on their agenda. Indeed, countervailing power is often exercised through a multitude of initiatives and is captured as activism and resistance (Baker and Chandler 2005). It is furthermore characterized by networks and alliances where different groups are involved in common projects and, together, engage in a wide array of activities from traditional protests through mass demonstrations to modern internet-based campaigns designed as a new form of citizen activism (McCaughey and Ayers 2003). Building up advocacy with professional organizations, however, is never a straightforward process, because many professionals tend to side with business (see Dezalay and Sugarman 1995) and rarely have an independent status.

It should be remembered that the intention behind various campaign activities – at least in some civil society organizations – is not necessarily to engage in a kind of formal relationship with other public or private actors but rather to use their leverage in the context of agenda-setting and decision-making processes from the outside. The reason is because access is officially denied by intergovernmental agencies and because participation is rejected by various bodies in the business world where these have authority, or because civil society organizations see a risk of being compromised once they enter such arrangements and share responsibility for public policy.

Under these circumstances, however, the formation of alliances is highly relevant. Countervailing groups form part of larger alliances with professional organizations and assist in the formation of epistemic communities (Haas 1992), or find ways to cooperate with advisers or the media (Carpenter 2001). Some are based entirely on mass actions or run by a group of committed experts without any proper constituency, or entail a combination of both. Some are adopting a very pragmatic strategy, whereas others have a more radical bent. This diversity gives rise to new outfits, such as Transparency International investigating private and public corruption (Hodess 2001), ATTAC (The Association for the Taxation of Financial Transactions for the Aid of Citizens) proposing a new global tax order, and Global Witness, a watchdog initiative monitoring the diamonds business but also with a general focus on natural resources.

Protest and open resistance by citizens can be a preferred mode of action and not merely a second-hand option in cases where recognition fails (Edwards and Gaventa 2002; Held and McGrew 2002), but formal participation in the work of intergovernmental organizations is often sought. It is not clear, however, whether the distinction between the "affirmative" and "resistant" globals (Rosenau 2003: 118) fully captures this cleavage because there exists a large group of civil society organizations that have not surrendered to globalization but seek through a participatory strategy to critically redirect these processes.

There is definitely no single objective for all organizations, initiatives and alliances. Where participation is a primary goal, the granting of consultancy status cements their role as serious and accountable organizations; it gives them access to important information, improves their tactical skills and timing, and provides better opportunities for influencing policy processes and policy outcomes.

Many civil society organizations are also long-time participants to intergovernmental organizations, and, as illustrated earlier, serious reforms further institutionalize participation. When officially recognized, civil society organizations must invest more resources and build a strong capacity to follow developments more closely and to negotiate with international bureaucrats and other nongovernmental organizations, including those from the business side. To the extent that civil society organizations become an integral part of the global rule-making apparatus, the literatures on intergovernmental organizations on the one hand and civil society organizations and non-governmental organizations on the other are hardly distinguishable (Charnowitz 1997; Willetts 2000).

Although civil society organizations are recognized in many institutional contexts and are active in many policy fields, related studies tend to concentrate on specific issues and sectors. Thus, only some clusters of civil society organizations have been carefully examined and held as the archetypes of civil society – namely those in the areas of environmental politics, human rights, relief work and development, poverty alleviation, gender issues, and related fields. Furthermore, organizations are examined in their relation to oppressive states rather than in their relation to business. In other words, only some organizations that take an active interest in economic issues are reviewed. Furthermore, the story of non-participation in intergovernmental agencies dealing with macroeconomic issues or the regulation of the financial industries is clear (Coleman and Porter 2000; Scholte and Schnabel 2002; Porter 2005), although reforms have softened resistance toward civil society participation (Mason 2002).

Fads and fashions take researchers in some directions and leave other paths untrodden, but lack of scholarly consideration is in no small part attributable to the fact that some civil society action simply takes the form of protest rather than participation. Indeed, only if both civil society organizations and the bureaucracies of intergovernmental organizations find cooperation relevant and mutually attractive does formal participation become a true object of scrutiny. The changing role of policy fields and the related opportunity structures also matter. Many conflicts center round environmental issues; it requires a special effort to examine environmental policy, creating today a key battleground in global public policy where environmental movements have succeeded to organize themselves and voice their interests. This claim, however, is rarely advanced in environmental studies, and many other policy fields deserve consideration and can provide a more varied picture of global public policy.

The role of civil society organizations in public policy is interesting not only in relation to intergovernmental organizations but also in relation to business directly where specific industries or corporations are targeted. As outlined earlier, strong resistance is voiced and cooperation is anathema to a large extent. However, corporations and their associations are also seen as potential partners in a dialog (Doh and Teegen 2003). Although the majority of contributions on self-regulation and other private projects depart from a corporate rather than from a countervailing force perspective, we have already won some experiences about civic participation – as will be illustrated later. There is, however, no systematic evidence of whether the same organizations are involved in the more traditional forms of public policy-making and in arrangements with business, or whether those participating in both these forms of policy-making are making up a coherent group distinguishable from those organizations standing completely outside.

If such a division really exists, then we are speaking roughly of a dichotomy between organizations participating and organizations protesting; on the basis of existing research, however, it is difficult to establish such rigid categories. Contingency-based explanations suggest that much depends on the opportunities that are available within a given issue or within a given industry at a certain time of building policy arrangements. To compare these patterns of participation we need both a common treatment of this problematique and a synthesis of existing research; but so far the study of civil society organizations in global politics is rooted in different branches of political science and sociology, whereas the study of civil society involvement in direct cooperation with business is treated by a heterogeneous group of scholars across a somewhat broader landscape of disciplines.

Business is facing a number of dilemmas in exchanging with civil society organizations and building policy arrangements, and the same can be said for various countervailing forces. Thus, civil society organizations must seriously consider whether core interests and ideas advanced by them are genuinely taken care of, or whether their participation is primarily nominal and used by business largely to legitimize arrangements. In the civil community there is usually a lack of trust in business; therefore much skepticism about proposing or participating in such schemes must be overcome – yet support does not always rest on solid ground. This third-party involvement by interested agents also requires that countervailing forces build an independent capacity to monitor arrangements and do not depend on information provided by corporate sources. As arrangements with business can be fragile and may provoke cleavages within civil society organizations because different opinions about the quality of regulation are expressed, organizations must be particularly alert that arrangements work according to proclaimed rules and values.

Research only occasionally reports regulatory weakness, however. A probable reason is that stories regarding private arrangements are told about corporations and industries with a record of successful implementation. Cases where arrangements fail or are folded can be harder to identify, and from a public policy point of view are of course less fascinating – although it is exactly this kind of knowledge that is needed to critically assess the true potential of private forms of policy-making in public policy.

Key countervailing forces in the economy and in politics – labor and consumers

Countervailing forces are mainly seen as public interest groups that represent or at least proclaim to speak for wider societal concerns. Most of these groups are very large and are confronted with a number of severe collective action problems outlined in the classic interest group literature (Olson 1965). Unlike business groups that are much smaller – and in terms of associability therefore regarded as "privileged" – large groups should face a substantial degree of free-riding, and hence are more difficult to establish and sustain. They have limited resources and are outnumbered by business interest associations. Without disputing this principal argument, empirical evidence shows that many countervailing groups are, indeed, organized for political action. The view that countervailing organizations are structurally weak is challenged, and it is argued that in some respects they are advantageous and operate more skillfully than others in global politics and that business is also characterized by weaknesses (Kellow 2002; Fuchs 2005).

Not all civil society organizations referred to in the previous sections are actively involved in countervailing activities, and not all organizations with such a potential develop it fully. As with business, these organizations are not making up a uniform actor category either in terms of origin or in terms of political strategy. Therefore, we shall first identify those candidates in the diverse population of civil society organizations that are, at first glance, most likely to become countervailing forces vis-à-vis business in the context of global public policy, outline their different backgrounds, and then discuss other categories of countervailing organizations.

To become a major countervailing force, a key role must first and foremost be secured in the marketplace. Here the centrality of some actors is evident as they pose a fundamental economic challenge to business hegemony. The strong position of business, often held by a handful of firms in the marketplace, can be countered by restraints "not on the same side of the market but on the opposite side, not with competitors but with customers or suppliers" (Galbraith 1952: 118). However, these countervailing forces are not entirely self-generating: "In the light of the difficulty in organizing countervailing power, it is not surprising that the assistance of government has repeatedly been sought in this task" (Galbraith 1952: 133).

On an individual or collective basis, corporations respond to this politico-economic situation,[2] enter into negotiations, form agreements and sign contracts that regulate a large number of issues in the relationship between employers and employees and between producers and consumers.

This countervailing power can manifest itself in the market, but also in the political process when legislation is enacted. This proximity is politically exploitable and gives labor and consumers a qualitatively different position than many other countervailing organizations that are not directly involved in economic transactions with business. However, in the literature on countervailing powers in global politics, little attention has been directed toward these two encompassing groups, although the analysis on global unions can to some extent draw on comparative investigations (Harrod and O'Brien 2002).

Borrowing and adapting a term from the early public choice literature – another group of civil society organizations can be characterized as non-market organizations in the proper sense of the word,[3] because these are not directly involved in economic transactions. But as will be shown later, they are in some cases heavily involved in the setting of rules and standards; in addition, by monitoring the compliance of business with international conventions, they become indirectly involved in economic transactions. These organizations become recognized as political players drawn into the economic sphere, unlike labor and consumers that emerge from the economic sphere. In other words, in the case of civil society organizations different paths lead to global politics, and each of these must be analyzed to fully appreciate the role of countervailing power.

As an example of non-market-based organizations we find a range of environmental groups. They have received significant attention, and they sometimes appear to have far greater leverage than labor and consumer organizations – either because they are powerful actors in setting agendas, or because they are relevant partners of those corporations and industries that need and prefer some kind of third party participation to implement and solidify arrangements. In other words, countervailing activity can be particularly important if it is economically related to business and it is worthwhile for civil society organizations representing labor and consumers to link up with these groups in political agenda-setting, build alliances that enjoy broad credibility and also bank on their images as watchdogs.

One aspect that merits particular attention in the context of global public policy is the complex and fluctuating relationship between actors and policy fields. Although some kind of specialization exists between these two categories of countervailing powers – the market- and non-market based as outlined earlier – it is certainly not a very rigid one.

Labor and consumer organizations typically grapple with traditional problems in the labor and consumer markets, but they also expand activities and move into new areas, for instance, through campaigns or boycotts and by targeting a broad spectrum of labor standards (Braithwaite and Drahos 2000: 236–7; Harrod and O'Brien 2002; O'Brien 2002: 230; Haworth *et al.* 2005). Also in various initiatives launched by, for instance, Health Action Network, Pesticides Action Network or Climate Action Network, the economic and political behavior of business is targeted in different policy fields that tend to coalesce and require a concerted effort on the part of civic groups.

Indeed, labor and consumer organizations add new dimensions to and redefine established domains, but they also embrace new policy fields. To represent workers and consumers, they also tackle ethical issues that in the past were either neglected or represented through other organizations. The same kind of dynamic characterizes other countervailing powers. Thus, environmental and human rights organizations are increasingly involved in issues that were traditionally seen as outside their core field of operation. Although countervailing organizations are not uncritically conquering more and more policy fields, because they must still master their "own" field, they move into and out of new areas. Such diligent moves are propelled by the complex nature of many economic and social problems that must be approached in an integrated fashion and often simultaneously by different organizations. These developments pose a great challenge to business political action.

Sectors and policy fields – variation in arrangements

Global public policy is formulated at many different levels. In some cases public policy focuses on issues that are of general relevance to business, and consequently business must coordinate interests across a large number of industries and represent these in a dialog with intergovernmental agencies and occasionally with civil society organizations. Indeed, influential and encompassing business interest associations are granted consultative status and routinely participate in the work of intergovernmental organizations; some have a historical record of authorizing rules in the global business community. In such cases, private rule-making becomes a functional equivalent of regulation adopted by public regulators, and commerce has a long historical record of such arrangements (Cutler 2003).

Intergovernmental organizations develop policy in which they identify and prioritize problems, and in doing so they receive input through exchanges with available and often rather specialized business interest associations. They also structure the ways in which business is organized and formulates policy; for its part, business is represented through relevant interest associations that reflect the various properties of the specific industries concerned, but organizations also develop strategies to influence public policy by mediating heterogeneous interests in the membership.[4]

Finally, public policy can also be directed at or produced by single corporations; this is rarely the case however, especially in a global context where few, if any, producers will have such a single clear dominant position. Adding to this pattern of public policy is the acclaimed and institutionalized practice of intergovernmental organizations of not dealing with individual corporations.

If we seek to understand aggregates such as industries in the context of the concrete policy fields in which they operate, other bodies of work must be consulted. As testified by the individual chapters of this book, it is also at the sectoral level that we find a significant activity by global industries, either to influence intergovernmental agencies or to engage in private rule-making. A rich literature shows that much policy is actually dealing with international and global problem-solving. Although much literature exists on the sectoral organization of business and public policy, there are policy fields that are well researched as well as policy fields and issues that are rarely dealt with in scholarly work (Deacon *et al.* 1997; Bernauer 2003; O'Rourke 2003). Global public policy can furthermore be examined by departing from specific industries or sectors of business, and other aspects of policy-making will be discovered when studying – for instance agriculture (Coleman 2001), chemicals (Martinelli 1991), telecommunications, and the internet (Mueller 2002), intellectual property rights (Sell 2003) or finance (Porter 2005).[5]

Interesting as well is the high degree of political action above the level of single corporations and below the level of peak associations. At this meso-level, specific industries or product groups find collective action relevant and feasible, and this form of collective business action often fits certain policy fields in cases where public regulation is directed toward particular industries. In this context, the organization of public policy and the organization of business interests can be interpreted as a sophisticated relationship stimulated by mechanisms of regulatory requests and demands – but these developments cannot be understood fully without analyzing the simultaneous efforts of civil society.

Although configurations of international agencies, business and civic groups can be analyzed within large policy fields that cross the domains of several intergovernmental agencies, institutional and highly specialized innovations, such as the Forest Stewardship Council and the Marine Stewardship Council, cover large ecosystems and delve into many complex aspects of global public policy. The same attention is given to the Global Alliance for Vaccines and Immunization, Medicines for Malaria Venture and the Global Alliance for TB Drug Development. Around these initiatives, cooperation among drug companies, intergovernmental organizations and civil society organizations has emerged. Indeed, there are many examples of smaller certification projects and labeling schemes that are either led by industry or driven by independent forces outside business (see Domask 2003), and to which professional and technical expertise is attached (Sinclair 1999). Indeed, a variety of interests and actors are involved in issue-based problem-solving, and there is no single and celebrated model of policy-making.[6] These undertakings may be extremely valuable as a form of public policy organized beyond traditional public institutions but, as will be discussed later, there is no guarantee that they acquire this high quality.

For their part, many civil society organizations are specialized, but this fact does not suggest that these organizations are involved in exactly the same policy sectors as organized business. In terms of their countervailing capacity, civil society displays an organizational immaturity because important regulatory issues are covered by business as well as by intergovernmental organizations in a range of policy areas, whereas civil society has neither established relevant organizations, nor won a degree of expertise sufficient to enable it to deal with these same issues and to respond to new challenges in a timely manner.

On behalf of civil society organizations, this outcome indicates a certain policy specialization, the problematic side of it being that they stand outside some core areas where business takes a key interest and where it hosts significant expertise to influence public policy. Contrariwise, there are also some advantages for civil society. This alternative specialization may be used to target business in areas where business is usually weaker and less well equipped to address public policy, such as in the areas of human rights and child labor. The relative weight carried by business and countervailing forces, however, is dynamic: it may vary significantly across policy fields and may change over time.

All in all, existing research provides some important clues on business political matters across different fields of public policy, and on how public policy creates an institutional framework that integrates relevant business players. Furthermore, each industry faces a key set of problems: product profiles vary; different regulation applies and from the perspective of countervailing forces, industries also differ in terms of political saliency. Given these backgrounds and pressures, each section of business must rise to the occasion and find appropriate strategies to deal with public authority and countervailing powers. In a volatile environment, however, the implementation of such strategies raises some perennial questions in the business community. Can business interest associations or other collective formats influence traditional public policy? Will they voluntarily take upon them the responsibility of running policy arrangements alone, or will they include certain segments of civil society? It also raises questions about where such new initiatives emerge. One interesting possibility is that intergovernmental organizations, business and the countervailing powers of civil society may use such arenas as conferences with an economic, social or environmental agenda as a platform for joint action.

Arenas – platforms for dialog and collaboration

In addition to direct negotiations across states, various conferences, meetings, summits and forums have traditionally played an important part in the formation of public policy at international levels (see Schechter 2005). The growth of these arenas is characterized by great diversity in terms of participation, procedure and purpose.

The fact that the number of these conferences, meetings, etc., has skyrocketed over the least decades suggests that these venues are important in the formation of global politics. Indeed, the greater access of all sorts of private interests to these arenas is an interesting feature in today's global public policy. They have brought together states but, increasingly, also business and countervailing groups.[7] Participation has been democratized and made more affordable to these groups. Delegates meet and have an opportunity to seek a common understanding and even create new alliances. To use a classic concept from the study of organizations, life at these conferences is the "micropolitics" of global public policy (Burns 1961).

This diversity is encouraged by intergovernmental organizations hosting these conferences and other media events, promoting the reforming of the current landscape of global policy-making. However, some conferences are alternatively run by private organizations outside the domain of public authority. Consequently, procedures must account for this diversity. The integration of private interests at different stages of the events and their active involvement in panel hearings and committee work produce more varied rules. Finally, the express purpose of these conferences and other events is to influence public policy through many different channels and not necessarily to arrive at formal decisions to be implemented by international organizations and states. Other related goals are, for instance, to bring attention to neglected issues and set alternative agendas, create new alliances, and foster a dialog between conflicting interests.

High-profile summits run by the UN and its specialized agencies (Willetts 1989) have called the attention of the world community; these are examples of public driven arrangements that seek to include civil society. Following the experience of UNCED (United Nations Conference on Environment and Development) in Rio de Janeiro, where the participatory element loomed large, stronger emphasis is now placed on integrating civil society into the decision-making of intergovernmental agencies and on having a balanced representation of affected interests. The WSSD (World Summit on Sustainable Development) in Johannesburg in 2002 was a further important arena in bringing states and NGOs together and designing new forms of global governance.

In the spirit of the Global Compact initiative launched by the UN General Secretary in 1999, the formation of partnerships between business and civil society is welcomed, and this new technology is employed also in the context of global conferences (Hemmati *et al.* 2002). It is a rather open and flexible strategy that allows for cooperation and agreement between private parties under the auspices of intergovernmental organizations, but it also envisages direct bilateral or multilateral cooperation on a private basis, which is applied in many contexts and discussed at many conferences.[8] It is a format known from different territorial levels and not applied in global politics only (Lober 1997).

Beyond the UN we also find intergovernmental organizations that are involved in the development of public policy; besides, a further number of private organizations run conferences and meetings that serve as a forum for deliberation and compromise. In addition to these and other global conferences, various counter summits or supplementary forums, such as the Global People's Forum and the business based World Business Council for Sustainable Development Forum, are set up. There is a possibility, however, that even here nascent dialogs emerge because civil society and business find cooperation fruitful and move beyond confrontation. In the pharmaceutical industry, major generic producers and certain civic groups host conferences and – encouraged by the WHO – design new projects with the concrete goal of combating AIDS.

By definition, these arenas are at the same time both solid and elusive – because some conferences are serial and highly institutionalized, whereas other activities are one-time events. Most arenas, however, have an infrastructure that facilitates the production of public policy, or at least the formulation of strategies that can eventually become a part of public policy. Thus, some arenas can be regarded as policy arrangements in their own right either because they already have become an element of public policy, or because they host a potential to produce future arrangements to which both business and countervailing powers subscribe.

Some arenas have a broad thematic focus and seek to coordinate initiatives across policy fields, whereas others are closely related to specific policy fields. Therefore, some policy fields establish their "own" arenas closely tied to specific organizations, whereas other arenas lack a specific organizational basis and are linked to a variety of public or private organizations.

Arenas can become a distinct symbol of sectoral politics, such as in the environmental debate on atmospheric changes (Hurrell and Kingsbury 1992) or in environmental issues more generally (Seyfang 2003), when crucial issues are addressed and when serious attempts of agenda-setting are made; however, most conferences cover only parts of a larger policy field (Clark *et al.* 1998). Indeed, many issues are handled in the less spectacular day-to-day work of intergovernmental agencies, and here the growing conference life is often less spectacular.

In the context of this book, arenas are not limited to the formal conference machinery of the UN. Private conferences and forums, however, are dealt with in research. In the main, these activities are scrutinized from the broad perspective of social forces that take part in conferences rather than from the perspective of categorizing conferences, and we need clear taxonomies of these forums. When disaggregated, these forces operate both as "insiders" and "outsiders"; they are concretely analyzed as civil society organizations, transnational movements, advocacy groups, nongovernmental organizations, social movements, grass root movements or merely spontaneous *ad hoc* activity through street protests. These initiatives surround ordinary conference activity, and they are often juxtaposed to either conferences between states in the context of intergovernmental organizations, or business-led conferences in which civic groups are disinterested or simply excluded. The policy fields that are covered by this highly fragmented private conference system are by and large the same as those discussed in public conferences, but alternative approaches are offered in regard to trade agreements, patent rights, poverty alleviation, global warming and related fields (Fisher and Ponniah 2003).

Arenas dominated by business have been subjected to less intense scientific inquiry than others. In general, activities are run by stable organizations, they are more routinely operated, and they tend to be less spectacular. In this domain, conference activity is often restricted almost exclusively to regular annual conferences of individual business interest associations, does not include business on a cross-sectoral basis, and does not call attention to outside business. Given the economic and political globalization of business, these initiatives are both numerous and important. The high-profile World Economic Forum (WEF), covering a long list of current global issues, is, among other things, also a place where relations to civil society are deliberated and, to some extent, tested. At the same time, it is an arena that triggers significant protest (Houtart and Polet 2001).

In sum, arenas offer an excellent opportunity to address key issues in today's global public policy and involve different actors in problem-solving. Thus, in cases where intergovernmental organizations host conferences, participatory strategies are implemented in a way that allows for and facilitates new alliances between business and countervailing groups. In these contexts, business and countervailing powers may also find ways to contribute to a climate of collaboration instead of one of entrenchment. In cases where private conferences can be arranged, strategies can be formulated and initiatives can be adopted to bridge cleavages in an attempt to solve problems of mutual interest. Under these circumstances new policy arrangements may emerge.

Exchanges between public authority, business and civil society organizations

Having laid out some important prerequisites for analyzing global policy arrangements, we can now turn to the organization of various forms of global public policy. They include composites of public authority in the form of intergovernmental agencies, as well as a multitude of concerned business actors and civil society organizations that demonstrate a countervailing activity, yet are prone to pragmatic solutions.

With these key actors involved in problem-solving, two basic types of policy arrangements are discernable: public driven and private driven arrangements. However, the real world of policy arrangements is modified in several interesting ways, and research has grappled with these complex public–private interactions and, in some cases, offered a typology to classify arrangements.

To understand policy arrangements in further detail, much inspiration can be drawn from theories on pluralism, corporatism, policy networks, advocacy coalitions among others, but to varying degrees these theories carry with them certain connotations from the territorial context in which they were originally developed and have hitherto been applied. Prudence is therefore required when transplanting approaches and concepts from comparative politics to the international and global realm. Otherwise, we fail to recognize the specific exchange patterns typical of global politics.

The most rewarding strategy is to critically draw on these disparate theories, extract and transfer elements that are neutrally applicable, and use these as building blocks in the analysis of global public policy. In other words, we confront relevant theories with the present state of affairs in global politics. A significant number of private actors, for instance, represent their interests on the global scene and struggle for influence; however, as the existence of countervailing powers suggests, there is no monopoly on power, although there can be many asymmetries in the distribution of influence – some of which can be sustained over time.

These patterns of plurality, albeit modified, are most likely to be further corrected by the selection of relevant partners in these arrangements. As already shown, intergovernmental organizations selectively choose, recognize, and exchange only with a subset of the vast population of business and civil society organizations. In a similar vein, those organizations that have the vision and capacity to run various sorts of private driven arrangements, and those recognized by public authority in this capacity, must be limited in number because not all organizations or alliances fulfill the essential, yet unspoken, criteria to be backed up. Given these interactions, a range of insights from the neo-corporatist tradition can be helpful in understanding global public policy.

Studies on policy networks have also emphasized that a wide category of public and private actors are integrated through different policies, and that there networks show a strong similarity with the theoretical framework found in pluralism and that found in neo-corporatism. However, it is problematic to deal only with actors and their many interactions in a way that neutralizes or ignores their concrete actor qualities – in our case intergovernmental organizations, and business and civil society organizations. Each operates according to a unique set of rationales and properties.

Finally, experiences from the advocacy coalition framework can be exploited, in particular when analyzing the ways in which countervailing powers in the early stages of the policy process build agendas and form alliances to influence public policy in its more traditional forms. Given this public policy focus, this framework seems not well suited to investigating direct bilateral collaboration between business and civil society,[9] because global public policy includes many other forms, constituting the basic theme of the global governance literature.

This brief presentation highlights a few elements from theories primarily associated with comparative politics, elements that may also be utilized in the study of global politics. Before we return to the discussion of the essential features of public driven and private driven policy arrangements, and to which the earlier theories contribute, it is imperative to discuss some recent theories and works that have independently grappled with these international and global arrangements – without drawing on and reproducing some of the basic thoughts sketched earlier. Those theories that are most interesting for our purpose seek each in their way to formulate an integrated approach embracing both public and private actors in the global realm. Let us in turn consider three such approaches and their potential for analyzing global policy arrangements, namely regimes, networks and partnerships.

The regime approach that emerged in the late 1970s and early 1980s grapples with the problems of new or less-observed forms of international and global policy-making, in which various public and private actors focus on specific policy fields, including many socioeconomic issues (Krasner 1983). Indeed, this start was very promising, and the approach recognized that international relations and problem-solving were not a matter exclusively for states but included more actors in the formulation and implementation of rules through various sorts of multilateral agreements. These problem-solving mechanisms can emerge, for instance, through the participation of nongovernmental organizations in intergovernmental organizations (Young 1989; Levy *et al.* 1995; Zacher and Sutton 1996; Hasenclever *et al.* 1997; Rittberger and Zangl 2006), although this is not always the outcome.

Today, regime studies, although less in vogue than in the past, focus mainly on the interplay between states, and the role of nongovernmental organizations is largely filtered away. In a few cases, however, attempts have been made to attribute a greater role to nongovernmental organizations (Haufler 1993; Cutler 2002), but although this has met with some approval it has not been profoundly echoed in the regime tradition. Where the approach is employed it has, however, not seriously investigated the role of antagonized interests, such as business and countervailing, and how they may relate to each other, and eventually lead to some kind of negotiated settlement, which is the theme of this book. Inspired by regime analysis, an empirically broad and conceptually diverse group of private governance studies has become attentive to the role of nongovernmental organizations as rule-making and norm-setting institutions, but has moved beyond the conceptual framework once advanced in the regime literature.

While the regime approach has faded, network theories have flourished in the social sciences as a whole. They are useful in characterizing many new forms of policy-making involving a variety of non-state actors in both domestic and global politics, but they also carry some disadvantages. First, studies of policy networks aim, in principle, to analyze actors and linkages in the entire network, whereas our task is to focus entirely on key intergovernmental agencies, business and countervailing groups and not map the totality of relations. In cases, however, where organizations are not a direct part of a conflict but acquire a mediating role, for instance by producing reports and sharing knowledge that can be used by the conflicting parties and eventually form the basis of an agreement, these other actors will be given due attention.[10]

Second, most studies on policy networks have not established an explicit division of labor in their cast of actors. Policy networks do not reveal in depth whether arrangements are shaped by public or private initiatives, but in the context of our analysis it is important to study how arrangements emanate and who controls these schemes.

Third, studies on networks emphasizing the role of civil society organizations commonly restrict their understanding of networks to precisely this actor category. Shared interests and values of advocacy groups (Keck and Sikkink 1998; Nelson 2002), expressed through campaigns such as the World Rainforest Network or through professional and academic groups (Charle *et al.* 2004) or through the cooperation between movements and science, are investigated (Haas 1992). Usually, there is little or no room for the role played by business, but instead of sidelining economic interests and defining policy networks down to civil society, business must form an integral part of the study on global politics.

Fourth, relatively few studies concentrate on global policy networks per se (Coleman and Perl 1999; Cerny 2001; Stone 2004; Schneider and Hyner 2005), drawing on concepts from comparative politics. Other and related concepts that are only barely distinguishable from policy networks have also been introduced to analyze global politics. Especially the advocacy coalition framework, that borrows analytically and conceptually from the study on coalitions in domestic politics (Sabatier 1999), has been employed. In such cases we still need, however, to qualify what is typical when both business and countervailing groups contribute to global policy-making, and what characterizes the leverage of different coalitions.

These different approaches and lines of research all harbor a potential for analyzing global policy arrangements involving business as well as countervailing forces, but few of them actually take up this challenge. The primary research problem is not the conceptual elusiveness of, for instance, networks and advocacy coalitions, but rather the strong and prevailing compartmentalization in the study of these two groups of private actors. A more overarching challenge is that only parts of the networks and the coalitions are scrutinized, or cases are examined where either business or civil society organizations are deliberately not engaged or are forgotten.

An approach that has emerged more recently deals with the formation of private–public partnerships in the economy and in politics, especially with regard to the process of privatization (see Rosenau 2000). As with the majority of the perspectives mentioned earlier, this approach has wide applications and is not restricted to the global scene. Although, it is mainly used in domestic contexts and employed in studies on public sector reforms, the approach has also found its way into a number of intergovernmental organizations as a management tool. According to the UN Global Compact, partnerships may include UN-bodies and corporations as well as civic groups. Unlike the other approaches presented, it has not emerged in a scholarly environment, and it is characterized by much diplomatic jargon and bureaucratic newspeak of public management. The approach does not seek to accumulate existing empirical and theoretical experiences of the role of private organizations in politics, but rather to place concrete projects and their implementation under scrutiny.

To varying degrees, some of the other approaches discussed earlier also fail to address what is already advanced in parallel theories and how theoretical and conceptual duplication can be avoided. Given its bureaucratic offspring, however, this lapse is particularly strong in this strand of research. It is true that many forms of collaboration can hardly be accommodated within already existing theories and concepts, but this fact alone does not speak for organizing these under the emerging PPP-vocabulary.

However, contributions utilizing elements of the PPP-language are useful in our framework. For instance, global public policy is shaped neither through public agencies, nor through private organizations alone, and it is necessary to account for all the multifarious relations between private and public actors relating to concrete projects and agreements as well as to more stable institutions (Börzel and Risse 2005). Parts of this regulatory continuum, ranging from relations at the individual corporations to those at industries and national economies, have previously been dealt with in studies of corporatist problem-solving: private actors deliver important inputs into public institutions that to some extent also assist in the structuring of organizations and their strategies, but the influence of private interests on the formulation and implementation of policy varies significantly across countries, policy fields and issues. Whereas analyses in the neo-corporatist tradition typically emphasize the associational factor in politics and the guidance of public authority, there is, however, no specific actor focus in the PPP-literature but rather a willingness to be all-inclusive, or at least not give any group of private actors advance preferential treatment.

The corporatist paradigm has also been transferred to the global realm in the study of the interactions between public authority on the one hand, and conflicting private interests on the other (Ottaway 2001). This complex distribution of power at the global level occasions the establishment of trilateral institutions of exchange or joint schemes encompassing an even wider cast of interested parties (Doh 2003). Of course, a classic example of a global corporatist-like arrangement is the International Labour Organization (ILO), which is designed not only as a meeting place of states but also as a forum for business and countervailing powers. In a somewhat similar vein, many new arrangements exist and are constantly emerging – both with and without the directing hand of public authority.

Caution is required everywhere in the delicate process of transferring theories and concepts, but some elements in these disparate, yet parallel literatures, can be utilized in the study of global policy arrangements. According to the corporatist tradition, for instance, private and representative organizations are integrated in policy-making and can have a strong and sometimes independent problem-solving capacity. Policy networks and advocacy coalitions, at least programmatically, include many public and private actors and leaves the possibility open that public policy can become effective and legitimate at more disaggregated levels. Whereas some network-orientated studies stress the horizontal character of policy-making, those guided by coalition approaches and collective action theories are more inclined to recognize the conflicting interests involved, a recognition helpful in understanding the relations between business and countervailing powers. Arguments stressing actor plurality can also be found in the small but growing literature on partnerships and privatization, but here a greater role is attributed to the steering power of public bureaucracies in cases where they are encouraged by intergovernmental organizations.

Experiences from these research traditions can be saved for and benefit the study on new global policy arrangements, but a real synthesis is hardly achievable; used in isolation, each of the paradigms and conceptual clusters presented earlier carry many connotations. Given the emergence of new initiatives to bring public authority together with business and civil society organizations and given the independent efforts of business and civil society, the concept of policy arrangement is therefore wheeled in to account for the variety in today's global public policy.

Global public policy – public and private driven policy arrangements

The concept of "policy arrangement" has been used in an *ad hoc* fashion and generally without much substance in political science. In a few and more recent cases briefly reviewed later, however, attempts have been made to enrich this concept by relating it to governance problems and coalition behavior.

For instance, it has been suggested that "governance arrangements" offer an alternative to state and market at the same time as they enjoy a symbiotic relationship with these modes of problem-solving. Arrangements are seen as licensed by public authority but working horizontally between those private actors involved. Arrangements include many categories of actors representing different constituencies, but they usually include a careful selection of opposing interests of which the weaker parties are encouraged or even sponsored by public authority to balance interests so as to become more widely accepted in society (Schmitter 2002). It follows that conflicts are solved in a legitimate fashion when the major interested parties participate in the formulation and implementation of policy. This does not imply an equal distribution of resources among the concrete participants to these arrangements, but it does suggest mutual recognition with decision-rules and practices based on principles of compromise.

Another approach to policy arrangements, which is less elaborate theoretically but is helpful when analyzing the role of business and countervailing groups in global politics, draws on the policy network perspective and bears some resemblance to the advocacy coalitions framework, but it adds new elements to policy-making by analyzing policy within policy domains, such as environmental policy (van Tatenhove *et al.* 2000). A number of different actors participate in these arrangements, but they typically form conflicting coalitions, each having common goals and projects rooted in core interests and specific discourses. According to this interpretation, actors must in general adopt a set of formal rules for arrangements to function, while informal rules are no less important and reflect the dominant political culture that they must comply with.

Again important inspiration can be found in such treatises on the organization of policy arrangements, but in our context the emergence of arrangements and the role of public authority lack some precision. In the former view, the initiator of governance arrangements is clearly public authority, whereas in the latter perspective this question is answered more ambiguously. No doubt public agencies can be important in breathing life into policy arrangements, but a strong and unilateral emphasis on public authority rules out or reduces the creative forces of private actors.

Mindful of the conceptual diversity associated with the concept of policy arrangements and of the ensuing theoretical challenges, a reformulation is required to analyze arrangements within global public policy – given the more recent initiatives to renew policy through intergovernmental organizations and organizations representing business or civil society. Policy arrangements entail different problematiques. We may first distinguish between two basic sets of arrangements, namely the public driven and private driven arrangements, and then move on to show how this typology can be softened in various ways to account for the real world of policy-making.

Public driven arrangements are established under the auspices of intergovernmental organizations, where contacts are formalized on the one hand between these agencies and a selected number of recognized private groups more generally, and on the other hand between business and civil society organizations that operate within a given policy field. Specific participatory strategies are designed to integrate private groups into policy-making and to enhance legitimacy through the creation of a certain degree of representational balance between opposing interests. The ordinary work of intergovernmental organizations and the many conferences, events and projects that they host here provide a basic institutional framework. One important aspect is the public assistance given to countervailing groups that have limited resources and are difficult to organize, and need public support to represent interests coherently. In general, public arrangements tend to be relatively formalized, with public authority being able to coordinate in a hierarchical fashion.

Private driven arrangements are created and run by private actors as an alternative to traditional public regulation; but they have a problem-solving capacity and usually, but not always, reflect a compromise between affected interests. They include bi- or multilateral contacts between business and countervailing groups that have achieved a recognized status within a given policy field, or within more narrow and specific issues. Although the configuration of actors is complex and asymmetric because they play different roles in regulation, resources to control arrangements are invested by both parties. Private arrangements tend to be less institutionalized: some are created in an *ad hoc* fashion, for instance in the context of conferences, and initially take the form of a dialog that structures the behavior of the actors involved; others become highly institutionalized, leading to agreements and new rules in which permanent institutions are built to oversee arrangements effectively.

It is heuristically useful to keep these arrangements apart, but public agencies can play a decisive role in the creation of private arrangements, and private actors can also influence the formation of public arrangements. Let us take a closer look at these modifications. Actions through intergovernmental organizations from mild encouragement to direct pressure can bring private actors to adopt rules and install new arrangements, and in some cases authority is delegated to private organizations in exchange for the compliance with certain substantive and procedural rules typical of the public sector. However, the degree to which a rule system is already defined by public authority and is administered by private organizations must be empirically examined, and such practices of delegation are never consistent.

In turn, private initiatives may also influence public driven arrangements. Actions through business or civil society organizations, or perhaps even concerted efforts, may change the strategy of intergovernmental agencies and lead to the creation of new arrangements. However, manifest efforts are not always needed. Intergovernmental organizations gradually adapt to changing environments and, consequently, avoid major political conflicts. Under these circumstances, private influence on the emergence of public driven arrangements is sometimes crucial but nevertheless hard to locate and verify.

The distinction between public driven and private driven arrangements behind global public policy can also be softened when studied in an evolutionary perspective, and, hence, new interfaces will emerge in the process of formulating and implementing arrangements. Thus, as the notion "delegation" suggests, a public initiative is carried out in a private framework, because public agencies suffer from information deficits and cannot keep pace with processes of globalization (Reinicke 1998: 90). More stable nongovernmental organizations, rather than activist organizations with limited staff, will be able to police such arrangements.

In only some cases, however, do private arrangements originate through political institutions. They are also pioneered through independent private action and emerge without the prior or subsequent approval of intergovernmental agencies. Under these circumstances arrangements are voluntary and are administered by private bodies that often unite different functions typical of the legislative, executive and judicative branches of government to issue and implement rules and monitor and sanction behavior. These arrangements are not simply a second-best solution or an attempt following abortive public intervention. Although run by private concerns, business must be accountable to external interests and must think in strategic terms to sustain private regulation.

The same evolutionary perspective can be applied to public driven arrangements. Thus, a private initiative may be followed by public action and a decision to organize problem-solving under the umbrella of intergovernmental organizations or new public units created for that specific purpose. Business may be more reluctant to accept such solutions and experience a surrender of autonomy, whereas countervailing groups may find public regulation more satisfactory and reliable.

But countervailing groups may prefer purely private arrangements entered into with business – or perhaps even business self-regulation, although this is more likely to be viewed as a conspiracy – and see them as advantageous to traditional public regulation. Indeed, civil society organizations can take the lead, and if business is convinced or left with no other alternative, it will be forced to follow in their train. This option provides countervailing forces with an excellent opportunity to closely monitor corporate behavior and actively take part in the process of reprimanding and punishing firms. This can also provide a background for bringing broader public attention to problematic business practices.

Whether such arrangements can actually be hosted and administered by private institutions does not only hinge upon the preferences and capacities of business and countervailing groups but also depends on the ambitions of intergovernmental organizations and their trust in private arrangements. Functionally, the participation of civil society can to some extent be viewed as a proxy of public authority, although countervailing organizations consider themselves as independent actors with a public interest and not the instrument of governments.

There are reasons to modify the concepts of public driven and private driven arrangements not only in terms of their origin and maintenance but also in terms of their patterns of participation. As far as public driven arrangements are concerned, intergovernmental organizations do not, for instance, always reorganize their relations with the entire population of recognized associations, although such general reforms have been endorsed in recent years. Some reforms are primarily concerned about civil society and about giving civic groups better access. Other modest, and less inclusive, strategies aimed particularly at business are also endorsed. A change in the rules defining business–government relations, however, is also relevant from the perspective of political transformation and is useful in the context of our analysis. Although such changes do not necessarily deal with formal civil society participation, they may nevertheless impact global public policy and, therefore, merit our full attention.

In addition, certain private arrangements do not always allow for the participation of approximated civil society representatives. A plethora of self-regulatory bodies, agreements, schemes, codes and other entities exist and are not new (see Kline 1985), but large segments of business have shown a growing concern for their role in society. The concept of business self-regulation has been used to characterize regulation at the level of single firms, a selection of firms, and whole industries; in the latter case especially, private regulation can become a viable alternative to traditional public regulation because rules and norms pertain to all corporations within a given field of industrial activity.

This form of business self-regulation can be solidified in many ways through relations with civil society or with relevant public agencies, and regulation is rarely established in isolation of broader societal developments. Formally however, self-regulation can be run entirely by business and still be an ingredient in global public policy; but in such cases, stronger caution is needed simply because there is a fundamental difference between ruling oneself, as in the case of a straightforward business regulation, and ruling others, as when outside participation through interested parties or mediators is added.

These private arrangements may owe their existence to private or public initiatives, and authority can be delegated by intergovernmental organizations. Such arrangements will also have an impact on traditional business–government relations because broader and more legitimate arrangements sometimes render public regulation unnecessary (Teegen and Doh 2003). Although intergovernmental organizations may see some advantages in encouraging civil society participation, this is not always mandatory. Civil society organizations that counterbalance business interests effectively are, perhaps, not available nor given sufficient priority in the process of delegation. There is also the likelihood that otherwise capacitated civil society organizations prefer to stand outside such arrangements lest they lose identity and, ultimately, be cannibalized by business.

At the same time, business may find outside participation problematic and hard to accept – based on experiences with civic groups or the lack thereof. Some industries will see these organizations as not being genuinely interested in running joint self-regulatory schemes and rather see outside participation as a Trojan horse.

In other words, industry self-regulation is imaginable both with and without outside participation. Business self-regulation can therefore be a way of avoiding countervailing powers; or self-regulation can be a way of integrating countervailing forces, and narrow economic interest may blur in the face of broader concerns. In other words, our criteria for private driven policy arrangements can be relaxed because some cases of industry self-regulation may be extremely observant to demands and expectations in civil society organizations without formally including them.

The conditions for building global public policy on the compromise between opposing interests is, however, quite different from business self-regulation. But if left out of our analysis completely, many recent business initiatives and mechanisms of problem-solving would be ignored in advance, and a more inclusive, yet critical, research strategy recognizing the potential contributions of an enlightened industry self-regulation without any formal role attributed to countervailing groups is therefore preferable. Thus each case and its self-regulatory capacity must be critically examined.

Mindful of the public interest, many corporations and business groups today aspire to solve global problems, although they do not strive to encompass the whole industry or producer groups and do not produce pure public goods in a global context (Kaul 2001). In such cases, single corporations or a relatively small selection of corporations develop high standards, become accredited with larger schemes, bargain with stakeholders, define rules governing the behavior of corporations (Clapp 1998; Falkner 2003; Cashore *et al.* 2004; Potoski and Prakash 2005), and sometimes present these schemes as partnerships.[11] Unlike those forms of self-regulation where a public policy goal is formulated at the level of an industry, major undertakings to avoid or minimize free-riding are not made, and there are usually no strong mechanisms for monitoring and sanctioning non-compliant firms.

It is crucial that this lack of an encompassing order suggests that private regulation does not win authority, and it is becomes sub-optimal in relation to traditional public regulation. This underperformance can be related to many aspects, including such issues as the limited market shares of accreditation schemes or partnerships, the blatant neglect of the less responsible corporations, and the lack of government recognition.

These reservations should not, however, lead to the discounting of all partnerships, schemes and codes that do achieve general authority. It must be emphasized that although the overwhelming part of these small initiatives, fostered by single firms or a variety of committed corporations and, in some cases, including countervailing forces, do not produce regulation that is equivalent to public regulation or to the more advanced forms of industry self-regulation referred to earlier; however, they can still be valuable from the perspective of global public policy. They must also be seen as private driven policy arrangements in cases where they ambitiously move in this direction, spark new initiatives and eventually gain wider currency. In other words, we must see private arrangements, not in a static but in an evolutionary perspective.

However, the pace and consequence with which these moves are made vary enormously, and we must be indeed careful not to expand the concept of private driven policy arrangements beyond its natural boundary. Today, many studies with a management focus are too impatient about highlighting the societal role of business and exaggerate their real contribution to public policy. At the same time this research is seconded by ethical declarations, but on sober consideration these corporate advances may be less attractive from the angle of the public interest. Of course, if arrangements do not cover large groups of firms and if free-riding is not avoided or substantially reduced, the social and environmental responsibility of business is more limited and indeed also less relevant from the perspective of public policy.

In sum, all these public driven and private driven arrangements and their various modifications appear in different empirical settings. They can all be analyzed by including perspectives from intergovernmental organizations, business, and general countervailing groups, such as labor and consumers that participate in many such forms of policy-making. Turning to the more disaggregated levels of industries, policy fields and arenas, we see that a more comprehensive account can be offered of how attempts are made to renew global public policy. In the following, an outline of each chapter explains in further detail how this task is dealt with. The chapters draw upon concepts presented in the introductory chapter, but they add new angles and show that there is much variation and experimenting in the current development of global public policy.

The structure of the book

Chapters 2 and 3 focus on some classic and general countervailing powers and conflicts. Seen from the perspective of a given corporation, exchanges are made with key economic actors in the marketplace. Relations are established with labor within the corporation, and with consumers outside the corporation; relations also extend both beyond the individual corporation and the state or country. Globally, business must address significant issues within both labor market policy and consumer policy, and must build relations with organizations that represent – or claim to represent – these groups, while countervailing groups must find appropriate strategies.

In Chapter 2 Alex Diceanu and Robert O'Brien examine the labor movement's international and global attempts to counterbalance business interests in the global economy and in global public policy. They analyzes both a core of trade unions and surrounding nonunion labor associations, including research institutes, informal sector actors and peasant organizations. The chapter surveys labor's multiple strategies in the interstate system, in the world economy, and vis-à-vis global civil society. In the interstate system, labor is actively engaged in social democratic states and in some intergovernmental organizations – such as the ILO – but is marginalized in organizations, such as the World Bank. In the world economy, labor has pursued industrial disputes with multinationals beyond the borders of single states, built agreements with single firms, and assisted in the development of various corporate codes of conduct. In the civil society field, labor has been involved in building coalitions with civil society organizations in joint campaigns. This broader activity is important in limiting business prerogatives.

In Chapter 3 Karsten Ronit deals with the political activities of consumers, another key actor in the economy. Given their prominent position in the economy, we may at fist glance hypothesize that consumer groups are an important and integral part of the international machinery, building a regulatory framework in this policy field. Consumer groups have used two "voice" options: protest and participation. The former is fragmented; the latter is coordinated through the participation in some intergovernmental organizations. Examples of private arrangements with business groups are less frequent. The more established consumer organizations have used their participation in various international forums to influence policy, but they are confronted with serious problems of collective action. In principle, consumer organizations represent billions of consumers, but these are difficult to organize and represent properly. Furthermore, consumer interests must be defended in a rapidly increasing number of policy fields and institutional contexts, and here they both compete and cooperate with other civil society organizations.

Chapters 4 and 5 look at business and countervailing powers at a disaggregated level and analyze relations within policy fields and industrial sectors – finance and mining and minerals – where controversial issues must be solved. These fields have traditionally been characterized by either fragmented countervailing forces or by the lack of business or intergovernmental agencies to design and create relevant forums of participation. However, attempts have been made to bridge the cleavages and build new arrangements.

In Chapter 4 Tony Porter analyzes recent developments within global finance. This field is often seen as involving an expansion of fluid anonymous market interactions, but global institutionalization is manifest in the emergence of new structures of public authority, such as the committees of regulators at the Bank for International Settlements or the enhanced regulatory role of the International Monetary Fund. Despite various barriers to contestation, policies are challenged in important ways. First, global civil society organizations have become more knowledgeable and influential and have begun to develop more effective critiques of prevailing policies. Second, developing countries previously excluded from these processes are beginning to exert more influence over them. Third, conflicts among leading states and among powerful private-sector actors are becoming more open, forcing elite actors to justify their positions more aggressively and in more universal terms. Overall, this chapter paints a picture in which global financial policy-making is becoming more institutionalized, in turn bringing about new opportunities for institutionalized contestation.

In Chapter 5 Aynsley Kellow scrutinizes the role of the mining and metals industry and various countervailing powers – especially environmental groups – seeking to influence public policy. Not until 2001, however, was a comprehensive international nongovernmental organization formed to represent the mining and metals industry. The International Council on Mining and Metals (ICMM) was limited in scope, but managed to bring together all the key participants in the global non-ferrous metals industry, and it plays an active role in global policy development. Kellow argues that international business representation has been problematic because "the privileged position of business" does not easily translate to the international level. The industry has contributed to solving environmental problems and has been hard-pressed by countervailing forces. However, it is not primarily environmental movements or groups involved in development issues that have been the key adversaries of business. Many of the significant activities of these groups have represented a continuation by other means of more traditional struggles over issues like industrial relations.

Chapters 7 and 8 are devoted to conferences on global social, economic and environmental issues, and how these meetings lead to long-term or permanent forms of dialog within or outside the framework of intergovernmental organizations. At first glance, these arenas appear to be used for profiling and agenda-building purposes; on closer inspection we see that they host a potential for conflict resolution and institutional reform based on renewed dialog and negotiation.

In Chapter 6 Michelle Beyeler focuses on different types of summits that are important for the development of global public policy. The World Economic Forum (WEF) and the World Social Forum (WSF) of Porto Alegre display much variation. More than what most other sites of global governance do, including the numerous summits organizations by the United Nations and its special agencies, these forums represent two opposing discourses of neoliberalism and anti-capitalism. The chapter presents both a descriptive and an analytical interest in characterizing these discourses. First, a general overview of world conferences provides insight into the structural difference between the WEF and the WSF and compares these with the UN-centered world summits; it then presents a description of the history and development of both forums, prepares the ground for an analytical perspective on differences between, and commonalities of, both sites of the theme of global governance, and asks whether these conflicting interests also find room for cooperation and compromise in public policy.

In Chapter 7 Shannon K. Orr discusses the arena of global climate policy, with a particular emphasis on the role of business and environmental interests. The negotiations for both the United Nations Framework Convention on Climate Change and the Kyoto protocol with its follow-up negotiations involved a range of interest groups. She argues that interest groups participating in these negotiations do not just influence global policy – as is commonly assumed – but also fulfill their own diverse interests through networking, negotiating business contracts, raising the profile of their organizations, participating in protests, monitoring governments, disseminating research and establishing their own expertise. Important activities underpin the formation of alliances and policy arrangements. This chapter provides an analysis of United Nations' meetings in the field of climate policy by looking at the role of interest groups that are both recognized and integrated in the policy process and are, at the same time, using the United Nations to pursue their interests outside these forums.

Finally, Chapter 8 sums up the major findings of the book and discusses the role of different groups of countervailing powers in their exchanges with business, the sectoral variation across industries and policy fields, the use of arenas in addressing problems of major concern in business and civil society, and how these forums can be used as a platform for future cooperation. Together these experiences help us analyze where and under which circumstances public as well as private driven policy arrangements have emerged and how they may contribute to the development of global public policy, or where they fail and leave a more gloomy imprint of the new policy arrangements.

Notes

1 In the otherwise impressive work by Braithwaite and Drahos (2000), no such attempt is made.

2 The appearance of countervailing powers does not suggest the arrival of any equilibrium, but it indicates that several conflicting interests motivate the development of global public policy. Indeed, the role of states is here replaced by intergovernmental organizations that encourage the formation of relevant countervailing organizations. This is illustrated elsewhere in the introduction and in the individual chapters of this book.

3 Under the editorship of Gordon Tullock, the journal "Public Choice" started out as "Papers on Non-Market Decision Making."

4 This relationship between organizations and their environments has been applied to associations (Schmitter and Streeck 1981).

5 Braithwaite and Drahos (2000) also include the associative dimension, but their study is not designed to analyze business collective action per se.

6 As will be discussed later, another possibility of sectoral policy-making is the potential for either single corporations or industries to make policy that qualifies as public policy. In cases where multinational or transnational corporations design such innovative rule-systems, these initiatives only rarely span whole

industries. However, these studies do provide certain insights into some societal dimensions of corporate behavior.

7 When participation is through states, or restricted to states, civil society organizations can, however, deliver an important input through established channels at domestic levels. This is also accounted for in the theory on two-level games and its state-centred followers (Putnam 1988).

8 A database records the many agreements behind the partnerships, of which many come out of Johannesburg (see http://webapps.o1.un.org/dsd/partnerships/ search/browse/do).

9 Often studies on international networks include only some categories of actors and avoid others, so they do not map the total set of actors involved in a given issue. This, for instance, is the case in the study of advocacy coalitions (Sikkink 2002), and in the analysis of government networks (Slaughter 2004). A rare and interesting exception from these more limited tasks is the endeavor to include a variety of structures in global governance (Koenig-Archibugi 2002).

10 To solve the problems associated with the diamonds business in Africa, intermediary institutions have provided both information and the necessary tools to control trading with diamonds.

11 In the recent scholarly literature, partnerships or public–private partnerships, are sometimes juxtaposed to self-regulation (e.g. Pattberg 2005). In such treatises, self-regulation is understood as a pure business arrangement from which all outside participation is barred. However, self-regulation is a very complex form of regulation. Several mechanisms are in operation, sometimes including countervailing forces. In an older but still applicable piece of research, Boddewyn (1985) points to self-regulation with outside participation, and various contributions have since emphasized this feature. If we want to study current alternatives to traditional public regulation, it is essential that we recognize, reflect and build upon past achievements, yet accept demands for new concepts where new developments exhaust the old. Indeed, following the tradition of the study of self-regulation, we would in principle be able to describe and analyze all private arrangements in this study as self-regulation; however, our concept of private driven policy arrangements encompasses only cases of private regulation where a public goal is a key driver, and where, primarily, affected interests jointly design and run arrangements. This is certainly not the case with all forms of self-regulation.

References

Arts, B. (2002) " 'Green alliances' of business and NGOs. New styles of self-regulation or 'dead-end roads'," *Corporate Social Responsibility and Environmental Management*, 9: 26–36.

Ascoly, N. and Zeldenrust, I. (2002) "Working with codes: Perspectives from the clean clothes campaign," in R. Jenkins, R. Pearson and G. Seyfang (eds) *Corporate Responsibility and Labour Rights: Codes of Conduct in the Global Economy*, London: Earthscan.

Baker, G. and Chandler, D. (eds) (2005) *Global Civil Society. Contested Futures*, London and New York: Routledge.

Barnett, M. and Duvall, R. (2005) "Power in international politics," *International Organization*, 59 (1): 39–75.

Bartley, T. (2003) "Certifying forests and factories: states, social movements and the rise of private regulation in the apparel and forest products fields," *Politics & Society*, 31 (3): 433–64.

Bernauer, T. (2003) *Genes, Trade, and Regulation. The Seeds of Conflict in Food Biotechnology*, Princeton, NJ and Oxford: Princeton University Press.

Boddewyn, J. J. (1988) *Advertising Self-Regulation and Outside Participation: A Multinational Comparison*, New York: Quorum Books.

Boddewyn, J. J. and Brewer, T. (1995) "International-business political behavior: new theoretical directions," *Academy of Management Review*, 19: 119–43.

Börzel, T. A. and Risse, T. (2005) "Public–private partnerships: effective and legitimate tools of international governance?," in E. Grande and L. W. Pauly (eds) *Complex Sovereignty: On the Reconstitution of Political Authority in the 21st Century*, Toronto: University of Toronto Press.

Braithwaite, J. and Drahos, P. (2000) *Global Business Regulation*, Cambridge: Cambridge University Press.

Burns, T. (1961) "Micropolitics: mechanisms of institutional change," *Administrative Science Quarterly*, 6: 257–81.

Carpenter, C. (2001) "Businesses, green groups and the media: the role of non-governmental organizations in the climate change debate," *International Affairs*, 77 (2): 313–28.

Cashore, B., Auld, G. and Newson, D. (2004) *Governing through Markets: Forest Certification and the Emergence of Non-State Authority*, New Haven, CT: Yale University Press.

Cerny, P. (2001) "From 'iron triangles' to 'golden pentangles?' Globalizing the policy process," *Global Governance*, 7: 397–410.

Charle, C., Schriewer, J. and Wagner, P. (eds) (2004) *Transnational Intercultural Networks: Forms of Academic Knowledge and the Search for Cultural Identities*, Frankfurt: Campus.

Charnowitz, S. (1997) "Two centuries of participation: NGOs and international governance," *Michigan Journal of International Law*, 18 (2): 183–286.

Charnowitz, S. (2000) "Opening the WTO to nongovernmental interests," *Fordham International Law Journal*, 24: 173–216.

Clapp, J. (1998) "The privatization of global environmental governance: ISO 14000 and the developing world," *Global Governance*, 4: 295–316.

Clark, A. M., Friedman, E. and Hochstetler, K. (1998) "The sovereign limits of global civil society: a comparison of NGO participation in UN world conferences on the environment, human rights, and women," *World Politics*, 51 (1): 1–35.

Colas, A. (2002) *International Civil Society. Social Movements in World Politics*, Cambridge: Polity.

Coleman, W. D. (2001) "Policy networks, non-state actors and internationalized policy making: a case study of agricultural trade," in D. Josselin and W. Wallace (eds) *Non State Actors in World Politics*, London: Palgrave.

Coleman, W. D. and Perl, A. (1999) "Internationalized policy environments and policy network analysis," *Political Studies*, 47 (4): 691–709.

Coleman, W. D. and Porter, T. (2000) "International institutions, globalization and democracy: assessing the challenges," *Global Society*, 14 (3): 377–98.

Cutler, A. C. (2002) "Private international regimes and interfirm cooperation," in R. B. Hall and T. J. Biersteker (eds) *The Emergence of Private Authority in Global Governance*, Cambridge: Cambridge University Press.

Cutler, A. C. (2003) *Private Authority and International Affairs: Transnational Merchant Law in the Global Political Economy*, Cambridge: Cambridge University Press.

Cutler, A. C., Haufler, V. and Porter, T. (1999) "Private authority and international affairs," in A. C. Cutler, V. Haufler and T. Porter (eds) *Private Authority and International Affairs*, New York: State University of New York Press.

Deacon, B., Hulse, M. and Stubbs, P. (eds) (1997) *Global Social Policy – International Organizations and the Future of Welfare*, London, Thousand Oaks, New Delhi: Sage.

della Porta, D., Kriesi, H. P., and Rucht, D. (1999) *Social Movements in a Globalizing World*, New York: St. Martin's Press.

Deslauriers, J. and Kotschwar, B. (2003) "After Seattle: how NGOs are transforming the global trade and finance agenda," in J. P. Doh and H. Teegen (eds) *Globalization and NGOs: Transforming Business, Governments and Society*. New York: Praeger.

Dezalay, Y. and Sugarman, D. (eds) (1995) *Professional Competition and Professional Power. Lawyers, Accountants and the Social Construction of Markets*, London and New York: Routledge.

Drache, D. (ed.) (2001) "Introduction: the fundamentals of our time. Values and goals that are inescapably public," in D. Drache (ed.) *The Market or the Public Domain? Global Governance and the Asymmetry of Power*, London and New York: Routledge.

Doh, J. (2003) "Nongovernmental organizations: corporate strategy, and public policy: NGOs as agents of change," in J. P. Doh and H. Teegen (eds) *Globalization and NGOs. Transforming Business, Government, and Society*, Westport and London: Praeger.

Doh, J. P. and Teegen, H. (eds) (2003) *Globalization and NGOs. Transforming Business, Government, and Society*, Westport and London: Praeger.

Domask, J. (2003). "From boycotts to global partnership: NGOs, the private sector, and the struggle to protect the world's forests," in J. P. Doh and H. Teegen (eds) *Globalization and NGOs. Transforming Business, Government, and Society*, Westport and London: Praeger.

Edwards, M. and Gaventa, J. (eds) (2002) *Global Citizen Action*, Boulder, CO: Lynne Rienner.

Eschle, C. and Maiguascha, B. (2005) "Introduction," in C. Eschle and B. Maiguascha (eds) *Critical Theories, International Relations and "The Anti-Globalization Movement". The Politics of Global Resistance*, London and New York: Routledge.

Falkner, R. (2003) "Private environmental governance: exploring the links," *Global Environmental Politics*, 3: 72–87.

Fiorini, A. M. (2000) *The Third Force. The Rise of Transnational Civil Society*, Tokyo and Washington, DC: Japan Center for International Exchange and Carnegie Endowment for International Peace.

Fisher, W. F. and Ponniah, T. (eds) (2003) *Another World is Possible: Popular Alternatives to Globalization at the World Social Forum*, London: Zed Books.

Fox, J. A. and Brown, L. D. (eds) (1998) *The Struggle for Accountability: The World Bank, NGOs, and Grassroots Movements*, Boston, MA: MIT Press.

Fuchs, D. (2005) "Commanding heights? The strength and fragility of business power in global politics," *Millennium*, 22 (3): 787–824.

Galbraith, J. K. (1952) *American Capitalism. The Concept of Countervailing Power*, Boston, MA: Houghton Mifflin.

Glasbergen, P. (ed.) (1998) *Co-operative Environmental Governance: Public–Private Agreements as a Policy Strategy*, Dordrecht: Kluwer.

Grose, R. (ed.) (2005) *International Business and Government Relations in the 21st Century*, Cambridge: Cambridge University Press.

Guidry, J. A., Kennedy, M. D. and Zald, M. N. (eds) (2000) *Globalization and Social Movements: Culture, Power, and the Transnational Public Sphere*, Ann Arbor, MI: University of Michigan Press.

Haas, P. M. (1992) "Introduction: epistemic communities and international policy coordination," *International Organization*, 46: 1–36.

Hall, R. B. and Biersteker, T. J. (eds) (2002) *The Emergence of Private Authority in Global Governance*, Cambridge: Cambridge University Press.

Harrod, J. and O'Brien, R. (eds) (2002) *Globalizing Unions? Theory and Strategies of Organized Labor in the Global Political Economy*, London and New York: Routledge.

Hasenclever, A., Mayer, P. and Rittberger, V. (eds) (1997) *Theories of International Regimes*, Cambridge: Cambridge University Press.

Haufler, V. (1993) "Crossing the boundary between public and private: international regimes and non-state actors," in V. Rittberger and P. Mayer (eds) *Regime Theory and International Relations*, Oxford: Clarendon Press.

Haufler, V. (2002) *A Public Role for the Private Sector: Industry Self-Regulation in a Global Economy*, Washington, DC: Carnegie Endowment for International Peace.

Haworth, N., Hughes, S. and Wilkinson, R. (2005) "The international labor standards regime: a case study in global regulation," *Environment and Planning*: A., 37 (11), Nov.: 1939–53.

Held, D. and McGrew, A. (eds) (2002) *Globalization/Anti-Globalization*, Cambridge: Polity.

Hemmati, M., Dodds, F., Enayati, J. and McHarry, J. (2002) *Multi-Stakeholder Processes for Governance and Sustainability. Beyond Deadlock and Conflict*, London: Earthscan.

Hodess, R. (2001) "The contested competence of business and NGOs in public life," in Drache, D. (ed.) *The Market or the Public Domain? Global Governance and the Asymmetry of Power*, London and New York: Routledge.

Hollingsworth, J. R., Schmitter, P. C. and Streeck, W. (eds) (1994) *Governing Capitalist Economies: Performance and Control of Economic Sectors*, Oxford: Oxford University Press.

Houtart, F. and Polet, F. (eds) (2001) *The Other Davos: The Globalization of Resistance to the World Economic System*, London: Zed Books.

Hurrell, A. and Kingsbury, B. (eds) (1992) *The International Politics of the Environment: Actors, Interests and Institutions*, Oxford: Clarendon.

Jenkins, R., Pearson, R. and Seyfang, G. (eds) (2002) *Corporate Responsibility and Labour Rights: Codes of Conduct in the Global Economy*, London: Earthscan.

Jordana, J. and Levi-Faur, D. (2004) "The politics of regulation in the age of governance," in J. Jordana and D. Levi-Faur (eds) *The Politics of Regulation. Institutions and Regulatory Reforms for the Age of Governance*, Cheltenham and Northampton: Edward Elgar.

Josselin, D. and Wallace, W. (eds) (2001) *Non-State Actors in World Politics*, London: Palgrave.

Kaul, I. (2001) "Public goods: taking the concept into the 21st century," in D. Drache (ed.) *The Market or the Public Domain? Global Governance and the Asymmetry of Power*, London and New York: Routledge.

Keck, M. E. and Sikkink, K. (1998) *Activists Beyond Borders. Advocacy Networks in International Politics*, Ithaca, NY and London: Cornell University Press.

Kellow, A. (2002) "Comparing business and public interest associability at the international level," *International Political Science Review*, 23 (2): 175–86.

Khagram, S., Riker, J. V. and Sikkink, K. (eds) (2002) *Restructuring World Politics. Transnational Social Movements, Networks, and Norms*, Minneapolis, MN: University of Minnesota Press.

Kline, J. M. (1985) *International Codes and Multinational Business: Setting Guidelines for International Business Operations*, Westport: Quorum.

Koenig-Archibugi, M. (2002) "Mapping global governance," in D. Held and A. McGrew (eds) *Governing Globalization. Power, Authority and Global Governance*, Cambridge: Polity.

Krasner, S. (1983) *International Regimes*, Ithaca, NY and London: Cornell University Press.

Levi-Faur, D. (2004) "Comparative research design in the study of regulation: how to increase the number of cases without compromising the strengths of case-oriented analysis," in J. Jordana and D. Levi-Faur (eds) *The Politics of Regulation. Institutions and Regulatory Reforms for the Age of Governance*, Cheltenham and Northampton: Edward Elgar.

Levi-Faur, D. and Jordana, J. (eds) (2005) *The Rise of Regulatory Capitalism: The Global Diffusion of a New Order, The Annals of the American Academy of Political and Social Science*, vol. 598, March 2005.

Levy, M. A., Young, O. R. and Zürn, M. (1995) "The study of international regimes", *European Journal of International Relations*, 3 (1): 267–330.

Lober, D. J. (1997) "Explaining the formation of business-environmentalist collaborations: collaborative windows and the Paper Task Force," *Policy Sciences*, 30: 1–24.

McCaughey, M. and Ayers, M. D. (eds) (2003) *Cyberactivism. Online Activism in Theory and Practice*, New York and London: Routledge.

Martens, K. (1999) "The role of NGOs in the UNESCO system," *Transnational Associations*, 2 (99): 68–82.

Martinelli, A. (ed.) (1991) *International Markets and Global Firms. A Comparative Study of Organized Business in the Chemical Industry*, London, Newbury Park, New Delhi: Sage.

Mason, M. (2002) "Representing transnational interests: new opportunities for non-governmental access to the World Trade Organization," *Environmental Politics*, 13 (3): 566–89.

Mueller, M. L. (2002) *Ruling the Root: Internet Governance and the Taming of the Cyberspace*, Boston, MA: The MIT Press.

Nelson, P. J. (2002) "Agendas, accountability, and legitimacy among transnational networks lobbying the World Bank," in S. Khagram, J. V. Riker and K. Sikkink (eds) (2002) *Restructuring World Politics. Transnational Social Movements, Networks, and Norms*, Minneapolis, MN: University of Minnesota Press.

Noelke, A. (2004) "Transnational private authority and corporate governance," in S. A. Schirm (ed.) *New Rules for Global Markets. Public and Private Governance in the World Economy*, London: Palgrave.

O'Brien, R. (2002) "The varied paths to minimum global labour standards," in J. Harrod and R. O'Brien (eds) *Theory and Strategies of Organized Labour in the Global Political Economy*, London and New York: Routledge.

O'Brien, R., Goetz, A. M., Scholte, J. A. and Williams, M. (2000) *Contesting Global Governance: Multilateral Economic Institutions and Global Social Movements*, Cambridge: Cambridge University Press.

Olson, M. (1965) *The Logic of Collective Action: Public Goods and the Theory of Groups*, Cambridge, MA: Harvard University Press.

O'Rourke, D. (2003) "Outsourcing regulation: analyzing nongovernmental systems of labor standards and monitoring," *Policy Studies Journal*, 31: 1–29.

Ottaway, M. (2001) "Corporatism goes global: international organizations, nongovernmental organization networks and transnational business," *Global Governance*, 7 (3): 265–92.

Parker, A. R. (2003) "Prospects for NGO collaboration with multinational enterprises," in, J. P. Doh and H. Teegen (eds) (2003) *Globalization and NGOs. Transforming Business, Government, and Society*, Westport and London: Praeger.

Pattberg, P. (2005) "The institutionalization of private governance: how business and nonprofit organizations agree on transnational rules," *Governance*, 18 (4): 589–610.

Piciotto, S. and Mayne, R. (eds) (1999) *Regulating International Business: Beyond Liberalization*, London: Macmillan.

Porter, T. (2005) *Globalization and Finance*, Cambridge: Polity.

Potoski, M. and Prakash, A. (2005) "Green clubs and voluntary governance: ISO 14001 and firms' regulatory compliance," *American Journal of Political Science*, 49 (2): 235–48.

Prakash, A. (2000) *Greening the Firm. The Politics of Corporate Environmentalism*, Cambridge: Cambridge University Press.

Putnam, R. D. (1988) "Diplomacy and domestic politics: the logic of two-level games," *International Organization*, 42 (3): 427–60.

Reinicke, W. H. (1998) *Global Public Policy. Governing without Government?*, Washington, DC: Brookings Institution Press.

Ritterger, V. and Zangl, B. (2006) *International Organization. Polity, Politics and Policies*, London: Palgrave.

Ronit, K. (2006) "International governance by organized business – the shifting roles of firms, associations and intergovernmental organizations in self-regulation." in W. Streeck, J. R. Grote, V. Schneider and J. Visser (eds) (2006) *Governing Interests: Business Associations Facing Internationalization*, London and New York: Routledge.

Ronit, K. and Schneider, V. (eds) (2000) *Private Organizations in Global Politics*, London and New York: Routledge.

Rosenau, J. N. (2003) *Distant Proximities. Dynamics Beyond Globalization*, Princeton, NJ and Oxford: Princeton University Press.

Rosenau, P. V. (ed.) (2000) *Public-Private Policy Partnerships*, Cambridge: The MIT Press.

Sabatier, P. A. (ed.) (1999) *Theories of the Policy Process*, Boulder, CO: Westview Press.

Schechter, M. G. (2005) *United Nations Global Conferences*, London and New York: Routledge.

Schirm, S. A. (ed.) (2004) *New Rules for Global Markets. Public and Private Governance in the World Economy*, London: Palgrave.

Schmitter, P. C. (2002) "Participation in governance arrangements: Is there any reason to expect it will achieve 'sustainable and innovative policies in a multi-level context?',*" in J. R. Grote and B. Gbipki (eds) *Participatory Governance. Political and Societal Implications*, Opladen: Leske and Budrich.

Schmitter, P. C. and Streeck, W. (1981) *The Organization of Business Interests. A Research Design to Study the Associative Action of Business in the Advanced Industrial Societies of Western Europe*, IIM/LMP 81 – 13, Berlin: International Institute of Management.

Schneider, V. and Hyner, D. (2005) "Security in cyberspace: governance and transnational policy networks," in M. Koenig-Archibugi and M. Zürn (eds) *New Modes of Governance in the Global System: Explaining Publicness, Delegation, and Inclusiveness*, London: Palgrave.

Scholte, J. A. and Schnabel, A. (eds) (2002) *Civil Society and Global Finance*, London and New York: Routledge.

Sell, S. K. (2003) *Private Power, Public Law. The Globalization of Intellectual Property Rights*, Cambridge: Cambridge University Press.

Seyfang, G. (2003) "Environmental mega-conferences – from Stockholm to Johannesburg and beyond," *Global Environmental Change*, 13: 223–28.

Sikkink, K. (2002) "Restructuring world politics: the limits and asymmetries of soft power," in S. Khagram, J. V. Riker and K. Sikkink (eds) *Restructuring World Politics. Transnational Social Movements, Networks, and Norms*, Minneapolis, MN: University of Minnesota Press.

Sinclair, T. J. (1999) "Bond-rating agencies and coordination in the global political economy," in A. C. Cutler, V. Haufler and T. Porter (eds) *Private Authority and International Affairs*, New York: State University of New York Press.

Skjelsbaek, K. (1971) "The growth of international nongovernmental organization in the twentieth century," in R. O. Keohane and J. S. Nye (eds) *Transnational Relations and World Politics*, Cambridge, MA: Harvard University Press.

Slaughter, A. M. (2004) *A New World Order*, Princeton and Oxford: Princeton University Press.

Smith, J. and Johnston, H. (eds) (2002) *Globalization and Resistance. Transnational Dimensions of Social Movements*, Lanham, MD: Rowman & Littlefield.

Smith, J., Chatfield, C. and Pagnusco, R. (1997) *Transnational Social Movements and Global Politics. Solidarity Beyond the State*, New York: Syracuse University Press.

Stone, D. (2004) "Transfer agents and global networks in the 'transnationalization' of policy," *Journal of European Public Policy*, 11: 545–66.

Strange, S. and Stopford, J. (1991) *Rival States, Rival Firms*, Cambridge: Cambridge University Press.

Streeck, W. and Schmitter, P. C. (1985) "Community, market, state – and associations? The prospective contribution of interest governance to social order," in W. Streeck and P. C. Schmitter (eds) *Private Interest Government. Beyond Market and State*, London, Beverly Hills, New Delhi: Sage.

Streeck, W., Grote, J. R., Schneider, V. and Visser, J. (eds) (2006) *Governing Interests: Business Associations Facing Internationalization*, London and New York: Routledge.

Tatenhove, J. van, Arts, B. and Leroy, P. (eds) *Political Modernization and the Environment: The Renewal of Environmental Policy Arrangements*, Dordrecht: Kluwer.

Teegen, H. and J. P. Doh (2003) "Conclusion: globalization and the future of NGO influence," in J. P. Doh and H. Teegen (eds) (2003) *Globalization and NGOs. Transforming Business, Government, and Society*, Westport and London: Praeger.

Willets, P. (1989) "The patterns of conferences," in P. Taylor and A. J. R. Groom (eds) *Global Issues in the United Nations Framework*, New York: St. Martins Press.

Willetts, P. (ed.) (1996) *"The Conscience of the World"*. *The Influence of Non-Governmental Organizations in the UN System*, London: Hurst and Company.

Willetts, P. (2000) "Representation of private organizations in the global diplomacy of economic policy-making," in K. Ronit and V. Schneider (eds) *Private Organizations in Global Politics*, London and New York: Routledge.

Young, O. (1989) *International Cooperation. Building Regimes for Natural Resources and the Environment*, Ithaca and London: Cornell University Press.

Zacher, M. W. and Sutton, B. A. (1996) *Governing Global Networks: International Regimes for Transportation and Communications*, Cambridge: Cambridge University Press.

2 Labour and business on a global scale

Alex Diceanu and Robert O'Brien

Introduction

Business and labour groups are engaged in a never ending struggle over the distribution of profits and conditions of work. As economic activity has increasingly globalized over the past thirty years, so has the struggle between labour and business. Transnational businesses based in the developed world have been increasingly successful in pushing for global reregulation putting labour on the defensive worldwide. This chapter focuses upon one aspect of that contest – efforts to influence global policy arrangements in the area of labour rights and working conditions. The struggle over global policy arrangements takes places in two key spheres – interstate (negotiated between states) and in the global economy (mixture of firms, industries, and civic associations including labour). This chapter argues that business strategy has been to enshrine corporate rights in the interstate sphere while relegating social and labour rights to the private economic sphere. This business advocated form of 'selective regulation' has enjoyed considerable success, but its status remains contested.

This chapter is divided into four sections. The first section discusses key concepts that clarify the contest between labour and business over global policy arrangements. The second section reviews the structure of selective regulation in the interstate arena. The third section focuses on the attempt to develop and contest mechanisms of private authority in the global economy arena. The conclusion argues that global policy arrangements surrounding labour rights are fluid and unstable because the two main actors continue to advocate rival policy prescriptions.

Key concepts

There are a number of key concepts that help us understand labour's engagement with business in the field of global policy arrangements. This chapter draws upon the concepts of countervailing power, double movement, social movements, policy politics triangle (supremacy, contestation, and hegemony), selective regulation, and private authority. The first three concepts refer to different approaches to understanding the relationship between contending social forces (countervailing power, double movement, and social movement), the policy politics triangle differentiates conditions in battle for ideas (supremacy, contest, or hegemony) while the final two terms (selective regulation and private authority) refer to modes of regulation.

Let us begin with three possible approaches to understanding the relationship between the social forces represented by business associations and labour unions. One approach, the starting point for this book, is the idea of countervailing power. John Kenneth Galbraith (1952) developed his theory of countervailing power as a critique and a supplement to liberal economic theories of power. The liberal view was that concentrations of economic power were eroded by competition between sellers. The power of dominant firms would be undermined by the activity of its rivals. Galbraith argued that while this was true in some cases, in many other cases economic power was held in check by the development of countervailing power by other actors. Concentration of economic power leads other actors to take action to dilute that power. For example, suppliers might organize against retailers or workers against employers.

With regard to labour, Galbraith argued that the most advanced labour organizations would be found in industries where there was the greatest concentration of power. Powerful large corporations brought into existence powerful labour unions. Galbraith argued that the concentration of power in, for instance, the steel industry brought forth the United Steel Workers. In contrast, industries which lacked large employers, such as agriculture, would also lack unions. In retrospect, the deterministic aspects of Galbraith's arguments are not very persuasive. They certainly do not map on to today's union structures. Large concentrations of economic power still exist in the United States, but unionization rates have plummeted to only 8 per cent in the private sector. Unions have been on the defensive for the past thirty years and are nearly extinct in many parts of the United States. Industry structure does not automatically call forth a successful union response. Concentration of power may provide a motivation for labour activity, but does not ensure its development.

Galbraith's argument echoes the now often quoted work of Karl Polanyi. Polanyi (1957) argued that marketization of societies led people to take steps to protect themselves from the devastation wrought by liberal economic forces. In his view, the rise of Fascism, Communism, and the New Deal were all responses by societies against the ravages of the market. Some observers have suggested that recent moves to spread neoliberal forms of globalization have brought forth similar social upheaval and moves to self-defence in the form of the global justice movement (Gill 2000).

Both Galbraith and Polanyi's theories offer interesting insights into why labour might be motivated to respond to changed economic structures, but they are too deterministic in predicting successful social responses to corporate and market power. Rather than being an automatic or inevitable process, labour influence is highly contingent upon the action of labour groups themselves and the nature of the obstacles they face.

While deterministic perspectives might suggest that there is an inevitable following of labour regulation after capital, social movement literature argues that movements and groups of civic associations have a large role in influencing their own success or failure. In his text *Power in Movement*, Tarrow (1998) argues that external opportunities and constraints shape the field of operation for social movements, but their ability to employ a repertoire of collective action, forge or frame an identity, and create structures for mobilization, heavily influence social movement outcomes. For example, social movement studies chronicling the demise of the Knights of Labour in the United States in the nineteenth century demonstrated how labour groups were undermined both by their own shortcomings and the immense economic and state power of their corporate antagonists (Voss 1999).

This chapter combines the insights of Galbraith, Polanyi and Tarrow by suggesting that while structural factors may provide incentives for labour organizations to tackle business inspired policy arrangements on a global scale, the success of such challenges is highly contingent.

Turning our attention to forms of regulation, two concepts are particularly useful. The first is selective regulation and the second is private authority. Selective regulation refers to a system of interstate regulation which entails elaborate mechanisms and enforcement procedure for corporate rights and weak or non-existent mechanisms for social rights (O'Brien 1998). It is public economic regulation, but only in selective areas. A good example is the World Trade Organization's (WTO) strict enforcement of intellectual property rights on behalf of transnational corporations (TNCs) (Sell 2003) and its lack of jurisdiction over labour standards. While economic globalization requires increased regulation to create and maintain the rules of the global marketplace, the goal of business is to shape that regulation so it furthers corporate rights but does not strengthen the rights of other non-state actors such as labour unions or civic associations.

The concept of private authority captures the state of affairs where firms exercise decision-making power over a particular issue area and this activity is viewed as legitimate by other actors, such as the state. It entails both the 'the capacity to set standards recognized and adhered to by others' (institutional market authority) and 'acceptance of market-based decision-making' (normative market authority) (Biersteker and Hall 2002: 218). Mechanisms for exercising private authority include: industry norms, coordination service firms (e.g. bond rating), production alliances, cartels, business associations, and private regimes (Cutler *et al.* 1999). Studies of the telecommunications industry, insurance business, accountancy, and cartels supports the notion of private authority (Strange 1996). With regard to labour standards the goal of TNCs is to have this issue dealt with in the realm of private authority rather than by states.

In terms of the political and intellectual struggle over policy arrangements it is helpful to think of a policy politics triangle. One point of the triangle represents supremacy, a second, contestation, and a third, hegemony. Policy arrangements that are the expression of supremacy are those that are imposed without negotiation and with little concern about opposing views. Particular actors are so powerful that they can simply impose their preferred options upon other elements of society (Gill 1995). An example is the liberal restructuring adopted by much of the developing world in the wake of the 1980s debt crisis. An environment where rival groups espouse conflicting policy options and there is no mechanism for resolving these differences is one of contestation. The ongoing debate about public access to lifesaving drugs versus the intellectual property rights of pharmaceutical companies is an example. A third possibility is that of hegemony. In this state, dominant actors have been able to persuade others that the policies they propose are in the general interest rather than in the specific interest of those who propose them (Cox 1983). Dominant actors secure the consent of others to policy arrangements. The trade and financial arrangements which governed international economic relations between Western state from the end of the Second World War until the early 1970s is an example of US hegemony (Figure 2.1).

The applicability of these concepts to business–labour policy arrangements on a global scale is that we have witnessed a shift from the politics of supremacy in the 1980s and to an era of contestation in the mid-to-late 1990s to an effort of creating a new hegemony in the twenty-first century. The content of the supremacist era was neoliberal restructuring which denied any corporate accountability for social ills. The era of contestation was, and is, characterized by a vigorous resistance by social and labour groups to neoliberal principles and practices. The effort to create a new consensus and hegemony focuses upon creating a system of selective regulation which pushes labour rights and social issues into the arena of private authority. Labour groups have been strong enough to resist

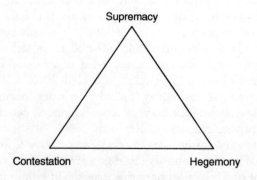

Figure 2.1 Policy politics triangle.

corporate supremacy, but are unable to advance an alternative and are in danger of succumbing to a selective regulation hegemony. The result is a volatile and unstable set of global policy arrangements regulating work and employment.

The following two sections of the chapter examine these trends by focusing upon the global policy arrangements in two spheres – the interstate and the global economy. It argues that interstate agreements have been marked by a proliferation of voluntary mechanisms at the same time that private arrangements to deal with labour issues have greatly expanded greatly. Private arrangements now overshadow state efforts and may become the basis of a new hegemony of selective regulation.

Selective regulation in the interstate arena sphere

The liberalization and transnationalization of economic activity has resulted in the growth of international economic regulation. Contrary to neoliberal visions of less regulation, increased international exchange necessitates explicit formulation and enforcement of rules to govern market activity. The goal from a business perspective has been to foster regulation which protects corporate rights while avoiding or weakening regulation which advances the interests of other economic groups, such as labour. This section reviews the ongoing contest.

The struggle over labour regulation in the interstate sphere is taking place primarily on two levels. One is the multilateral level which includes organizations with near universal state membership such as the International Labour Organization (ILO) and the World Trade Organization (WTO). Within this sphere there is a range of interest representation. Many interstate organizations such as the WTO only provide for state representation. However, some organizations such as the ILO provide for formal representation of other interests such as business and labour in their operational and governing structures. A second level is the regional level where economic agreements among a smaller number of states such as the European Union or the North American Free Trade Agreement (NAFTA) may or may not address labour issues.[1]

Multilateral level

The issue of multilateral regulation of labour standards re-emerged on the international agenda with the creation of the WTO and its first ministerial meeting in 1995. Prior to that date, trade relations had been overseen by the General Agreement on Tariffs and Trade (GATT) and labour standards issues were chiefly confined to the ILO. The WTO's creation was significant because the new institution's scope and depth greatly exceeded its predecessor. The WTO had a greater scope in that it brought in new areas of economic activity such as services and intellectual property rights. Its depth was enhanced because a new dispute settlement mechanism held out the promise of successfully enforcing the institution's rules amongst states.

As a result of its new prominence the WTO became the arena for intense corporate and labour activity. Northern TNCs scored a major victory when they were able to have the WTO take over enforcement of intellectual property rights from the World Intellectual Property Organization (WIPO). Labour lobbied to have the WTO enforce labour standards as well. In the run up to the first meeting of WTO ministers in Singapore in 1995 the International Confederation of Free Trade Unions (ICFTU) argued that the WTO should incorporate a social clause into its mandate. The social clause would commit members to ILO conventions on core labour rights: 87 and 98 on freedom of association and the right to bargain collectively; 29 and 105 on the abolition of forced labour; 111 and 100 on the prevention of discrimination in employment and equal pay for work of equal value; and 138 on the minimum age for employment (prohibition of child labour). Violation of these standards in export industries would result in sanctions in the same way that violation of intellectual property rights triggers investigation, hearings, and sanctions.

A coalition of business groups, neoliberal, and authoritarian states in the North and the South blocked any linkage of trade and labour standards (O'Brien *et al.* 2000). The enforcement power of the WTO's dispute settlement mechanism was guarded for serving the interests of corporations and states. While the WTO and its members offered rhetorical support for labour standards, they indicated that the issue should be confined to the operation of the ILO. The ICFTU's fallback position has been to argue that the WTO should strike a working group to examine the relationship between trade and labour standards (ICFTU 2005). The hope is that this could evolve into some further movement on the labour issue in the future.

Keeping labour issues out of the WTO focused attention on the rather moribund ILO. States were eager to demonstrate that they could do something to advance labour interests in response to public protests about the WTO. Business groups were interested in using the ILO to fend off mandatory regulation, while labour groups jumped at the chance to put some life back into an international organization in which they had a formal role and voice. The ILO initiated four steps to reassert its prominence in the labour rights field. First, the ILO bundled the core labour rights into a new binding Declaration which applied to all states. The 1998 *Declaration on Fundamental Principles and Rights at Work* committed all member states to respect and promote ILO conventions in four key areas: freedom of association and collective bargaining; the elimination of forced or compulsory labour; the abolition of child labour, and the elimination of discrimination in employment (ILO 1998). Second, the ILO broadened its policy agenda by adopting the rhetoric of 'Decent Work' (ILO 2005). Decent work covers areas such as fair incomes, employment security, social protection, social integration, freedom to express views and organize, and equality of opportunity and treatment for all women and men. It allows the ILO to address issues of informal employment as well as broad policy debates around social security and public policy.

As a third step the ILO tried to influence the global public discourse on labour and globalization issues through the appointment of a high profile international commission. In 2002 the ILO drew on the services of twenty-six high profile people from government, business, labour, and academic fields to create the World Commission on the Social Dimension of Globalization (WCSDG). Business leaders participating in the Commission included a Vice Chair of Rand Corporation, Chair of the Board of Toshiba, and President of the International Organisation of Employers (IOE). Organized labour had two Commissioners, the President of the AFL – CIO and the General Secretary of the Congress of South African Trade Unions (COSATU). Other non-state interests had voices on the Commission through the participation of prominent parliamentarians, academics, and social activists. The Commission's report did not challenge the general trend of existing globalization, but it did highlight problems in global economic governance and called for changes to ensure more equitable development (ILO 2004). Similar to the UN's Millennium Development Goals, the ILO Commission was an effort to shift the economic agenda and focus attention on poverty and development.

Fourth, the ILO attempted to influence the policy of the major international economic institutions. Although the ILO had been an integral part of planning for the post-1945 international economic architecture it had become increasingly marginalized compared with the International Monetary Fund (IMF), World Bank (IBRD), and World Trade Organization (WTO) (Wilkinson 2002). These later institutions had been pushing policy prescriptions that had serious labour market implications since the 1980s, but the ILO was not a player in the formulation or implementation of those institution's policies. In response to this lack of communication and protest from civil society groups, including labour, the ILO established formal inter-institutional channels of communication with the financial institutions and attempted to participate in their activities. In terms of policy, the ILO is attempting to influence other organizations' view on labour related subjects. For example, the ILO has tried to influence the content of Poverty Reduction Strategy Papers used by the World Bank and IMF to determine loans to heavily indebted countries (ILO 2002).

While this activity has raised the profile of the ILO and influenced discussion about labour issues and globalization, the ILO remains a body which must rely upon force of argument rather than legal enforcement or financial incentive. Despite its active agenda, the ILO faces an uphill struggle in markets structured to value profit over worker protection.

Another response came from the Organization for Economic Cooperation and Development (OECD). The OECD is a club of advanced industrialized nations (Japan, the United States, Canada, West European states) which has given selective access to a few newly industrializing countries (Mexico, Korea). Its role is to provide policy advice to governments. In response to the issue at the WTO and in member states the OECD reinvigorated its *Guidelines for Multinationals*. These guidelines had originally been developed in the 1970s as TNCs and Western states sought to pre-empt the emergence of tougher, enforceable regulations being developed by the UN Commission on Transnational Corporations (UNTNC) (Rowe 2005). The resulting guidelines were indeed ineffective, but their weakness left the OECD exposed when the issue of labour standards and social rights exploded onto the international agenda in the 1990s.

In an attempt to once again make itself relevant on labour issues the OECD revised its guidelines in 2000. The major change was that OECD states were obliged to establish national contact points (NCPs) which would allow interested parties to air disputes. NCPs may be located in government departments or consist of government–civic association bodies. Workers in a country where a TNC is operating can lodge a complaint with the NCP in the company's home country. For example, Sri Lankan workers could make a case against a South Korean TNC in Seoul. This form of transborder attempt at accountability is potentially significant, but is undermined by the voluntary nature of the guidelines and the diversity of interest in NCPs across states. A NCP in France is more likely to exert pressure upon French companies than an NCP in Korea because the French state is more open to labour's influence than the Korean state. Although NCPs are mandatory, the guidelines themselves are still voluntary. The result is that the OECD revised guidelines join a long list of instruments for pressuring TNCs, but steer away from enforcing good behaviour (Bohmer 2004).

Another initiative sponsored by an interstate organization is the Global Compact (UN 2005). It was developed by the Secretary General's office of the United Nations in consultation with business and civic groups (including labour). The compact now includes six UN agencies – The United Nations High Commission on Human Rights (UNHCHR), the United Nations Environment Programme (UNEP), the International Labour Organization (ILO), the United Nations Development Programme (UNDP), the United Nations Industrial Development Organization (UNIDO), and the United Nations Office on Drugs and Crime (UNODC). It also includes numerous business associations (e.g. International Chamber of Commerce (ICC) and International Organisation of Employers (IOE), over 2300 corporate participants (e.g. BP, De Beers, Rio Tinto, etc.) some trade union confederations (e.g. ICFTU) and numerous civic associations (e.g. World Wide Fund for Nature (WWF) and Oxfam). While corporations have signed up by the thousands, labour's response has been much more hesitant. For example, only three of the 3 of 10 international industrial union federations or Global Union Federations (GUFs) are members. This reflects scepticism in some labour quarters about the utility of such voluntary measures.

The compact asks corporations to incorporate nine principles drawn from the *Universal Declaration of Human Rights*, the *ILO's Fundamental Principles on Rights at Work* and the *Rio Principles on Environment and Development* into their corporate practices. The compact does not monitor corporate practice nor does it assess corporate performance. It is designed to identify and disseminate good practices. The Global Compact asks leaders of some of the world's most prominent corporations (including many with battered reputations for social rights) to publicly commit themselves to good labour and environmental practices.

The compact's significance lies in a number of areas. First, it moves beyond interstate arrangements by bringing in corporate and civic actors to advance global policy arrangements in the field of labour and environmental rights. This creates a hybrid structure of private and public authority. Second, it is a voluntary agreement with no enforcement mechanisms. The hope is that corporations will live up to the key principles out of enlightened self-interest. A third relevant point is that the fact that key actors felt something like the Global Compact was needed highlights the failure of other institutions such as the ILO and the WTO to adequately address labour rights issues.

The business community through organizations such as the International Chamber of Commerce has been successful in maintaining the voluntary nature of labour regulation in both the *OECD Guidelines* and the Global Compact (Bruno and Karliner 2002; Rowe 2005). Official documents even deny that these are regulatory instruments. For example, the OECD comments that the UN's Global Compact 'is not a regulatory instrument – it does not "police," enforce or judge the behaviour of companies – it relies on public accountability, transparency, and the enlightened self-interest of companies…' (OECD: 2005: 6). The *OECD Guidelines* have a bit more of a regulatory flavour through the national contact points, but implementation is at the pleasure of individual states. There is no transnational oversight – each state may choose to develop NCPs or let them languish. States have signed on to or encouraged the proliferation of voluntary regulation which leaves compliance largely in the hands of private interests.

Regional level

At the same time that multilateral regulatory structures are responding to labour issues, regional integration initiatives also confront the same topic. Indeed it is possible that global practice on labour issues may conform to a series of regional agreements. In many cases they responded in similar ways. For example, in the Asia Pacific Economic Cooperation (APEC) mechanism labour rights were simply ignored. While labour issues have gradually crept on to APEC's agenda they have been under the auspices of human resource management (Haworth and Hughes 2002).

An alternative strategy of pre-empting regional and/or global regulation is to rely upon national enforcement of national standards. This is the strategy adopted in North America's economic constitution. In response to public criticism over the terms of NAFTA in the United States, labour and environmental side accords were added to the agreement. The North American Agreement on Labour Cooperation (NAALC) was particularly weak in two areas. First, rather than harmonizing standards upward along continental standards, it simply urged the three signatories (Canada, the United States, and Mexico) to faithfully apply existing laws. Second, the scope of issues in which governments may be fined is very limited. Relevant violations are confined to the issues of minimum wage, child labour, and health and safety. The core labour rights of freedom of association, collective bargaining, and freedom from discrimination are not covered by this 'hard law' section of the agreement (Compa 2001). States must be shown to have tolerated a persistent pattern of failing to enforce regulation in these areas. While the NAALC has stimulated substantial cross border union activity, its limited legal and practical impact pales in comparison to the corporate rights enshrined in NAFTA (Ayers 2004). The most dramatic of these is 'chapter 11' which gives corporations the right to sue member governments in the event that public policy initiatives threaten corporate profits!

European integration has always contained a more social democratic and explicitly political element than other integration projects, but progress on labour issues still faces large obstacles. The rejuvenation of the European project in the mid-1980s centreed around the liberalization of economic activity required to build a single market. The strict deflationary discipline of the Mastricht Treaty and implementation of intrusive national requirements for monetary union contrast with a EU Social Protocol which left national regulation of labour affairs largely intact (Stevis 2002). Social directives on parental leave, part-time, and contract work have made some progress while the major development was the initiation of European Works Councils (EWCs) (Wills 2004). The EWC Directive of 1994 required that all companies of more than 1000 employers that had at least 150 located in more than one country must establish a forum for consulting employees across Europe. These forums have enjoyed different rates of success. While they have provided workers with a chance to communicate with each other and gain information, they are a long distance from facilitating transnational collective bargaining.

While European workers feel the pressure for labour deregulation at the national level and defences at the regional level have been meagre, multilateral regulation continues to pose a threat. For example, when EU bureaucrats, in the wake of the Enron scandal, proposed that corporate social responsibility (CSR) should be pursued through EU regulations, the European Round Table of Industrialists (ERT) and the Union of Industries of the European Community (UNICE) both argued that such regulation was unnecessary given the existence of global initiatives such as the Global Compact and the *OECD Guidelines* (along with the ILO Tripartite Declaration) (Greenwood 2003). It is thus possible that weak global policy arrangements can be used as an excuse for not taking policy initiatives at the national or regional level.

In general, attempts at securing labour rights in a global context through interstate enforcement mechanisms have been successfully repulsed. The effort to link labour rights with WTO enforcement has been defeated. The voluntary approach of the ILO has been replicated in the *OECD Guidelines*, Global Compact and in regional agreements. Labour groups have not given up the interstate option, but attention has increasingly shifted to dealing with the private regulation of labour standards. This regulation may or may not involve trade unions depending upon its form.

Privatizing labour standards and the struggle for hegemony

Non-state or private-based mechanisms for dealing with labour conditions have taken on increased significance in recent years. Corporations have advanced their own private solutions to pre-empt public state regulation while labour groups have tried to make use of such mechanisms as stepping stones to state regulation. The goal from the corporate view is to prevent public authorities from enacting rules which would force compliance with labour codes. This section examines corporate initiatives and labour's response.

The corporate initiative

The response by most corporate leaders to an upsurge in public interest in labour standards and labour rights has been to argue that such concerns are best addressed within the private economic sphere through self-regulation. Self-regulation refers to corporations setting and monitoring their own rules. This could take place either through the actions of an individual corporation or through the activities of business associations in a particular sector. The strategy has been to relieve the state of a labour enforcement role by privatizing labour standards.

The concept and practice of Corporate Social Responsibility (CSR) has been the primary rejoinder to those arguing for state-based regulation. The European Commission provides a useful definition of CSR as a concept 'whereby companies integrate social and environmental concerns in their business operations and in their interaction with stakeholders on a voluntary basis' (Greenwood 2003: 56). It has also come to be known as 'the triple bottom line' or 'corporate citizenship' signifying the responsibility of companies to create wealth, pursue sustainable development and enhance the lives of their employees and the communities in which they locate. As Chris Thomas, a corporate reputation consultant, writes, 'CSR is a prudent adaptation to changing circumstances: countering the increased ability of stakeholders to scrutinize corporate activities and motives with openness and complementary action' (Thomas 2003). CSR policies have been put into practice by many firms, epically those caught in the sweatshop scandals.

While TNCs and business organizations suggest that CSR will advance social rights, critics contend that CSR has been developed as a substitute and diversion for action (Justice 2002). For example, one analyst argues that 'In plain terms, business "talks the talk" *so as not to* "walk the walk"' (Rowe 2005: 144) (emphasis in the original). In this view CSR is a public relations ploy. The main targets are average consumers who may have encountered anti-corporate campaigns but are not particularly engaged with the issue and therefore largely ignorant of the ongoing situation on the company's factory floors. The goal is 'to solve guilty consumer consciousness' rather than to improve working conditions (Brooks 2005: 134).

In response to scepticism over in-house company codes of conduct many TNCs have been forced to support a number of third-party or joint corporate–NGO initiatives. In addition to numerous partnerships between firms and NGOs, the most prominent response has been the creation of a number of multi-stakeholder initiatives in the United States and western Europe such as the Fair Labour Association (FLA), and the Ethical Trade Initiative (ETI), industry-based initiatives such as the Worldwide Responsible Apparel Production (WRAP), and the emergence of third-party certification providers such as Social Accountability International (SAI). All these institution were made to avoid traditional state-based regulation. For example, the FLA was created after sweatshop scandals in the United States in the early 1990s raised industry fears that Congress would pass tougher regulation (Jenkins 2002). Voluntary initiatives claim to support labour standards through a mix of cooperation between key actors, learning networks, 'enlightened company self-interest', benchmarking, internal and external monitoring and enforcement through market sanctions (O'Rourke 2003). The serious weaknesses of these private regulatory approaches have been well documented and, not surprisingly, it is increasingly apparent that they do not serve as an effective substitute for traditional labour regulation (Haufler 2001, 2002; Jenkins *et al.* 2002; O'Rourke 2002, 2003).

Numerous organizations have sprung up to support the corporate response to labour and social issues. For example, in the United Kingdom the following organizations exist: Business in the Community (the UK member of CSR Europe), Common Purpose, the Institute of Business Ethics (IBE), and the Prince of Wales International Business Leaders Forum (PWBLF) (Greenwood 2003).

Most major TNCs belong to more than one such organization in addition to having their own CSR committees. These initiatives are supported by academics within corporate-funded business schools across, who advocate CSR and carry out research to improve its practice and effectiveness. The vast majority of their focus is on how TNCs can use CSR to respond to anti-corporate activism, protect corporate reputations and brand names, and encourage a 'business-friendly' regulatory environment (Jenkins *et al.* 2002; John and Thomson 2002; Hartman *et al.* 2003). Nationally based initiatives in the advanced industrialized countries such as the United Kingdom or the United States have an impact upon global arrangements because their activity influences home corporations which have a global reach. One element of global policy arrangements can be the regulatory activity of national actors which impacts upon localities in other parts of the world.

At the same time that businesses adopt CSR they draw upon both liberal–economic and cultural–nationalist arguments which suggest that movement to enforceable labour standards may hurt development. Many neoclassical economists argue that regulation and codes of conduct reduce wealth and harm the very workers labour activists are attempting to help. In 2000 a letter signed by over 250 economists was sent to US university presidents at a time when the FLA and the Worker's Rights Consortium (WRC) were quickly gaining university memberships. According to these economists the codes of conduct promoted by the FLA and WRC would cause employment in the developing world to shift away from the poorest workers. They also argued that regulation was unnecessary as TNCs already pay higher wages than the 'prevailing market wage' (Wells 2004). The economists' intervention offered comfort to TNCs trying to avoid meaningful codes of conduct, much less effective regulation.

Echoing arguments made by some developing country leaders (such as Mahathir Mohamad, the former Prime Minister of Malaysia), corporations have been able to argue that their hands off approach to labour issues respects national sovereignty and cultural diversity. For example, some members of the Toy Manufacturers of America, when faced with demands to live up to the ILO's universal standards argued that they did not want to be seen as imposing 'Western values' on non-Western cultures (Justice 2002).

A key element of CSR engagement is the emphasis on partnerships between firms and their NGO opponents. The concept of partnership has 'become an orthodox public affairs strategy' (Greenwood 2003: 54). From a PR perspective it is an attempt to protect brands plagued by mistrust by associating with NGOs which enjoy a higher level of trust (Hatcher 2003). This strategy has come to be known as 'greenwashing' in relation to partnerships between environmental NGOs and TNCs. More recently anti-corporate activists have coined the term 'bluewashing' to describe partnerships between TNCs and the UN, such as the Global Compact.

The Global Compact mentioned earlier has been attacked as a prominent case of 'bluewashing' (Bruno and Karliner 2000). Some examples of partnerships between TNCs and/or employers' associations and NGOs linked to labour rights include: Gap and the National Labour Committee (NLC); Fairtrade Foundation (FF) and Sainsbury's; the Co-operative Wholesale Society (CWS), World Federation of Sporting Goods Industry (WFSGI) and Save the Children, and the FLA and the ETI.

The literature on business–NGO partnerships in the environmental field is more developed that the work on labour issues and one could expect to see similar dynamics in the labour field. This literature suggests that corporate–NGO partnerships may result in demobilization of social movements as they become more involved in implementing policy and less involved in campaigning (John and Thomson 2002). The end result is a moderation of goals and tactics with the hope, from a corporate point of view, that accommodation now be achieved without a radical challenge to corporate interests. One PR representative has suggested that the corporate goal is 'to isolate the radicals, "cultivate" the idealists and "educate" them into becoming realists, then co-opt the realists into agreeing with the industry' (John and Thomson 2002: 44).

One aspect of this strategy that is particular to the global labour standards struggle is that TNCs have at times engaged with non-union NGOs as a way of avoiding and thus marginalizing the trade union movement (Justice 2002). Some non-union NGOs have been more open than unions to using private approaches to regulation. In some cases codes developed by corporations and NGOs omit labour rights such as the right to organize and the right to bargain collectively. By offering concessions to some NGOs representing consumer or environmental interests rather than labour rights, corporations have been able to isolate the demands for core labour rights from other demands for social responsibility.

The attempt to co-opt opposition and marginalize radicals also has an economic facet. Companies are able to use their tremendous financial power to influence moderates and marginalize less pliant opposition through a variety of tactics such as offering employment to NGO 'professionals', funding moderate NGOs and/or funding 'partnerships' with moderate NGOs while excluding more radical groups and working with NGOs to develop 'green' products. For example, when the United Students Against Sweatshops (USAS) set up the WRC as an alternative to the FLA, Nike withdrew 50 million USD from three universities that had joined the WRC instead of the FLA. In this way Nike used its economic weight to support a weaker initiative supported by moderate NGOs (and some business-friendly NGOs or business associations) and to marginalize a stronger alternative and the less pliant NGOs that support it (Jenkins 2002).

Labour response

Social forces opposing business inspired selective regulation such as workers' rights NGOs and organized labour have also actively shaped developments in the struggle over global policy arrangements. They have responded to the TNC strategy by engaging in 'a war of position' through a policy of 'contestation and reform'. As a result they have been able to make some modest gains while also risking becoming participants in a new hegemony of privatized labour standards.

The term 'war of position' was coined by Antonio Gramsci (Gramsci 1989) to describe a strategy used by subordinate groups attempting to challenge dominant groups that already control the state and other centres of power in civil society. It denotes a long-term strategy, carried out across multiple arenas (e.g. the state and civil society) and across multiple dimensions (e.g. the political, economic, and cultural). It involves lengthy efforts at gaining allies, building consensus around an alternative or counter-hegemonic worldview and gradually increasing political and economic power. The goal is to build a counter-hegemonic bloc armed with the necessary material and cultural 'forces' capable of challenging the power of the hegemonic or dominant bloc (Cox 1983; Levy and Egan 2003).

Civic associations working on labour issues cover a wide spectrum from traditional trade unions to labour NGOs in the informal sector (Harrod and O'Brien 2002; Waterman 2005). This diversity of actors, themselves products of diverse histories and national contexts ensures that different tendencies will exist side by side within labour groups.

However, this chapter deals primarily with those groups pursuing a strategy of engagement labelled 'contestation and reform' (Starr 2000).[2] This involves a mixture of public campaigning and working for reform of the transnational state apparatus. These groups seek to change current international institutions towards some kind of a global Keynesian framework capable of carrying out effective economic and social regulation or what Howitt calls 'the construction of an international legal framework which will engender genuine accountability for corporate behaviour' (Howitt 2002: xv). Several modest but important achievements of this approach can be identified.

One early achievement coming on the heels of anti-sweatshop activism by NGOs and trade unions is what some researchers have identified as a rise in the expectations and standards of corporate behaviour (Jenkins *et al.* 2002). The time when TNCs could publicly claim they have no social responsibility in their overseas operations beyond the legal minimum and expect little public backlash seems to be over. One of the most important examples is the double acknowledgement by most TNCs of their responsibility for labour standards internationally and for working conditions among employees working for contractors and subcontractors (Hale and Shaw 2002; Justice 2002). For years TNCs did not acknowledge any responsibility for labour standards internationally and also claimed they were not responsible for the working conditions of workers that did not work directly for them. However, this position proved to be unsustainable in the face of consistent activism. Responsibility for international labour standards and for the labour rights of subcontracted workers is now a common feature of most codes of conduct. These changes makes the new codes 'new' and represent two goals long held by the trade unions (Justice 2002). This establishes an important norm (an ideational victory for the opposition) that in the future might potentially lead to more effective (legal) transnational obligations for TNCs.

A second achievement is the establishment of the ILO's core labour standards as the eminent standards to be pursued. Labour unions have feared that codes would ignore ILO rights such as the freedom to organize and bargain collectively. Company codes tended to 'cherry-pick' from established international standards excluding those they disagreed with and choosing those with the highest public relations value (Blowfield 2002). After deciding to engage with the new codes, organized labour's 'overriding consideration was how the new codes could promote the application of good laws and how they could be used to help workers join or form trade unions' (Justice 2002: 93). Trade unions' response was to prevent TNCs from setting their own codes and instead ensure codes of conduct were based on the universally recognized standards of the ILO. The importance of ILO core standards is that they are based on a body of jurisprudence and thus not simply a company statement. It thus provides a link to the established international regulatory framework that labour groups hope to strengthen.

A third achievement has been the overall improvement in the content, implementation, and enforcement of codes of conduct. Many significant problems still exist with codes, many of which are structural and thus difficult if not impossible to overcome. However, compared with the company codes that TNCs originally put in place, todays' arrangements force companies to meet a higher standard. In addition to including the ILO core labour standards, many codes are also independently monitored and verified and increasingly allow for participation by outsiders. However, once companies adopted company codes in the wake of Levi's 1992 decision, 'the seeming success of getting labour standards onto corporate agenda was offset by the enormous challenge of ensuring that this was more than a public relations exercise' (Hale and Shaw 2002: 103). While the challenge is ongoing and codes remain fraught with serious weaknesses, today's codes are not the codes TNCs had in mind when they began developing them in the early 1990s.

A fourth development has been the establishment and growth in recent years of agreements between particular TNCs and the international trade union bodies representing workers in particular sectors, the Global Union Federations (GUFs). These agreements known as Global Framework Agreements (GFAs) represent a reassertion of the primary role of unions as the legitimate representatives of workers. GFAs acknowledge the importance of trade unions in articulating worker's concerns about labour issues and bargaining on their behalf. GFAs go beyond codes of conduct by establishing a formal ongoing relationship between business and labour and thus are a step closer to collective bargaining and the traditional union–company relationship than company codes and multi-stakeholder initiatives (Wills 2002; Torres and Gunnes 2003; Riisgaard 2004). GFAs are organized labour's attempt to consolidate the gains from codes of conduct within the more representative and familiar territory of collective bargaining (Hale and Shaw 2002).

A fifth example of how labour groups have attempted to outmanoeuvre TNCs in their war of position is the use of codes to enforce national legislation and local organizing. This is an attempt to take codes, designed by TNCs as substitutes for state regulation and union organizing, and instead use them as one more tool in the fight for workers' rights at the national level.

Codes have been used in women workers' rights national campaigns in Central America as a means of raising awareness and pressuring governments. In Nicaragua, the Movimiento de Mujeres Trabajadoras y Desempleadas Maria Elena Cuadra (MEC) was able to have its Ethical Code adopted by the national government (Prieto *et al.* 2002). Women Workers Worldwide (WWW), the Clean Clothes Campaign (CCC), and other NGOs have consulted with workers in the developing world as to how codes might be designed and used to enforce local labour laws and support local organizing (Dent 2002; Hale and Shaw 2002). On several occasions the Accor-GFA framework agreement has also been helpful to local organizing efforts (Wills 2002). Although these are limited gains, the use of codes to enforce national labour laws and local organizing is significant because it is a step in opposition to the privatization of labour standards using the very tool intended by TNCs to privatize labour regulation.

Conclusions

The global policy arrangements around labour rights have a tentative and precarious outline. Enforceable labour rights have been omitted from interstate economic agreements and most of the activity has taken place in the area of private authority, market mechanisms, and self-regulation. The various private driven policy arrangements are tentative because they have not been accepted as legitimate by many actors and continue to be the object of much debate and agitation. The era of supremacy by neoliberal forces in the 1980s yielded to an intense contestation in the 1990s. The early years of the twenty-first century witness corporations trying to create a new hegemony or consensus around voluntary policy arrangements while labour groups are struggling to move from voluntarism to state-based regulation.

For labour groups a key question is whether participation or engagement in private regulatory initiatives implicitly supports the privatization of labour standards regulation. As mentioned, although the opposition has been able to build some links between private initiatives and the traditional national and international regulatory frameworks, it is still operating on neoliberal 'terrain' or engaging in 'politics via markets'. This refers to the use of market mechanisms to regulate market activity. In the context of global labour standards this means the use of consumer pressure by the opposition to try and align the economic incentives of business so that they are compatible with workers' rights. Lipschutz (Lipschutz 2005) contrasts 'politics via markets' to 'politics and the political' by which he has in mind a politics similar to participatory democracy although he also includes aspects of traditional liberal democracy. The danger is that labour and NGO participation in private regulation initiatives legitimizes 'politics via market' and the privatization of regulation and thus works to undermine binding regulation and the kind of deliberative and participatory politics that give rise to state regulation.

To the degree that participation enhances the perceived or real effectiveness and acceptance of private regulation, demands for state regulation may be weakened. Improvements to codes of conduct brought about by labour activists may actually strengthen the view that private regulation is effective and thus adequate. Participation by unions and NGOs also adds increased legitimacy to corporate labour regulation increasing the firm's normative market authority. As one analyst suggests 'the primary cost of supporting voluntary codes is precisely what global civil society hopes to gain through them: the binding regulation of transnational politics' (Rowe 2005: 123).

However, labour groups have not accepted a private regulatory approach as the only 'realistic' way forward for the improvement of global labour standards. Groups that participate in such initiatives see them as a building bloc for more elaborate and enforceable regulation. In some cases, far from leading to demobilization, engagement with private regulatory initiatives has led to increasing alliances and campaigns among the different groups involved at various points along TNCs' supply chains (Ascoly and Zeldenrust 2002; Dent 2002; Hale and Shaw 2002; Justice 2002; Riisgaard 2004). More importantly, while the opposition has decided to participate in private regulatory schemes it has done so with a clear awareness of the limitations of private regulation and with the intent to shift the agenda back towards public forms of regulation as was demonstrated previously.

In addition, the longer private mechanisms have existed, the more they have come under criticism especially as labour's allies within academia and in non-union NGOs have focused upon them. The result has been renewed calls from a broad section of civic actors to move beyond the self-regulation paradigm (Rowe 2005). For example, Christian Aid (CA) (Aid 2004) has produced a study arguing that corporate social responsibility should be replaced by corporate social accountability. Corporations should be held legally accountable for their impacts upon people and the environment. Using case studies of British American Tobacco, Shell, and Coca Cola it offers ten arguments why public regulations must replace voluntary arrangements. A move away from CSR and towards a reaffirmation of the need for 'corporate accountability' as defined earlier can also be seen by the NGO response to the UN Global Compact. This took the form of the creation of the *Citizens Compact on the United Nations and Corporations* whose first principle states: 'Multinational corporations are too important for their conduct to be left to voluntary and self-generated demands. A legal framework, including monitoring, must be developed to govern their behavior on the world stage' (Bruno and Karliner 2002: 143).

The global policy arrangements around labour issues continue to be the source of considerable struggle between business and labour groups. Because interstate arrangements have been limited in their effectiveness and the shortcomings of market-based initiatives are clear, it is likely that we will see continued contestation over policy arrangements rather than either a new hegemony or a reassertion of supremacy by neoliberal supporters. The central unanswered question is whether the general public will buy into the concept of selective regulation and private authority mechanisms for dealing with labour issues or whether they will continue to be swayed by labour arguments for enforceable regulations. If private authority becomes the new common sense we will see the implementation of global policy arrangements that are hegemonic. If scepticism endures one can expect increased contestation.

Notes

1 A third and as yet relatively underdeveloped area is the prosecution of home state TNCs for their violation of labour rights overseas.
2 Other elements of the anti-corporate movement pursue strategies of 'globalization from below' and 'delinking, relocalization, and sovereignty' (Starr 2000). In practice groups may mix elements of all three strategies depending upon the time frame and issue.

References

Aid, C. (2004) *Behind the Mask: The Real Face of Corporate Social Responsibility*, London: Christian Aid.

Ascoly, N. and Zeldenrust, I. (2002) 'Working with codes: perspectives from the clean clothes campaign', in R. Jenkins, R. Pearson, and G. Seyfang (eds) *Corporate Responsibility and Labour Rights: Codes of Conduct in the Global Economy*, London: Earthscan.

Ayers, J. (2004) 'Power relations under NAFTA', *Studies in Political Economy*, 74 (Autumn): 101–23.

Biersteker, T. and Hall, R. B. (eds) (2002) *The Emergence of Private Authority in Global Governance*, Cambridge: Cambridge University Press.

Blowfield, M. (2002) 'ETI: a multi-stakeholder approach? Corporate responsibility and ethical trade: codes of conduct in the global economy', in R. Jenkins, R. Pearson, and G. Seyfang (eds) *Corporate Responsibility and Labour Rights: Codes of Conduct in the Global Economy*, London: Earthscan.

Bohmer, A. (2004) 'The revised 2000 OECD Guidelines for Multinationals: challenges and prospects after 4 years of implementation', *Policy Papers on Transnational Economic Law*, 3.

Brooks, E. (2005) 'Transnational campaigns against child labour', in J. Bandy and J. Smith (eds) *Coalitions Across Borders: Transnational Protest and the Neoliberal Order*, Lanham, MD: Rowman & Littlefield.

Bruno, K. and Karliner, J. (2000) *Tangled up in Blue: Corporate Partnerships at the United Nations*, Oakland: Transnational Resource and Action Centre.

Bruno, K. and Karliner, J. (2002) *Earthsummit.biz: The Corporate Takeover of Sustainable Development*, Oakland: Food First Books.

Compa, L. (2001) 'NAFTA's labor side agreement and international labor solidarity', in P. Waterman and J. Wills (eds) *Place, Space and the New Labour Internationalisms*, Oxford: Blackwell.

Cox, R. W. (1983) 'Gramsci, hegemony and international relations: an essay in method', *Millennium: Journal of International Studies*, 12 (2): 162–75.

Cutler, A. C., Haufler, V., and Porter, T. (eds) (1999) *Private Authority and International Affairs*, Albany, NY: State University of New York.

Dent, K. (2002) 'The contradictions in codes: the Sri Lankan experience', in R. Jenkins, R. Pearson, and G. Seyfang (eds) *Corporate Responsibility and Labour Rights: Codes of Conduct in the Global Economy*, London: Earthscan.

Galbraith, J. K. (1952) *American Capitalism: The Concept of Countervailing Power*, Boston, MA: Houghton Mifflin Company.

Gill, S. (1995) 'Globalization, market civilization and disciplinary neo-liberalism', *Millennium: Journal of International Studies*, 24 (3): 399–423.

Gill, S. (2000) 'The post-modern prince', *Millennium: Journal of International Studies*, 29 (1): 131–41.

Gramsci, A. (1989) *Selections from the Prison Notebooks*, New York: International Publishers.

Greenwood, J. (2003) 'Trade associations, change and the new activism', in S. John and S. Thomson (eds) *New Activism and the Corporate Response*, New York: Palgrave.

Hale, A. and Shaw, L. (2002) 'The emperor's new clothes: what codes mean for workers in the garment industry', in R. Jenkins, R. Pearson, and G. Seyfang (eds) *Corporate Responsibility and Labour Rights: Codes of Conduct in the Global Economy*, London: Earthscan.

Harrod, J. and O'Brien, R. (eds) (2002) *Global Unions? Theory and Strategies of Organized Labour in the Global Political Economy*, London: Routledge.

Hartman, L. P., Arnold, D. G., and Wokutch, R. E. (2003) *Rising Above Sweatshops: Innovative Approaches to Global Labor Challenges*, Westport, CT: Praeger.

Hatcher, M. (2003) 'Public affairs challenges for multinational corporations', in S. John and S. Thomson (eds) *New Activism and the Corporate Response*, New York: Palgrave.

Haufler, V. (2001) *A Public Role for the Private Sector*, Washington, DC: Carnegie Endowment for International Peace.

Haufler, V. (2002) 'Industry regulation and self-regulation: The case of labour standards', in A. F. Cooper, J. English, and R. Thakur (eds) *Enhancing Global Governance: Towards a New Diplomacy?*, New York: United Nations University.

Haworth, N. and Hughes, S. (2002). 'International labour and regional integration in the Asia-Pacific', in J. Harrod and R. O'Brien (eds) *Global Unions? Theory and*

Strategies of Organized Labour in the Global Political Economy, London: Routledge.

Howitt, R. (2002) 'Preface', in R. Jenkins, R. Pearson, and G. Seyfang (eds) *Corporate Responsibility and Labour Rights: Codes of Conduct in the Global Economy*, London: Earthscan.

ICFTU (2005) *Final Trade Union Statement on the Agenda for the 6th Ministerial Conference of the WTO*, Press Release.

ILO (1998) *ILO Declaration on Fundamental Principles and Rights at Work*, Geneva: International Labour Organization.

ILO (2002) *Poverty Reduction Strategy Papers (PRSPs): An Assessment of the ILO's Experience*, C. o. E. a. S. Policy, Geneva: International Labour Organization.

ILO (2004) *A Fair Globalization: Creating Opportunities for All*, Geneva: International Labour Organization.

ILO (2005) Available http://www.ilo.org

Jenkins, R. (2002) 'The political economy of codes of conduct', in R. Jenkins, R. Pearson, and G. Seyfang (eds) *Corporate Responsibility and Labour Rights: Codes of Conduct in the Global Economy*, London: Earthscan.

Jenkins, R., Pearson, R., and Seyfang, G. (eds) (2002) *Corporate Responsibility and Labour Rights: Codes of Conduct in the Global Economy*, London: Earthscan.

John, S. and Thomson, S. (eds) (2002) *New Activism and the Corporate Response*, New York: Palgrave.

Justice, D. (2002) 'The international trade union movement and the new codes of conduct', in R. Jenkins, R. Pearson, and G. Seyfang (eds) *Corporate Responsibility and Labour Rights: Codes of Conduct in the Global Economy*, London: Earthscan.

Levy, D. L. and Egan, D. (2003) 'A neo-gramscian approach to corporate political strategy: conflict and accommodation in the climate change negotiations', *Journal of Management Studies*, 40 (4): 803–29.

Lipschutz, R. (2005) *Regulation for the Rest of Us? Globalization, Governmentality and Global Politics*, London: Routledge.

O'Brien, R. (1998) 'Shallow foundations: labour and the selective regulation of free trade', in G. Cook (ed.) *The Economics and Politics of International Trade*, London: Routledge.

O'Brien, R., Goetz, A. M., Scholte, J. A., and Williams, M. (2000) *Contesting Global Governance: Multilateral Economic Institutions and Global Social Movements*, Cambridge: Cambridge University Press.

OECD (2005) *The UN Global Compact and the OECD Guidelines for Multinational Enterprises: Complementarities and Distinctive Contributions*, Paris: Organization for Economic Cooperation and Development.

O'Rourke, D. (2002) 'Monitoring the monitors: a critique of third-party labour monitoring', in R. Jenkins, R. Pearson, and G. Seyfang (eds) *Corporate Responsibility and Labour Rights: Codes of Conduct in the Global Economy*, London, Earthscan.

O'Rourke, D. (2003) 'Outsourcing regulation: analyzing nongovernmental systems of labor standards and monitoring', *Policy Studies Journal*, 31 (1): 1–29.

Polanyi, K. (1957) *The Great Transformation: The Political and Economic Origins of our Time*, Boston, MA: Beacon Press.

Prieto, M., Hadjipateras, A., and Turner, J. (2002) 'The potential of codes as part of women's organizations' strategies for promoting the rights of women workers: a Central America perspective', in R. Jenkins, R. Pearson, and G. Seyfang (eds) *Corporate Responsibility and Labour Rights: Codes of Conduct in the Global Economy*, London: Earthscan.

Riisgaard, L. (2004) *The IUF/COLSIBA-CHIQUITA framework agreement: a case study*, Working Paper 4. Geneva, International Labour Office.

Rowe, J. K. (2005) 'Corporate social responsibility as business strategy', in R. Lipschutz and J. K. Rowe (eds) *Globalization, Governmentality and Global Politics: Regulation for the Rest of Us?*, London: Routledge.

Sell, S. (2003) *Private Power, Public Law: The Globalization of Intellectual Property Rights*, Cambridge: Cambridge University Press.

Starr, A. (2000) *Naming the Enemy: Anti-Corporate Movements Confront Globalization*, London: Zed Books.

Stevis, D. (2002) 'Unions, capitals and states: competing internationalisms in North American and European integration', in J. Harrod and R. O'Brien (eds) *Global Unions? Theory and Strategies of Organized Labour in the Global Political Economy*, London: Routledge.

Strange, S. (1996) *The Retreat of the State: The Diffusion of Power in the World Economy*, Cambridge: Cambridge University Press.

Tarrow, S. (1998) *Power in Movement: Social Movements and Contentious Politics*, Cambridge: Cambridge University Press.

Thomas, C. (2003) 'Cyberactivism and corporations: new strategies for new media', in S. John and S. Thomson (eds) *New Activism and the Corporate Response*, New York: Palgrave.

Torres, L. and Gunnes, S. (2003) *Global Framework Agreements: A New Tool for International Labour*, Oslo: Fafo.

UN (2005) Available http://www.unglobalcompact.org

Voss, K. (1999) 'The collapse of a social movement: the interplay of mobilizing structures, framing, and political opportunities in the Knights of Labor', in D. McAdam, J. D. McCarthy, and M. N. Zald (eds) *Comparative Perspectives on Social Movements: Political Opportunities, Mobilizing Structures and Cultural Framings*, Cambridge: Cambridge University Press.

Waterman, P. (2005) 'Talking across difference in an interconnected world of labour', in J. Bandy and J. Smith (eds) *Coalitions Across Borders: Transnational Protest and the Neoliberal Order*, Lanham: Rowman & Littlefield.

Wells, D. (2004) 'How ethical are ethical purchasing policies?', *Journal of Academic Ethics*, 119–40.

Wilkinson, R. (2002) 'Peripheralizing labour: the ILO, WTO and the completion of the Bretton Woods project', in J. Harrod and R. O'Brien (eds) *Global Unions? Theory and Strategies of Organized Labour in the Global Political Economy*, London: Routledge.

Wills, J. (2002) 'Bargaining for the space to organize in the global economy: a review of the Accor-IUF trade union agreement', in *Review of International Political Economy*, 9 (4): 675–700.

Wills, J. (2004) 'Re-scaling trade union organization: lessons from the European front line', in R. Munck (ed.) *Labour and Globalisation: Results and Prospects*, Liverpool: Liverpool University Press.

3 Modes of consumer participation and engagement in the making of global consumer policy

Karsten Ronit

Introduction

With the internationalization and globalization of economies the stage is set for the making of a global public policy in a variety of issues relating to the marketplace (Reinicke 1998), including consumer affairs.[1] Together with labor, consumers belong to the immediate environment of business, and firms must sell their products and services to customers to survive and thrive. Given this prominent position of consumers in the economy, we may, at fist glance, hypothesize that consumer groups are an integral part of the international machinery, building a regulatory framework in this policy field. Not only do consumers have important rights to represent, but they also have experiences that can contribute to the formulation and implementation of regulation and, thus, assist intergovernmental organizations as well as business in standardizing rules.

At the same time, associated with the process of globalization, there exists the free and, in some industries, almost unrestricted movement of capital. This point is stressed both in scholarly expositions and in an abundant "airport literature" on the global economy. A second and different reading scrutinizing state–market relations, therefore, gives rise to a different hypothesis that consumers are long subdued and that business dominance has become ever more prevalent. The leading role assumed by business has led to a decline of public authority at the national and international levels and the forces marshaled to defend consumers and other under-resourced societal groups have become weaker. In sum, the global scene is surrendered to business that prefers a minimum of regulation and is not inclined either to negotiate rules or consult with the diverse landscape of nongovernmental organizations that have become disenfranchised in the process of globalization.

Although the power of the market is recognized as a key driver in the globalization process, the extreme version of the freely expanding market is today less in vogue. Attempts are made to accommodate the different views presented above (e.g. Vogel 1996; Levi-Faur 2005). On the one hand, many voices acknowledge the intervention of states and intergovernmental organizations in the development of global public policy, the rising influence of civil society, and the need to establish rules regulating ever more complex economic exchanges. On the other hand, due attention is also given to new imbalances between conflicting socioeconomic interests leveraging global public policy and generally leaving business with a stronger influence.

As an expanding policy field, however, consumer affairs are sidestepped in much of the literature. Consumers are rarely attributed an independent and countervailing role. Meanwhile, the literature on social forces acting through movements and NGOs shows that a variety of organizations contribute to solving a range of global problems, and that they host a huge governance potential alongside intergovernmental organizations. Whereas civic groups in, for instance, the humanitarian and environmental domain have received a fair amount of thought, social movement studies and analyses of the role of NGOs are inattentive to the specific role of consumers in global politics.

Maybe they have fallen into oblivion because they have hardly any role to play; perhaps they are in fact smoothly integrated into the decision-making structures of many international organizations and welcomed by corporations and business interest associations alike; or maybe they are struggling to be heard and are taking up the form of protest – as do many other social movements – as an alternative or a supplement to a participatory strategy.

In this chapter we analyze these questions by first taking a close look at the position of consumers in global politics. We begin by asking the more fundamental question as to whether it is at all possible for such a large group to organize coherently within a collective framework and how action is shaped and constrained. Furthermore, we discuss some of the basic properties of consumer policy as a complex policy field and how this may impact on consumer action.

In this context, an important avenue of investigation is to study the concrete formats of organized consumers, how large organizations coexist with smaller initiatives, and how consumers build alliances with other organizations or movements to enhance their countervailing potential. An interesting feature is to analyze how traditional consumer organizations approach the expanding field of consumer policy, and at the same time to understand how other organizations move into the traditional and new areas of consumer policy and, hence, give rise to cooperation between different interest groups. These are pertinent problems because consumer policy is a somewhat amorphous area and overlaps many other policy fields. Core principles must be defended and central issues must be handled by relevant intergovernmental organizations and consumer organizations at the same time as new products appear in the changing and turbulent processes of globalization.

Next we examine whether consumer organizations have access to and have achieved an official status vis-à-vis those international bodies where consumer policy is primarily made. The issue of participatory rights is itself a key symbol of recognition; it is often an important constitutional battlefield because consultative status is only selectively granted to relevant private organizations. Under these circumstances, protest may cease to be the preferred mode of consumer action, and public driven policy arrangements involving key public and private actors may arise.

To study the possible ascent of consumers as an influential countervailing force, we shall examine the organization of consumers from a relational perspective, taking into account also the behavior of business. In the final section, therefore, we direct attention toward the institutionalized cooperation between business and consumer organizations, as well as other organizations with a consumer agenda. Parts of this cooperation can be structured through private driven policy arrangements where intergovernmental organizations are not completely sidelined but play a less significant role.

Theoretical sketches on the political organization of consumers

Various theoretical candidates are available when explaining the global organization and political activity of consumers. Although the following is not an exhaustive list of these candidates, theories focusing on key aspects should be consulted: first, the organization of consumers as a form of large-scale collective action; second, the role of the institutional environments in fostering consumer organization and third, the structure of public policy in which consumer issues are embedded.

Regardless of the definition of consumers, they represent an extremely large societal group. Intuitively, it is hard to imagine a group that is larger. In his seminal and often cited work, Mancur Olson emphasized the strong variation in the organization of small and large groups (Olson 1965). The rational assumptions underlying this analysis have been challenged in many different ways and factual evidence pointing to the existence of real-life big organizations have frequently been provided.

Without denying the actual organization of certain large groups, this argument stresses the significant extent of free-riding and the sub-optimal forms of collective action. In other words, some groups are less likely to emerge and stabilize as formal organizations, and to various degrees they fall short of representing the interest category they seek to organize. Consequently, these groups are generally underprivileged in terms of their collective potential. Business is a quite different story. Because business typically consists of a limited number of firms in a given area, these legal persons are much easier to organize than natural persons, and many industries have a comparative advantage representing interests.

Even in Europe, with a strong tradition of organizing consumers and where the European Union has in recent years strongly encouraged the participation of civil society, consumer organizations are seen as weaker than business (Pollack 1997). They are definitely not missing in the associational landscape but they carry a more limited weight, which is not least attributable to the problem of group size. On a world scale, collective action problems among consumers should be even further exacerbated.

Given these constraints, the global organization of consumers is likely to follow a different course. Very big organizations are less likely to emerge, and powerful members are difficult to attract. Instead, smaller and specialized organizations that represent a subset of consumer interests are imaginable. This line of reasoning suggests that consumer interests are represented either through a diverse array of small independent organizations or through large federated organizations constituted of small organizations that have their own identity, with each enjoying the advantages of mobilizing collective action (Olson 1965).

One characteristic is group size; another is the role of institutionalized political environments in shaping collective action. It is evident that even in countries where a strong tradition of freedom of associability prevails, associations can play a very different role. Comparative politics demonstrate this premise clearly by emphasizing the variation between the Anglo-Saxon countries on the one the hand, where a pluralist pattern of organizing interests is said to prevail, and continental Europe on the other, where a corporatist pattern has emerged, although interesting variation is demonstrated from North to South.

Strong variation can also be found in the degree to which independent civil society organizations can be distinguished in other parts of the world. Sometimes they are controlled by government, or are influenced from abroad. Of course, these experiences cannot be summarized in a few lines here, but it is permissible to maintain that the political environments in some countries and regions have a huge impact on the organization and representation of interests, including of course consumer interests.

Institutional factors in the political environment are, however, by no means reducible to the freedom of association. States can in numerous ways influence collective action through associations by encouraging their formation, funding them, seeking their advice, and establishing regular exchanges to the extent that certain forms of rule-making are delegated to private bodies. The neo-corporatist tradition 'especially' has scrutinized these interactions and emphasized the substantial impact exerted by the public authority on key associations in society, such as in business and labor groups. As far as consumers are concerned, we still know too little about how public authority influences their structure and behavior, but as with other groups, there are reasons to believe that this influence varies across countries.

Although we cannot say how intergovernmental organizations more concretely assist in the formation and life of global consumer groups, experiences won in the study of other territorial levels suggest that there is definitely information here worth exploring, something that would add to our understanding of the organization of global consumers. In principle, at least some states can assist consumers in the organization of domestic consumer interests, and this aid can be very helpful when national organizations meet to build global organizations. Last but not least, intergovernmental organizations may encourage the formation of global consumer organizations and assist in numerous ways those already established, and generally compensate for hardship facing the organizers of consumer interests.

A third perspective from which to study consumers is found in research on the role of consumers in public policy. Thus, a general typology of public policies – building upon earlier works on the influence of interest groups (Lowi 1969; Stigler 1971) – has been offered. It structures the outcome of policy according to costs and benefits to different groups in society (Wilson 1980: 364–72) as follows: when both benefits and costs are widely distributed (majoritarian politics); when benefits and costs are concentrated (interest-group politics); when benefits are concentrated while costs are widely distributed (client politics); and when benefits are widely distributed and costs covered by a small group in society (entrepreneurial politics).

Our concern here lies with the appropriate categorization of consumer policy. In cases where regulation is aimed at business in general and where all consumers are affected, we may with some justification talk about "majoritarian politics" – although of course even the entire business community is still a comparatively small group in a wider societal perspective. These cases are, however, qualitatively different from situations where only minor groups of firms are influenced by regulation.

Whereas "entrepreneurial politics" is not a very likely phenomenon in relation to consumer affairs, there can be cases of "interest-group politics" when only minor groups within business, and small segments within the encompassing group of consumers, are really affected. Consumer policy has mainly been conceived of as "client politics": small but well-organized industries influence and enjoy the benefits of public regulation, while consumers as a large but weakly organized group are disadvantaged. There are, however, ways to compensate for these weaknesses.

The emergence of "watchdog" or "public interest" associations that have devised ways of maintaining themselves without having to recruit and organize the people who will be affected by a policy is an important feature of some forms of "client politics" (Wilson 1980: 369).

In cases, where "watchdog" organizations are active – whether through protest or participation – the typical asymmetry of "client politics" – and even other types of public policy – is in part corrected.

Some glimpses into these theoretical debates suggest that consumer interests are extremely difficult to organize in a coherent way, and especially at the global level. The organization of consumers is certainly possible, but a high degree of free-riding and of fragmentation in the representation of interests is expectable. However, through a federation with no direct membership, a global organization can build upon existing national organizations of consumers. Indeed, comparative studies are keen to emphasize the strong institutional variation in the public recognition of interest groups, and it is likely that these patterns will affect the global organization of consumers and their goal formation. Finally, the public policy perspective briefly outlined earlier points to the under-supply and possible fragmentation of consumer involvement in the very broad areas of "client politics," and the strengths of business political action. However, some policy fields are also characterized by a certain propensity to establish the so-called watchdog organizations that do not need to organize in an encompassing fashion but, nevertheless, are broadly recognized as speaking for these groups.

As far as consumer action is concerned, theories point to some of the inherent problems of large-scale collective action, and also show how these problems can be overcome. Empirical research, however, gives us fewer hints as to the concrete manifestations of consumers. We may therefore ask whether consumer organizations have to be comparatively large and organize all those they really claim to represent, or whether smaller and more specialized units that operate within narrow areas, and consequently aim to organize and represent a smaller group of concerned consumers but with stronger interest intensity, are a possibility. We may also take an interest in the patterns of participation. Some organizations will most likely give priority to protests and not strive to become part of any international rule-making machinery, whereas other organizations will seek formal cooperation with various international agencies, and perhaps even with business. Because public policy is highly complex, and because consumer policy intersects with environmental policy, development policy, social policy and others, we may also ask whether consumers through alliance-building can meet the new and diverse challenges. To discuss these issues, empirical studies are needed. In the chapters that follow we shall scrutinize the pattern of global consumer organizations, how coherently these are actually represented, which issues they address, and how participatory strategies are employed vis-à-vis intergovernmental organizations and the business community.

The organization of global consumers – territorial and issue-specific cleavages

At first glance the pattern of consumer organization contradicts some of the theoretical assumptions outlined earlier. Consumers should, presumably, not organize in a global context, because of their overwhelming size – they would face severe problems doing so. However, consumers have long ago established coherent associations: on a global scale, there is today one major consumer organization, namely Consumers International (CI). Founded in 1960 as the International Organization of Consumer Unions (IOCU),

CI is a stable expression of collective action, a very inclusive organization that seeks to represent all consumers irrespective of their country of origin and – almost – irrespective of the issue concerned. Its encompassing character sets it apart from practically all other consumer organizations.

On closer inspection, however, there is also much truth in the standard theory of collective action. Although several decades old, this leading organization of consumers was founded much later than some of the major international business interests associations that are involved in more or less the same issue areas, and collective action did not easily come about. It is also interesting to note that individual consumers are not directly affiliated with CI, and there is an extreme amount of free-riding. As a global organization, CI has made no serious effort to organize and represent the billions of individual consumers worldwide.

The quality of successful representation does not hinge on individual membership but rather on collective membership. Thus, CI is a kind of global federation whose members are national consumer organizations all structured along different lines. This kind of intermediate organization (Olson 1965) leaves it to the national organizations to design appropriate strategies to recruit members locally, a factor that facilitates collective action.

Although it aspires to be a truly global outlet, Consumers International cannot stretch out and claim to represent consumers aggressively in all parts of the world. The founding members and most resourceful members came from the industrialized countries; members from developing countries joined later, and today more than 250 organizations from about 115 countries are affiliated, with regional offices in Latin America and the Caribbean, Asia and the Pacific and Africa.

Consumers in developing countries, although by no means a uniform category, have comparatively few resources and are generally without effective organizations that either play a role in the domestic context, or assist the global organization in the formulation of policies relevant to these groups of consumers. Therefore, it is the official task of CI to help create national organizations in those parts of the world with weak consumer representation, and be attentive to issues that due to the incapacity of national organizations would otherwise be ignored in the global context.

Establishing some minimum regulation in these countries is also needed, as is an effort to push for higher standards in countries where consumer organizations have a far greater leverage on public policy. Evidently, the difference in origin between member organizations from the industrialized and developing countries suggests that they have different domestic experiences with consumer policy. They enjoy different degrees of recognition in the policy-making process and – what is crucial in a global context – give different priority to issues. Many cleavages have a territorial background, because country- or region-specific traditions and preferences structure choice.

Apart from Consumer International, we find many other global organizations involved in consumer policy. These do not aspire to represent consumer interests across a vast number of policy fields but are instead organized around specific agendas, such as the cooperative movement through the International Cooperative Alliance (ICA), or around sectors and policies. Thus, consumers are also represented through, for example, Health Action International (HIA) that acts as a spokesperson for consumers of drugs and patients vis-à-vis the pharmaceutical industry and public health systems. In air transport, we find the International Airline Passengers Association (IAPA), that gives the otherwise dispersed community of airline passengers around the world a voice – but the association takes no interest in more general consumer issues. In relation to food, an organization like the Organic Consumers Organization has emerged. Food however is a mundane commodity; as well, the CI is highly active in food policy.

In an even further number of sectors we find different groups and networks of consumers. Organizations, that do not view themselves as genuine consumer organizations, occasionally participate in consumer policy – though lacking the ability to coordinate with core consumer organizations more permanently. Environmental organizations, federations of trade unions, and human rights associations are sometimes involved in consumer issues, and it is often difficult to know which type of organization takes the lead role (Kellow 2003).[2]

Some initiatives and campaigns are distinctly related to sectoral issues and agendas. New issues give rise to new formats, such as Genetic Resources Action; in addition, increased outsourcing to Third World countries in textiles has created the Clean Clothes Campaign to regulate sweatshop garment manufacturing. In many cases, such initiatives are virtually unaware of each other's existence; some are not concerned even about participation in the work of intergovernmental organizations, expressing themselves mainly through protests or consumer choice in the market.[3] Unlike the organizations depicted earlier, these initiatives are relatively unstable – they come and go, and enduring alliance-building is difficult to achieve.

It has been debated whether consumer movements in some policy areas are single-issue campaigns or long-term reform-oriented movements (see Mintzes and Hodgkin 1996); in consumer policy, evidence points in both directions. The CI is definitely a reform-based pragmatic organization, but campaigns are increasingly launched to back up activities when issues are tabled in various forums. At the same time, we find organizations with a single issue, or a high degree of specialization, but they are not necessarily extremely ideological.

In sum, the organization of consumers at the global level displays a mixed pattern of action. Together with the uniformity of interest representation provided by the CI, the diversity of collective action becomes manifest through the high degree of specialization in the form of smaller interest groups. As pointed out in the literature, large-scale collective action is complicated, but the intermediate character of CI – together with the advantage of small committed groups with a special identity – facilitate action.

Consumer involvement in policy fields

As a specific area of public policy, consumer policy is not easily delineated. Although we should not be paralyzed by this ambiguity, we must account for this complexity in consumer policy. Like many other fields of public policy, consumer policy is ill-defined and ill-structured (Chisholm 1987); its boundaries are indeed blurred; and it is not institutionalized in any significant way. Other areas of public policy have "their own" intergovernmental organizations, programs, projects, agendas and financial resources, and they are based on an established policy tradition. In all these respects, consumer policy is less independent and less mature.

The major reason for this elusiveness is not simply the drawback of the consumer perspective in global public policy. As a matter of fact, consumer issues have reached the agendas of many international conferences and intergovernmental organizations, and international business must increasingly respond to consumer demands. Without having a very strong set of core institutions, however, this policy field has developed along two lines: first, some issues in consumer policy are of a horizontal nature and are of general relevance to business and consumers and second, some issues have a vertical makeup and are only dealt with in the context of certain industries and consumer groups.

There is no single and specialized intergovernmental organization – backed up by a community of business and civil society organizations – exclusively devoted to consumer affairs. Accordingly, this policy field is defined on the one hand at a general level by the United Nations, that by virtue of its universal character is "responsible" for all sorts of global public policy, and on the other hand by key consumer organizations that have tried to define what consumer policy really is.

The *UN Guidelines on Consumer Protection* consensually adopted by the UN General Assembly in 1985, and supported by Consmers International, has served as a guide for its own activities and for global consumer policy in general; it was expanded in 1999 to include the promotion of sustainable consumption (UN Assembly 1999). The definition entailed in the universal consumer guidelines emphasizes the broad character of consumer policy; but these general principles are implemented through special agencies, and here we move from the horizontal to the vertical level.

At the vertical level, consumer policy blends with other policy fields. This interpenetration includes competition policy, trade policy, development policy, environmental policy, human rights policy, social policy, gender policy, health policy, and food policy; each field having its own history and focal points and organized around one or more intergovernmental organizations active in the development of global public policy.

Notwithstanding a solid and consistent core, consumer policy has always been in a state of flux. The development of new consumer goods has constantly raised new regulatory problems, and public discourse has been directed toward new economic, social, and ethical aspects of consumer policy. These changes are again reflected in the work of consumer organizations, as well as in the work of intergovernmental agencies involved in the regulation of consumer affairs.

Although consumer rights are by no means at the center of all these policy fields briefly listed, consumer organizations often make an energetic effort to carve out an underlying consumer dimension in each of these fields. Therefore, the changing tectonic structures can lead to new alliances between consumer groups and other countervailing powers when common interests are discovered; for their part, consumer organizations can use this interaction as a vehicle to advance otherwise dormant or forgotten consumer interests.

However, a new policy mix can also create conflicts when different agendas are raised and when goals are essentially different. It is evident that whenever consumer groups enter into new fields where they lack strong traditions and competencies, recognized organizations and movements that specialize in the fields and do not define themselves as consumer organizations proper are more likely to take the lead role.

In some cases, however, policy fields merge in new and interesting ways that are relevant not only to the various patterns of consumer protest and participation but to a wider group of actors that likewise have no established tradition. The GMO issue is such an example. Here food policy, environmental policy and consumer policy meet with trade policy and create a policy hybrid (Krissoff *et al.* 2002). It is neither the exclusive "property" of consumer organizations nor the domain of environmental organizations, and this new amalgam requires a high degree of coordination. The setting of priorities very much depends on the efforts of consumer organizations in the initial stages of agenda formation, and today the consumer perspective forms part of an integrated approach to GMOs by critical countervailing powers.

It should be stressed that the development of countervailing power can be seen from a slightly different angle from that offered by public policy, where consumer action is analyzed in relation to specific policy fields. Countervailing action can also be analyzed in relation to specific sectors of the business community (Schmitter 1990).[4] Indeed, some consumer activities are horizontal in the sense that they are directed toward the business community at large, whereas other activities aim at particular industries and, perhaps, even single corporations and products. As we shall see later, this diversity of focus also gives rise to different public and private policy arrangements.

This understanding of policy is complementary rather than competing with the taxonomy previously offered in the public policy perspective, where policy was categorized according to its implications for various groups in society. Accordingly, the study of global consumer policy may depart from the analysis of specific industries and the public policy that develops around them. In the case of the global pharmaceutical industry, for instance, regulation emerges in different intergovernmental agencies, centered on both consumer policy and health policy among others. Indeed, more specialized consumer organizations also monitor specific industries and corporations, basing some of their strategies upon departure from analyses on a diversity of regulatory problems that are relevant to some groups of consumers. This point will be further discussed later in relation to industries where some cooperation has already been established between business and countervailing groups, and where some degree of consumer participation has been secured in the new policy arrangements.

Taken together, consumer organizations have given priority to a wide range of issues. The field of consumer policy has always been elusive and, therefore, organizations' engagement includes both areas where consumer protection is already established, and areas where consumer concerns are only of minor importance – and only slowly gaining attention. These patterns demonstrate both weakness and strength on behalf of the consumers.

Consumer action is complicated because of the many policy fields and industries where consumers can potentially act as a countervailing force. Given the complex character of consumer policy, consumer interests are not represented just through the large or small or highly specialized consumer organizations, or even the many campaigns that they launch. Opinions are also expressed through many other organizations that basically focus on other issues but that from time to time integrate the consumer perspective.

Consumer participation and engagement in public policy arrangements

No intergovernmental organization is designed to handle consumer affairs per se. The task is divided across numerous organizations, working groups and conferences, and the idea to establish a single organization specializing in consumer affairs has never been approved.[5] Consequently, consumers must find their way into a number of intergovernmental organizations, where the recognition of consumer organizations varies considerably.

Intergovernmental agencies dealing with macroeconomic problems, competition policy, and trade issues have been extremely slow in recognizing the consumer interest. They have shown a preference for either avoiding interest-group participation altogether and leaving the scene exclusively to member states, or including business interests while ignoring countervailing powers, such as consumers. Thus, key organizations like the

World Trade Organization (WTO), the World Bank (IBRD) or the International Monetary Fund (IMF) have not facilitated strong cooperation with international consumer organizations (e.g. Nelson 1995; Scholte 2002; Porter 2006). At the same time, countervailing forces have not targeted business but have often seen these institutions as captured and dominated by business agendas, directing their protests against them or pointing to their lack of legitimacy when civil society is excluded.

As an organization focused on private sector interests and having special committees with a clear business agenda, the Organization for Economic Cooperation and Development (OECD) has taken an interest in consumer policy since the late 1960s, operating a Consumer Policy Committee in which consumer organizations participate. The OECD has hosted some conferences, for instance the 1994 conference on *A Global Marketplace for Consumers* at which globalization was discussed from consumers' point of view. It has also issued a number of guidelines, especially its *Guidelines for Multinational Enterprises*, to direct business activity in ways that enhance consumer protection. This initiative followed the *UN Code on Transnational Corporations* which sparked the adoption of a number of new and consumer-relevant declarations, rules and principles in intergovernmental organizations such as the International Labor Organization (ILO), United Nations Conference on Trade and Development (UNCTAD), World Health Organization (WHO) and Food and Agriculture Organization (FAO).

The major economic organizations are involved in regulation of importance to consumers worldwide. Participation in forums for these regulations would be a highly useful platform for consumer influence at the global level; consumer organizations have also struggled for consultation rights where invitation has not been granted, but they have been only modestly successful. Investigations by the CI have resulted in a number of detailed recommendations to reform the institutional structure of some intergovernmental organizations in the firm belief that better access is essential for the consumer cause.

Without any solid accreditation of countervailing powers, the WTO, with the adoption of the Marrakesh Agreement establishing the organization, has allowed some civil society involvement: that is greater access to documents, registration at ministerial conferences, briefings with relevant NGOs, and participation in symposia – but not always with an eye to bringing business and civil society together more systematically in the field of consumer policy. All NGOs – those representing business, and those representing civil society – are however excluded from the various councils, bodies, and committees, as well as from the dispute settlement process. Therefore, the small steps taken toward greater civil society participation should not be overestimated.

This arrangement does not necessarily suggest that consumer interests have been excluded from the higher levels of decision-making, because participation has instead been achieved at national levels, where they assist governments in formulating negotiation and other strategies (Putnam 1988). International relations theories of a realist brand explain this form of decision-making by reference to the national interests attached to these issues and the prerogatives of states in "high politics" areas. In other words, interest groups can be important, but not at the international level.

States do not always transport consumer-friendly positions into global politics, however. Some states can block consumer issues – often with the support of business interests – leading possibly to other private initiatives. Thus, after a failed attempt to have the UN Commission on Transnational Corporations adopt guidelines for global business, CI released in 1995 its *Consumer Charter for Global Business*, that was aimed at transnational corporations in particular. In other words, this private consumer initiative was fostered by the weakness of public action, but so far it has not been a really successful alternative (Braithwaite and Drahos 2000: 202).

Some consumer organizations, most notably Consumers International, have been granted consultative rights in a number of intergovernmental organizations, but we must also search for consumer participation at other territorial levels. In some areas of consumer policy, there is a formal or informal division of labor between national and regional organizations on the one hand, and global organizations on the other hand. Organizations in large countries, such as Consumers Union or Public Citizen in the US, or regional organizations such as the recognized The European Consumers' Organization (BEUC) in the European Union are occasionally involved in inter-regional or global issues.

Consumer regulation varies significantly across countries and intersects with other policy fields in a variety of interesting ways (Vogel 1995). In some cases, a national or a regional consumer organization has the needed expertise and can take the lead role in building a case in a global context, although such an organization typically does not have formal access to global agencies. This applies, for instance, to the Transatlantic Consumer Dialogue (TACD), that was established in 1998 and has relations with both the US and the EU administration (Bignami and Charnowitz 2001). The creation of the TACD is a vivid illustration of the regionalization of consumer policy within the context of globalization, a regionalization that includes a participatory dimension – because the TACD has become an accepted player through public authority.

Theoretically, severe problems are associated with large-scale collective action sketched earlier in this chapter, and regional constituencies can become an appropriate way to avoid organizing global consumers. However, the regional outfits can also launch their own initiatives. Global consumer organizations can either actively encourage such a division of labor or tacitly accept it. In a period of globalization and increasing demands for international rule-making however, the question remains as to whether such strategies are sufficient to represent consumers. No matter how subtle labor is divided, the presence of global consumer organizations shows that global consumer policy is not merely the sum of national actions.

This premise is illustrated by turning to some intergovernmental organizations in which global consumer policy is an integral part of the policy program and in which participatory rights have voluntarily been granted to consumer organizations. Consumers International has an observer status at, for instance, the United Nations Economic and Social Council (ESOSOC), and in special agencies like the FAO (Food and Agriculture Organization), United Nations Conference on Trade and Development (UNCTAD), the United Nations Industrial Development Organization (UNIDO), the World Health Organization (WHO), and the International Labor Organization (ILO).

Sometimes participation dates back several decades, such as in the case of FAOs Codex Alimentarious Commission, founded in 1962 by FAO and WHO, which is an important body in food safety regulation and handles questions of both nutrition and health. Participation was evaluated in 2002 to improve the traditional slow process of implementation and to change the criteria for accreditation in 2005 after a revision took place in 1999. FAO also has a tradition of including civil society organizations more generally into its various technical committees. Since the mid-1990s, UNCTAD has had a competition and consumer policy committee and various forms of producer–consumer cooperation have been mapped. Stronger efforts by the WHO are a more recent reality, although formal accreditation schemes are decades old. In 2001 the WHO launched *the WHO Civil Society Initiative*, the first of its kind in the organization. Although not all events are necessarily moving in a direction beneficial to consumers and civil society at large, greater awareness of consumer issues results in new institutional arrangements in which corporate players also are involved (Oliviero and Simmons 2002).

Intergovernmental organizations dealing with food, health, development, environment and other issues intersecting with consumer policy have a quite different historical record than that of the economic and financial institutions, and the consumer voice is stronger. However, these organizations are by no means captured by civil society; business representation is significant also, whereby many public driven policy arrangements involve business as well as countervailing forces.

Consumer organizations, however, are but one group out of many civil society organizations, and the agenda of these agencies is not primarily consumer policy. Without overdoing their role in these institutional contexts, participating consumer organizations must ensure that the consumer perspective is embodied in discussions and negotiations and that it does not seriously conflict with the goals of other parts of civil society. Indeed, there is a great potential for alliance-building in these contexts, but the flip side of the coin is that the formulation of a common civil society approach can be extremely complicated.

Also the more consumer-friendly intergovernmental organizations have adopted strict and general principles regarding consultation status. Preferential treatment is given to internationally encompassing organizations from civil society and business, and although organizations claiming to represent the very same interest category are not accredited, there are still many organizations with a consultative status.

Numerically, the business world everywhere is better represented in consumer-friendly agencies and there is no ambition to create any kind of parity; but if we include other countervailing forces, this imbalance is to some extent corrected. Consequently, public policy is arranged against the backdrop of the inputs from a plurality of conflicting interests whose participation is to some degree influenced by relevant public authorities.

Participatory rights have the character of a strategic commodity, because participation is not simply a matter of the "bottom-up" energy, willingness, and priority of private organizations but very much hinges on the "top-down" initiatives of intergovernmental organizations. They do not simply accept the existing landscape of private organizations but they help structure it by selecting some organizations and by directly or indirectly encouraging and disciplining organizations to cooperate or merge.

As far as the participating consumer organizations are concerned, we can distinguish between the general organizations that claim to represent consumers worldwide and in all policy fields, and specific organizations that also claim to represent consumers worldwide but are only concerned with consumer affairs in a certain field or in relation to a specific product group or industry. Thus, some consumer organizations are represented only in one of these intergovernmental organizations, whereas others have been granted consultation rights in several agencies.

As a consequence, general consumer organizations, especially the CI, must apply general principles in specific issue areas, whereas the more specialized organizations and, for instance, environmental organizations must understand that the solving of sometimes narrow questions has a bearing on consumer policy generally. However, there are also organizations, movements, networks and initiatives that have not gained access to these forums. Either they do not have the necessary resources and are not sufficiently representative, or they have adopted strategies of protest and institutional disengagement. It becomes a great challenge for all parties when these strategies conflict with those consumer organizations that actually participate and invest much energy in public driven policy arrangements.

In sum, consumer organizations have, to different degrees, access to and been granted consultative rights by intergovernmental organizations, freedoms essential to their engagement in public driven policy arrangements. From some agencies they are effectively sealed off, whereas in other contexts they participate alongside private organizations from business. In cases where they have been invited, the core activities of these intergovernmental organizations do not always center on consumer policy, and consumer concerns are integrated in many other agendas. Accordingly, consumer organizations must develop appropriate strategies to bring the consumer perspective into stronger focus. To that end alliances are forged with other consumer organizations as well as with organizations that have a different, yet compatible, point of departure.

Consumer action in relation to private driven policy arrangements

Under the auspices of intergovernmental organizations, business and countervailing groups, such as consumers, sometimes meet in fruitful collaboration. Apart from legitimizing public authority in various ways, conflicting interests, as a side effect, also experience certain bases for cooperation beyond the traditional public framework.

In other words, global consumer policy is not exclusively produced by states or intergovernmental organizations. Governance beyond government has increasingly been recognized in domestic and international settings (van Keersbergen and van Waarden 2004), when private organizations formulate and implement rules that become a valid alternative to traditional public policy (Ronit and Schneider 2000). Although this dimension of global consumer policy cannot always substitute traditional public regulation, privatization and various sorts of private driven arrangements have been identified as a paradigm shift (Asher 1998).

But examples of private regulation have not emerged just recently – they have long been recorded in many areas of business activity. As a private business interest association, the International Chamber of Commerce (ICC), for instance, has been active in marketing and advertising, areas where patterns of self-regulation are documented (Boddewyn 1994). In principle, these private initiatives may replace public rule-making or make it redundant, but these arrangements are generally run independently by the industries and rarely involve such non-industry organizations as those representing consumers. Even if business interest associations do not invite countervailing forces to take part in the building and monitoring of arrangements, several business initiatives are triggered by civil society protests; these are particularly valuable for consumers in cases where effective monitoring is introduced, and where free-riders are sanctioned in ways that contribute to strengthening private rules.

In addition, some arrangements directly involving consumers have a historical tradition. Consumers International and other consumer organizations are taking part in the work of nongovernmental standard setting organizations, encountering numerous business interest associations. The International Organization for Standardization (ISO) and the International Electrotechnical Commission (IEC) are the two most important of their kind; in the main they are industry-sponsored bodies. In 1979 the two organizations issued a joint statement emphasizing the need to include all relevant stakeholders, including consumers, into their work, and ISO has since adopted a code of ethics going in the same direction. Even a special Committee on Consumer policy (COPOLCO) is entitled to focus on the consumer dimension of standardizing rules.

Wherever regulation has been largely an industry matter, consumer organizations standing outside private arrangements have often been rather skeptical as to whether consumer concerns are taken seriously. In the field of standard setting, for instance, some civil society organizations will accept this regulation, and some will not (Mattli 2003: 254–7). It is evident that business has a strong self-interest in adopting consumer-friendly practices, but it is also clear that critical voices among consumers will bring new perspectives into these arrangements.

A more recent trend is manifested through private driven arrangements where business and countervailing powers meet outside the framework of intergovernmental organizations and the private standardizing organizations, and independently find ways of exchange (Doh and Teegen 2003).

Public authority, however, also stimulates some of these initiatives. The United Nations' most recent *Guidelines for Consumer Protection* stresses that public authority should encourage the formulation and implementation by business in cooperation with consumer organizations, of codes of marketing and other business practices to ensure adequate consumer protection. Voluntary agreements may also be established jointly by business, consumer organizations and other interested parties (United Nations 1999: 7)

Part of this work is also carried out in the special agencies, and UNCTAD, for instance, can play a role in this regard by bringing together government, business and consumer representative to clarify specific policy and regulatory issues relating to consumer protection in the context of a globalizing world (UNCTAD 2001: 13).

Further, the UN Global Compact has stimulated direct cooperation between business and civil society, although major emphasis is placed on visions and principles relating to human rights, labor conditions and the environment. Given the many policy linkages with consumer policy, however, these arrangements often entail a consumer dimension. The Global Reporting Initiative, a multi-stakeholder body related to the Global Compact, also includes consumer organizations.

Private policy arrangements may reduce the burden imposed on public authority that has limited resources to devise rules and monitor agreements. Seen from both a consumer angle and the broader angle of countervailing powers, such negotiations and arrangements are not always attractive and desirable. Some organizations do not really trust business; they develop protest as the preferred mode of action and see public regulation as the ultimate and only reliable goal. Such strategies are also premised on the fact that these organizations either do not want to become involved in often highly specific arrangements, or do not possess the means to act as effective off-shore watchdogs.

From a business perspective, cooperation with consumers can be a way of avoiding the intervention and constant policing from public bureaucracy and of selecting exactly those partners that are reliable and relevant and can help solidify agreements. A large group of countervailing organizations and opinions are available in principle, but some corporations and industry associations fear organizations that are too critical. The building of agreements, therefore, requires an analysis of the many motives underlying organized consumers, including those of the more radical and protesting movements (McMurtry 2002).

In some cases, consumers are not invited because they are not expected to provide significant and relevant input, but there is still a clear public policy goal. The Global Aviation Security Action Group (GASAG), for instance, unites many aviation-related organizations with the objective to solve a range of security problems relevant to consumers and outside the framework of public institutions (see GASAG 2005). Single corporations and business interest associations respond in many ways to consumer demands and expectations in the marketplace, and these private rules can acquire a regulatory quality without the direct involvement of consumers. In most cases, however, arrangements including consumers are not suitable alternatives to public regulation, because they include only some highly committed firms.

If we take a closer look at these bi- and multilateral arrangements that have emerged in recent years at the level of specific industries or products, we find that consumers are only occasionally welcomed. CI and other consumer organizations have developed alliances with various civil society organizations, and initiatives include for instance joint statements with farmers represented by the International Federation of Agricultural Producers (IFAP) and cooperation with the Agrobusiness Accountability Initiative (see Consumers International 2005).

It is common for the consumer perspective to be pushed somewhat in the background or integrated into environmental agendas, if it is not simply represented by environmental organizations instead. For instance, a number of voluntary agreements have been made that set environmental standards for firms; however, arrangements are usually interfirm-based rather than agreed on between industry and environmental organizations, or even consumer groups (Glasbergen 1998). Environmental organizations have been both more active and more successful in finding such compromises with industry than have consumer groups (Stern and Hicks 2000), and it can be more relevant and advantageous for an industry to find an agreement in sensitive issues with environmental organizations. These organizations are better known among the general public than are others, and they are in a position to use the protest option more effectively than many consumer organizations. The availability of such alternative forms of action can seriously influence the incentive structure of business. Corporate reputation, especially in countries where corporations are vulnerable and risk public exposure, is critical to maintain – an issue particularly for large corporations.

Consumers – when they are strong enough – can also act in powerful ways in the marketplace by encouraging firms to join accreditation schemes to raise standards to the benefit of the environment. This option has been well researched in forestry, for instance (Cashore *et al.* 2004), and in other fields also (Haufler 2002). Some outfits, such as the Global Ecolabelling Network (GEN) and, the Fairtrade Labelling Organizations International (FLO), encourage and record schemes, but operate outside of the general consumer organizations. Indeed, traditional forms of standard setting and the new voluntary schemes can stir conflicts.

A central issue, however, is whether consumers can effectively put pressure on an industry when they act in a kind of business-to-business relationship, or whether they have similar leverage when they act as end consumers more narrowly. Another crucial issue is whether these arrangements attract merely the pioneering firms in an industry – maybe through a system of self-accreditation picking the "winners" – and whether only a smaller group will eventually subscribe to them (Potoski and Prakash 2005). In this case, the public value is decimated but the symbolic value can be significant when ways are paved for more encompassing private driven policy arrangements, and are not restricted to small groups of elite consumers or elite firms.

A perennial problem for business is to avoid free-riding and ultimately make all firms within an industry comply so that agreements have the same quality as traditional public regulation. Business must invest huge resources in running such arrangements, but consumer organizations, whether formally included or not, can also play an important part in the monitoring process. Nonetheless, there is a marked difference between being part of the institutional infrastructure of an agreement and giving it formal support, and providing outside ad hoc-interventions. Indeed, some forms of consumer monitoring are done with the clear ambition of bringing private regulation "back" into public domains.

Conclusions

Although many problems in consumer policy are solved at national or regional levels, important issues are discussed and settled in a global framework – sometimes with the direct involvement of consumer organizations in global rule-making. Consumers face significant collective problems, but they are nevertheless organized in a framework characterized by centralization through Consumers International, the only global and encompassing organization, and characterized by decentralization through the many small organizations active in each policy field. An even wider group of organizations take an interest in consumer affairs temporarily, addressing these while focusing on their core issues.

Not only is there a relatively high degree of fragmentation in the organization of consumer interests, but also a multitude of issues demand attention. Consumer policy is a highly complex field, permeating social policy, food policy, environmental policy and development policy, among others. Consequently, consumer organizations seek to integrate these neighboring policy fields without losing sight of key consumer perspectives.

Thus, the inherent complexity of consumer policy adds to the difficulties of organizing consumers as a large and heterogeneous group. This difficulty is further exacerbated by the split between issues relevant to consumers in the developed countries and consumers in the developing world where they must handle more basic problems – a fact testifying to the uneven globalization of policy. Bridging all these cleavages is an immense task.

Consumer organizations, however, have been granted participatory rights and have reached a consultative status in many forums, but participation varies significantly across policy fields and intergovernmental organizations. Where consumer organizations have been relevant and pragmatic partners, they have gained access to some important decision-making structures; and where action has been weak, uncoordinated or perhaps too radical, integration has been fragile and problematic.

Recent reforms, however, have questioned institutional legacies and welcomed stronger participation of civil society, a step that has also benefited consumer groups although they are rarely specifically targeted. Consumer organizations that are not invited figure mainly as outsider pressure groups, whereas in other organizations they are recognized together with many other groups – all carefully selected. In these contexts they form part of the international machinery producing global rules, but the consumer interest is one out of numerous concerns. Nevertheless, there has been a movement toward creating more public driven policy arrangements including consumers and business but, given the current processes of globalization, this challenge is enormous.

Changes in public policy are also accomplished beyond the framework of intergovernmental organizations, and private driven policy arrangements are negotiated between smaller consumer groups and business. This form of governance is a more flexible vehicle to advance consumer interests; but, apart from standardizing, arrangements hardly ever encompass a whole industry and they do not have the same quality as traditional regulation, but some move in this direction. Attention to consumer protection is stronger when these arrangements include consumer organizations, but various alliances of business also foster important arrangements.

Examples are found across different industries and often have an environmental flavor. Countervailing organizations that are not flagged as consumer organizations are attentive to the consumer perspective and have a stronger position in many bilateral and multilateral arrangements than traditional consumer organizations. To the individual consumer this is of limited importance, but it emphasizes the complexity of organizing and representing consumer interests in the evolution of a global consumer policy. The smaller arrangements, however, seem to be decoupled from traditional forms of consumer policy, there is no general recording and oversight, and traditional and capacitated consumer organizations are not seriously involved. A major challenge in the further development of global consumer policy, therefore, lies in the creation of a strong institutional coherence and the weaving together of the many forms of participation in public and private arrangements.

Notes

1 The interaction between firms and consumers is regulated at a variety of levels. Thus, single corporations formulate strategies and adopt ethical, social or environmental programs to respond to the expectations and demands of consumers – sometimes in dialog with consumers. This kind of research is, in the main, focused on large corporations. It is also possible that business establishes rules and standards, occasionally through contacts or negotiations with civil society. Finally, and without presenting an exhaustive list of regulatory devices and levels, we find that relations between business and consumers are governed by public policy and expressed through national legislation or international conventions etc. Business and civil society usually deliver an input into these processes. To confine politics within its natural boundary, we are concerned mainly with the second and third aspect of consumer policy.

2 A casual observation of a few recent collections dealing with NGOs and social movements shows that the role of consumer organizations is largely sidestepped. The main emphasis is instead put on environmental organizations, human rights organizations, relief organizations and so forth. They appear to be more important and heroic, and are not viewed as "dusty" actors from a bygone age (Smith *et al.* 1997; Keck and Sikkink 1998; Boli and Thomas 1999; Guidry *et al.* 2000; Khagram *et al.* 2002; Smith and Johnston 2002; Baker and Chandler 2005; Bandy and Smith 2005). Many political economy studies on globalization tend to focus on the business side of exchanges rather than on the role of consumers, and some scrutinize specific industries or examine the changing boundaries between state and market. Finally, those analyses that take an interest in the role of consumer behavior, especially analyses in the different branches of business administration, view consumers as having different economic preferences and cultural backgrounds. They are analyzed in an individualized perspective in which little or no room is left for understanding them as a collective force in global politics.

3 Here "political consumerism" is not dealt with. Political consumerism is defined as "consumer choice of producers and products with the goal of changing objectionable institutional or market practices" (Micheletti *et al.* 2004: xiv). The type of consumer action dealt with in this line of research is an enlightened, intelligent or ethical behavior whereby consumer protests, campaigns, demonstrations, boycotts and so forth can be useful tools and change business behavior. Consumers use their economic muscle to bring about changes, and firms identify and adapt to changing perceptions and demands among consumers. Changes in

consumer action, however, are primarily manifested in their economic pattern of behavior as voice (Hirschman, 1970), and do not seem to affect public policy in the sense, for instance, that rights are extended to all consumers, or in the sense that all firms must comply with a given set of rules. In sum, the political consumerism perspective highlights forms of civic engagement rather than public policy and the processes leading to or following political decisions (Braithwaite and Drahos 2000).

4 Furthermore, or perhaps rather as an alternative strategy, consumer policy can be disaggregated into specific products (The Worldwatch Institute 2004) and be viewed at different stages in the production and consumption chain.

5 This cooperation is not always accomplished within formal intergovernmental organizations. States also build more flexible and network-like arrangements. One such example is the International Consumer Protection and Enforcement Network (ICPEN). Established in 1992 as the International Marketing Supervision Network (IMSN), it brings together the trade practices law enforcement authorities in the OECD countries and beyond.

References

Asher, A. (1998) "Going global: a new paradigm for consumer protection," *The Journal of Consumer Affairs*, 32: 183–203.

Baker, G. and Chandler, D. (eds) (2005) *Global Civil Society Contested Futures*, London and New York: Routledge.

Bandy, J. and Smith, J. (eds) (2005) *Coalitions Across Borders: Transnational Protest in a Neoliberal Era*, Lanham, MD: Rowman & Littlefield.

Bignami, F. and Charnowitz, S. (2001) "Transatlantic civil society dialogue," in M. A. Pollack and G. C. Shaffer (eds) *Transatlantic Governance in the Global Economy*, Lanham, MD: Rowman & Littlefield Publishers.

Boddewyn, J. J. (1994) *Global Perspectives on Advertising Self-Regulation: Principles and Practices in Thirty-Eight Countries*, Madison, WI: University of Wisconsin Press.

Boli, J. and Thomas, G. M. (eds) (1999) *Constructing World Culture. International Nongovernmental Organizations Since 1875*, Stanford, CA: Stanford University Press.

Braithwaite, J. and Drahos, P. (2000) *Global Business Regulation*, Cambridge: Cambridge University Press.

Cashore, B., Auld, G. and Newsom, D. (2004) *Governing Through Markets: Forest Certification and the Emergence of Non-State Authority*, New Haven, CT: Yale University Press.

Chisholm, D. (1987) "Ill-structured problems, informal mechanisms and the design of public organizations," in J. E. Lane (ed.) *Bureaucracy and Public Choice*, London: Sage.

Consumers International (2004) *2004 Annual Report*. London: CI.

Consumers International (2005) *Decision Making in the Global Market: Trade, Standards and the Consumer*, London: CI.

Doh, J. P. and Teegen, H. (eds) (2003) *Globalization and NGOs: Transforming Business, Governments and Society*, New York: Praeger.

GASAG (2005) *Industry Positions on Security Issues*, Issue 10, May 1, 2005.

Glasbergen, P. (ed.) (1998) *Co-operative Environmental Governance: Public-Private Agreements as a Policy Strategy*, Dordrecht: Kluwer.

Guidry, J. A., Kennedy, M. D. and Zald, M. N. (eds) (2000) *Globalizations and Social Movements. Culture, Power and the Transnational Public Sphere*, Ann Arbor, MI: The University of Michigan Press.

Haufler, V. (2002) *A Public Role for the Private Sector: Industry Self-Regulation in a Global Economy*, Washington, DC: Carnegie Endowment for International Peace.

Hirschman, A. O. (1970) *Exit, Voice and Loyalty. Responses to Decline in Firms, Organizations and States*, Cambridge, MA: Harvard University Press.

Keck, M. E. and Sikkink, K. (1998) *Activists Beyond Borders. Advocacy Networks in International Politics*, Ithaca, NY and London: Cornell University Press.

Keersbergen, K. van and Waarden, F. van (2004) "Governance as a bridge between disciplines: cross-disciplinary inspiration regarding shifts in governance and problems of governability, accountability and legitimacy," *European Journal of Political Research*, 43 (1): 143–71.

Kellow, A. (2003) *Privilege and Underprivilege: Countervailing Groups and the Trajectory of the Mining Industry at the International Level*, paper presented at the Australian Political Science Association Conference, Hobart 2003.

Khagram, S., Riker, J. V. and Sikkink, K. (eds) (2002) *Restructuring World Politics. Transnational Social Movements, Networks and Norms*, Minneapolis, MN & London: University of Minnesota Press.

Krissoff, B., Bohman, M. and Caswell, J. A. (2002) (eds) *Global Food Trade and Consumer Demand for Quality*, Plenum Pub. Corp. International Agricultural Trade Consortium.

Levi-Faur, D. (2005) "The global diffusion of regulatory capitalism," in D. Levi-Faur and J. Jordana (eds) *The Rise of Regulatory Capitalism: The Global Diffusion of a New Order*, The Annals of the American Academy of Political and Social Science, vol. 598: March 2005.

Lowi, T. J. (1969) *The End of Liberalism. The Second Republic of the United States*, New York: W.W. Norton & Company.

McMurtry, J. (2002) "Why the protestors are against corporate globalization," *Journal of Business Ethics*, 40 (3): 201–5.

Mattli, W. (2003) "Public and private governance in setting international standards," in M. Kahler and D. A. Lake (eds) *Governance in a Global Economy. Political Authority in Transition*, Princeton, NJ and Oxford: Princeton University Press.

Micheletti, M., Follesdal, A. and Stolle, D. (2004) "Introduction," in M. Micheletti, D. Stolle and A. Follesdal (eds) *Politics, Products and Markets. Exploring Political Consumerism Past and Present*, New Brunswick, NJ: Transaction Publishers.

Mintzes, B. and Hodgkin, C. (1996) "The consumer movement. From single-issue campaigns to long-term reform," in P. Davis (ed.) *Contested Ground: Public Purpose and Private Interest in the Regulation of Prescription Drugs*, Oxford: Oxford University Press.

Nelson, P. S. (1995) *The World Bank and Non-Governmental Organizations. The Limits of Apolitical Development*, London: Macmillan.

Oliviero, M. B. and Simmons, A. (2002) "Who's minding the store? Global civil society and corporate responsibility," in M. Glasius, M. Kaldor and H. Anheier (eds) *Global Civil Society 2002*, Oxford: Oxford University Press.

Olson, M. (1965) *The Logic of Collective Action. Public Goods and the Theory of Groups*, Cambridge, MA: Harvard University Press.

Pollack, M. (1997) "Representing diffuse interests in the EC policy-making," *Journal of European Public Policy*, 4 (4): 572–90.

Porter, T. (2006) Governance and contestation in global finance, in K. Ronit (ed.) *Global Public Policy: Business and the Countervailing Powers of Civil Society*, London and New York: Routledge.

Potoski, M. and Prakash, A. (2005) "Green clubs and voluntary governance: ISO 14001 and firms' regulatory compliance," *American Journal of Political Science*, 49 (2): 235–48.

Putnam, R. S. (1988) "Diplomacy and domestic politics: the logic of two-level games," *International Organization*, 42 (3): 427–60.

Reinicke, W. H. (1998) *Global Public Policy. Governing without Government?* Washington, DC: Brookings Institution Press.

Ronit, K. and Schneider, V. (2000) "Private organizations and their contribution to problem solving in the global arena," in K. Ronit and V. Schneider (eds) *Private Organizations in Global Politics*, London and New York: Routledge.

Schmitter, P. C. (1990) "Sectors in modern capitalism. Modes of governance and variations in performance," in R. Brunetta and C. Dell'Aringa (eds) *Labour Relations and Economic Performance*, London: Macmillan.

Scholte, J. A. (2002) "Civil society and the governance of global finance," in J. A. Scholte and A. Schnabel (eds) *Civil Society and Global Finance*, London and New York: Routledge.

Smith, J. and Johnston, H. (eds) (2002) *Globalization and Resistance. Transnational Dimensions of Social Movements*, Lanham, MD: Rowman & Littlefield.

Smith, J., Chatfield, C. and Pagnusco, R. (1997) *Transnational Social Movements and Global Politics. Solidarity Beyond the State*, New York: Syracuse University Press.

Stern, A. J. and Hicks, T. (2000) *The Process of Business – Environmental Cooperation*, New York: Qurom Books.

Stigler, G. J. (1971) "The theory of economic regulation," *Bell Journal of Economics*, Spring 2(1): 3–21.

The Worldwatch Institute (2004) *State of the World 2004. A Worldwatch Report on Progress Toward a Sustainable Society*, New York: W.W. Norton & Company.

UNCTAD (2001) *Consumer Protection, Competition, Competitiveness and Development*, Note by the UNCTAD Secretariat, TD/B/COM.1/EM.17/3. 20.08.2001.

United Nations (1985) *Guidelines for Consumer Protection*, Resolution 39/248. UN General Assembly, New York.

United Nations (1999) *United Nations Guidelines for Consumer Protection* (as expanded in 1999), New York and Geneva: United Nations.

Vogel, D. (1995) *Trading Up. Consumer and Environmental Regulation in a Global Economy*, Cambridge, MA: Harvard University Press.

Vogel, S. K. (1996) *Freer Markets, More Rules: Regulatory Reform in Advanced Industrial Countries*, Ithaca and London: Cornell University Press.

Wilson, J. Q. (1980) The Politics of Regulation, in J. Q. Wilson (ed.) *The Politics of Regulation*, New York: Basic Books.

4 Governance and contestation in global finance

Tony Porter

Introduction

Global finance is an issue area in which the question of whether aggressive international business initiatives are constrained to an appropriate degree has long been front and center. Many citizens and nongovernmental organizations have viewed global finance with suspicion, associating it with destructive speculation, undeserved profiteering, and the manipulation of governments by powerful financial elites, and they have been eager to restrict its activities. In contrast, many supporters of the globalization of finance have applauded the removal of regulatory constraints on financial business actors, portraying those seeking to constrain global finance as backward or as self-interested nationalists. The intensity of this debate and of the pace of the globalization of finance over the past quarter century makes global finance a useful case for understanding the central theme of this book, the relationships among global public policy, business, and the countervailing powers of civil society.

A challenge in analyzing these relationships is to distinguish the degree to which they are shaped by features of globalization or late modernity that are not unique to finance, and the degree to which variation across issue areas or industries makes the case of finance distinctive. International industries and issue areas vary enormously in the degree to which they stimulate countervailing activity by civil society. For instance global chemical, apparel, mining, pharmaceutical, petroleum, and agro-food industries have all been strongly challenged by civil society actors, while airlines, semiconductors, electrical machinery, furniture, and auto parts have generally not been.[1] Since each of these sets includes both new and old industries it is clearly not only the linkages of industries with the change that globalization brings that explains the opposition from civil society that some industries and issue areas stimulate.

This chapter starts with a conceptual discussion that aims to identify the factors that are likely to account for variation in the strength of the countervailing power of civil society across international industries and issue areas. It starts by looking at theoretical work done by those studying social movements, but it seeks to go beyond this work by considering factors associated with global industries displaying high levels of global private authority – factors that are often not considered in social movement literature that assumes that the key interaction is between social movements and national or subnational public authorities. In particular it introduces the concept of an "industry opportunity structure" and variations in "supply" and "demand" with regard to solutions for problems. The chapter then looks at the case of global finance, applying the theoretical points developed in the first section to this particular case. It will show that global finance involves the types of problems that in other industries and issue areas have created "demand" for solutions from civil society organizations, but that deficiencies in the capacity of civil society actors to "supply" those solutions, including not only with regard to factors identified by social movement theory, such as framing and political opportunity and mobilizing structures, but also due to the distinctive character of the industry opportunity structure in global finance. A challenge is the degree to which policy and regulatory processes are decentralized, informal, highly technical, and closely attuned to the needs and interests of business. Nevertheless some examples are provided of civil society overcoming these challenges and providing some countervailing power to business in global finance.

Conceptualizing countervailing power and private authority at the global level

The growth of the power of business at the global level in industries such as global finance makes timely a consideration of the issue of countervailing power at the global level, first raised by Galbraith (1952), more than half a century ago, in reaction to the growth of business power in the United States. At the global level the power of business is evident in the ability of individual firms and capital more generally to achieve their goals by lobbying, by threatening to leave jurisdictions that do not comply with their preferences, and by funding industry-friendly policy research. It is also evident in the growth of collaboration among business actors at the global level and the private authority that this can produce (Cutler *et al.* 1999; Ronit and Schneider 2000; Hall and Biersteker 2002). Although organized business actors often remain nationally focused (see Kellow 2006) there are cases where they have developed substantial capacity at the global level. For instance the International Accounting Standards Board is a private-sector body that develops international accounting standards, and its rules are recognized in a very large number of jurisdictions around the world.

In his original formulation, in addition to civil society groups such as consumer groups and labor unions, Galbraith devoted considerable attention to the countervailing power of industry groups such as chain stores that he saw as emerging to offset the oligopolistic power of firms that dominated particular parts of the production process, and he urged a change in anti-trust policy to allow more horizontal collaboration among weaker segments of the business community to offset the power of a few firms in other industry segments. However, in a rapidly changing global economic environment there is no guarantee that the enhancement of business collaboration that might initially appear to countervail a different set of business actors will not itself lead to market dominance that in turn requires further countervailing power. This deficiency in the idea of business as a countervailing power suggests that we must look to non-business civil society actors, and that is the focus of this chapter.

If we must look to civil society as the main source of countervailing power to business at the global level, then it is useful to turn to the body of scholarship that has sought to understand better the growth of civil society – social movement theory. There is a wide variety of research that can shed light on global civil society, including pluralist approaches to international relations that explore all types of non-state actors, analysis of transnational advocacy networks, and many specific case studies of nongovernmental organizations. However the literature that has most directly sought to explain variation in the strength and weakness of civil society is social movement theory. Social movement theory is not just concerned with social movements narrowly defined, but rather with all the actors, networks, groups, and formal organizations that together comprise a social movement, and it sees these various organizational forms as interrelated. Its domain, therefore, is very similar to the focus of this book: the countervailing role of civil society organizations.

Social movement theory has identified three main factors that account for the emergence and growth of social movements and civil society organizations – political opportunity structures; mobilizing structures, and strategic framing. I will look briefly at each of these in turn, including the significance of a shift to a transnational scale in social movement activities, before adding a fourth factor that is needed to understand the potential for civil society to act as a countervailing power to business and the financial industries more specifically: "industry opportunity structures". I will also develop the distinction between supply and demand with regard to countervailing power.

McAdam (1996: 27), in a review of the relevant literature, sets out a "highly consensual list of dimensions of political opportunity," each of which can be treated as a variable: (1) The degree of openness of the institutionalized political system; (2) The instability of elite alignments; (3) The presence of elite allies, and (4) The state's incapacity and or lack of propensity for repression. While the relationship between these variables and the emergence of social movements is complex, empirical research generally lends support to the idea that social movements emerge and grow when these variables are positive. If social movements are strong they can influence these variables to move further in a positive direction.

"Mobilizing structures" refers to the formal and informal organizational features of the social movement, including tactical and more strategic "repertoires" (McCarthy 1996: 141). Kriesi (1996: 153) distinguishes two axes on which mobilizing structures vary. The first axis runs from a professionalized organization such as an interest group or a group offering legal assistance through to institutions that involve the direct mobilization and participation of a movement's constituency. The second axis runs from groups that provide services to the social movement and groups that seek to influence policy-makers and other authorities. In general a theme that can be discerned in this literature is that successful movements develop a more pro-fessionalized aspect over time, but that professionalized, institutionalized activities can be complementary to more aggressive, radical, direct action when the latter motivates authorities to interact with professionalized actors that they find easier to talk to than the radicals (Smith 2006: chapter 4). The literature points to the importance of personal connections and networks in fostering the growth of social movements in their early stages.

"Strategic framing" refers to the efforts of social movements to create interpretations of grievances and demands that resonate positively with broader sets of values and beliefs in the population at large (Zald 1996). Social movements can use images, actions, metaphors, rhetoric, drama, and other techniques to evoke meaning. The mass media are especially impor-tant in framing processes, and they tend to favor visually dramatic events over more complex detailed analysis. A positive emotional response from members, donors, and sympathizers is likely to be provoked by framings involving testimonials about issues affecting the integrity of the body, along with issues that involve a denial of equal opportunity (Keck and Sikkink 1998: 27). Framing ties together political opportunities and mobilizing structures since it can identify and create opportunities where none were perceived before, and it can recruit support and strengthen the organization of a social movement.

While social movement theory began with a local or national focus, in more recent years it has been extended to include transnational dimensions (Keck and Sikkink 1998; Edwards and Gaventa 2001; Khagram *et al.* 2002; Clark 2003; Bandy and Smith 2005; della Porta and Tarrow 2005; Smith 2006). In noting three main movement forms – international civil society organizations (CSOs); CSO networks, and social movements (Clark 2003: 4–5) or formal transnational organizations, coalitions, and networks (Smith 2006: chapter 4) – other authors identify variation similar to Kriesi's emphasis on the degree of professionalization at the national level. It has been suggested that there are two generations of activism at the global level – one more professionalized and NGO focused, and a "second generation direct activism that embeds established NGO-centered networks in sprawling, loosely interconnected network webs" (Bennett 2005: 213), perhaps reversing the tendency in national social movements to become more professionalized over time (Tarrow and della Porta 2005: 241).

At the global level there are additional sources of tension within social movements with regard to North–South inequality, linguistic and cultural differences, gaps in technical capacities such as internet use, and the relationship of international CSO secretariats to national and local members (Bandy and Smith 2005: 237–40). The tension between the need for decisive speedy leadership and maintaining the sense of ownership of members is more severe at the international level where the environment is complex and volatile and distances between secretariats and members can be long (Clark 2003: 19–21) and the demands on leaders for communicating, translating, educating, and managing conflict are greater (Bandy and Smith 2005: 240–1).

Applying the insights of social movement theory to understand the sources of countervailing power to business

Social movement theory offers valuable insights into the reasons that resistance to prevailing configurations of power may arise or not but these insights need to be modified and integrated with other concepts in order to maximize their potential for understanding the issues that this book addresses. The configurations of power that social movement theory addresses are almost exclusively governments,[2] while this book primarily focuses on the role of business in global policies, whether this is expressed through public driven arrangements or private driven arrangements (see Ronit 2006). In the context of this book we can therefore apply the insights of social movement theory more fruitfully by adding a fourth variable, which can be labeled "industry opportunity structure." By understanding the factors that contribute to the emergence of countervailing power in one industry and not another we can better understand existing levels of countervailing power in any particular international industry, such as global finance.

A first step in developing the idea of industry opportunity structures is to consider factors on the business side that may contribute to the types of problems that demand responses from civil society organizations.[3] These demands can in part be encompassed by the notion of negative externalities: costs that are not incorporated into the prices involved in a transaction but instead fall on third parties, including citizens in general. This market-centric "market failure" approach should be supplemented with a more political approach that acknowledges the degree to which business can provoke resistance by engaging in activities that tend to be interpreted as involving unfair exploitation of people or the environment. These threats and risks are not just structural features of particular industries, but are also entangled with framing processes that define only some threats and risks as deserving to be opposed or offset. Opportunities for effective framing are likely to vary across industries since industries are already associated with particular meanings, such as "dirty," "high tech," "dangerous," "corrupt," "globalized," "big," "heavy," "health," and "fashionable."

When we add business power to state power as a form of power that needs to be countervailed, whether this business power is expressed through public driven or private driven arrangements, the opportunity structures for civil society organizations are likely to be more closed because there is a reduced expectation for public accountability; this closure is likely to involve very high barriers to entry, for instance from the costs involved in attending business conferences, the dispersed settings in which discussions occur, and the highly technical nature of many business policy or regulatory discussions. There is no expectation that business actors have an obligation to help finance or otherwise support the involvement of civil society actors, unlike public-sector institutions for which such involvement can be seen as important for their legitimacy. In general the degree of professionalization for civil society organizations to be successful is likely to be greater when they are seeking to challenge business actors than when they are seeking to challenge public-sector actors.

The challenges mentioned earlier increase the importance of revenue-generating opportunities other than donations and dues for civil society organizations. When the target of civil society actors is public-sector institutions dealing with non-business issues there are likely to be opportunities for revenue generation because of the compatibility of the public orientation of both public-sector institutions and civil society organizations. This could include civil society organizations receiving grants for producing information, or for delivering services, such as foreign aid. Although some such compatibilities may exist when the target is business actors, such as civil society organizations that generate income from certifying a product as environmentally friendly or a practice as socially responsible, such opportunities are likely to be more rare, at the same time that, as already noted, the need for revenue to keep up with developments in business dominated self-regulatory and policy processes is likely to be very high. Without opportunities to generate a stable revenue stream through donations, dues, or fees, civil society organizations alone will not be able to build a sustainable countervailing power to business.

The character of the countervailing power of civil society is also likely to be strongly affected by variations across industries and issue areas in the mediating or organizing role of public-sector actors and institutions, an aspect of political opportunity structure that is often not recognized. Public-sector actors and institutions can side with business or with civil society and this has an impact on the potential for the development of countervailing power to business. Hybrid combinations of public driven and private driven arrangements have become increasingly common in the making and implementation of global public policies. This involves a change in the role of the public sector from its monopolization of policy making in traditional international treaty negotiations or in the passing of laws in national legislatures.

Public-sector actors, including states and international organizations, foster and participate in a set of decentralized interactions with business and civil society actors (Reinicke and Deng 2000; Slaughter 2004). While these arrangements can be more open to civil society influence because of their decentralization and because of the important coordinating role played by technical knowledge rather than hierarchical commands, their informality and technical complexity can also make it difficult for civil society actors to know how to intervene effectively in policy debates.

This can negatively affect three of the elements of political opportunity structure identified earlier as important for the emergence of countervailing power: the institutionalized political system can become less open, elite alignments can become more stable, and elite allies become less likely. One solution is the creation by social movements of "rival transnational networks" (Smith 2006: chapter 2).

In looking at the earlier discussion of the four factors that are important in explaining variation in the emergence of a countervailing power of civil society it is useful to make one further distinction: between "supply" and "demand." "Supply" refers to the capacity of civil society organizations to supply solutions to problems such as the excessive power of particular firms, and "demand" refers to the intensity of the problems demanding solutions in public policy.

We may array these four factors and two distinctions as in Table 4.1. We can hypothesize that civil society organizations are more likely to develop effective capacity, including the capacity to act as a countervailing power to business, when both demand and supply are high: civil society organizations are unlikely to arise when there are no problems demanding solutions, if public authority alone can provide solutions, or when conditions make it impossible for them to organize.

The conceptual discussion mentioned earlier can be summed up in highlighting three factors that can explain variation in the strength of the countervailing power of civil society across industries and time: (1) The degree to which business initiatives generate the types of problems that *demand* responses from civil society; (2) The degree to which civil society has the capacity to *supply* countervailing power and engage in strategic framing to address these problems, and (3) The character of the international public-sector institutions and political opportunity structures that mediate between and organize the interactions between business actors and civil society, affecting both demand and supply. It should be noted that these propositions differ sharply from many prevailing approaches to the study of international relations, including state-centric approaches that neglect the role of both business and civil society actors; approaches that stress the autonomous power of business; and approaches that treat global civil society as a system-wide phenomenon that is an expression of globalization, rather than a phenomenon that varies across industries and issue areas.[4] In the next section I apply the conceptual points made so far to the

Table 4.1 Factors and supply/demand distinctions in the emergence of civil society
capacity, including its capacity to countervail business

	Industry opportunity structure	Political opportunity structure	Strategic framing	Mobilizing structures
Supply of solutions (factors that facilitate the organization of effective civil society opposition)	Retail presence (easy to pressure), simple technologies (easy to understand), concentrated structure (easy to target), lack of cross-border mobility (cannot flee)	Degree of openness of the institutionalized political system, instability of elite alignments; presence of elite allies; state's incapacity, and, or lack of propensity for repression (as per McAdam earlier)	Readily available stock of images, actions, metaphors, rhetoric, drama that can inspire support and participation in civil society activities	Readily available linkages, such as brokerage or relational, from this global issue area to other global and national issue areas where civil society organizations are well developed
Demand for solutions (factors associated with severity of problems)	High externalities, risks, and levels of economic and environmental exploitation	Failure of public sector institutions to countervail business power and risks, regulatory failures, public sector complicity in business exploitation	Readily available stock of images, actions, metaphors, rhetoric, drama that can frame problems as involving negative effects that demand responses	Problems are ones that fit with perceived mandate of civil society organizations in issue area

case of global finance. I look in turn at the degree to which problems in
global finance "demand" countervailing responses; the degree to which civil
society can "supply" countervailing power, and finally the mediating role of
public-sector institutions.

Problems in global finance and the demand for countervailing responses

As a set of industries global finance is surprisingly varied and differentiated,
with banking, securities, insurance, and other financial services such as

accounting, each displaying distinctive characteristics. For instance banking is focused generally on relatively short-term lending and deposits, and has always been closely monitored by governments for its impact on the monetary and payments system, while securities such as bonds and stocks are sold directly by governments or firms, with securities firms assisting in the underwriting and distribution. Since investors in securities markets are assumed to be more knowledgeable and able to take on risks than depositors in banks, governments have generally been less concerned about protecting them. The international financial system consists of many different private-sector actors, including huge internationally oriented banks, such as Citibank, small firms, such as local insurance brokers, and individual professionals, such as financial planners. Private-sector financial associations range from the Institute of International Finance (IIF), which is highly influential in global regulatory and policy processes, to the Certified Financial Planner Board of Standards (CFP Board), which trains and certifies professionals worldwide.

Most of the damage done by financial actors to citizens falls into three main categories. Each of these makes global finance prone to the types of problems that one might expect to stimulate opposition from civil society and thus the growth of countervailing power.

The first category involves problems of negative externalities in which damages or costs to citizens are not reflected in market prices of transactions but rather are arbitrarily imposed on actors that are not able to insist on compensation or mitigation of risk. This is in part due to the systemic role played by finance, where a financial crisis can lead to a broader economic crisis. It is partly due to the complex and intangible character of finance where the contingent costs of an arrangement such as a derivatives contract may easily be obscured. Financial crises can have catastrophic impacts on citizens who had no part in creating them. While financial damage is hard to quantify it is clear that it can be very significant. For instance a Bank of England working paper (Hoggarth *et al.* 2001) has estimated that cumulative output losses during periods of bank crisis average 15–20 percent of annual GDP. Fraud, in which unscrupulous financial actors cheat depositors or investors, as was the case with Enron, can involve widespread disruption in an economy as a whole, and can be included in this category. These are the types of problems that in other issues areas, such as the risks associated with toxic chemicals, have provoked a strong response from civil society.

Second, global finance is closely associated with the types of great social inequality that one might expect to provoke opposition from civil society. Not only are financial elites ostentatiously wealthy, but also their wealth has traditionally been seen by many as undeserved proceeds from speculation or from unnecessary activities that work against the real economy. Financial crises can exacerbate inequality. The International Monetary Fund (1998: 48) estimated that the countries most affected by the Asian financial crisis (Indonesia, South Korea, and Thailand) had an increase in the number of people in poverty between 11.4 and 33.6 million.

Third, and relatedly, financial problems touch on the types of existential issues that in other issue areas have inspired resistance. This includes the imposition of financial measures or markets on social processes in ways that undermine other values, such as when the IMF or bank creditors demand harsh cuts in social spending in order to ensure repayment on their loans. Finance is emblematic of commodification, competitive markets, and the dominance of pecuniary values over other human values. In this regard it has been charged with doing a similar type of damage to the human spirit and the human community as have other problematic business activities, such as those involved in the violation of labour standards or the destruction of human habitats through environmental degradation or urban development. Since violations of labour standards and destruction of habitats have provoked opposition from civil society, one might therefore expect a similar opposition to financial globalization.

The character of civil society and its capacity to supply countervailing power to business

Despite the types of problems created by global finance, which one might expect to provoke popular opposition, the countervailing power of civil society has been relatively weak in this issue area as compared with others like human rights or the environment (for analyses of global civil society and finance see also Edwards and Gaventa 2001: part 2; O'Brien *et al.* 2000; Porter 2005: chapter 9; Scholte and Schnabel 2002).

The primary focus of critics of global finance has been the structural adjustment policies of the IMF and World Bank. While the problem of structural adjustment can be traced back to the debt crisis of the early 1980s when developing countries had trouble repaying loans they had taken from commercial banks, the focus of the critics was the way in which the IMF and World Bank – two public-sector institutions – required indebted countries to cut back on social spending and implement market-oriented reforms in order to accumulate the financial resources needed to repay the banks if they wished to get the IMF and World Bank loans and their seal of approval needed for commercial banks to extend their loans. A great many civil society organizations, such as the European Network on Debt and Development (EURODAD), the Forum on Debt and Development (FONDAD), Oxfam, and the Committee for the Cancellation of Third World Debt (CADTM), highlighted the high personal costs for citizens of indebted countries of these structural adjustment policies. The problem lent itself to some degree to the types of testimonial knowledge and anger and denial of equal opportunity around which civil society organizations can mobilize.

A second focus of critics of global finance has been investment agreements, especially the failed negotiations on a *Multilateral Agreement on Investment* (MAI) (Smythe 1998) at the Organization for Economic

Cooperation and Development and the chapter 11 investor dispute provisions of the North American Free Trade Agreement (NAFTA). Both of these were seen as establishing strong international legal rules that gave private-sector investors unprecedented protection of their interests at the expense of other public policy goals without making them any more accountable for any negative externalities they might create. Chapter 11 came under fire for allowing foreign firms to treat environmental regulations as a form of expropriation for which they could demand compensation in a legal process lacking transparency or input from third parties that might be negatively affected. Civil society organizations played a key role in thwarting agreement on the MAI, and they have effectively highlighted the problems with chapter 11 cases.

A third focus of critics of global finance has been efforts to get governments to implement a "Tobin" tax on international financial transactions (Ul Haq *et al.* 1996). This tax would be a fraction of a percent on each transaction, and it would impose little burden on periodic long-term foreign investments but would become prohibitive for speculators moving quickly and frequently in and out of currencies. Many civil society actors concerned about North–South inequality favored the Tobin tax not just for the way it could dampen harmful cross-border financial volatility, but also for the revenue it could raise for development spending.

The Association for the Taxation of Financial Transactions for the Aid of Citizens (ATTAC), formed in 1998 (Muro 2003; Kolb 2005; Porter 2005: 145–6) grew in a few years to involve participants from 38 countries, generating a large number of popular and more analytical publications in support of the tax. ATTAC is an important example of the potentials and limitations of the countervailing power of civil society in global finance because it is the largest transnational group that focuses on the private-sector cross-border financial flows that are eclipsing official flows, such as those at the World Bank and IMF. Kolb (2005) provides a very interesting account of the initial failures to attract attention and members of ATTAC Germany, and the subsequent impressive successes that were linked to the organization's involvement in international protests, especially the 2001 G8 Summit in Genoa, and its skill in media relations. Muro (2003) comments on the relationship between ATTAC in France, where the organization was founded, and the transnational aspect of ATTAC. ATTAC appears to have had some success in developing a detailed technical analysis of the feasibility of the tax, in recruiting members, and in making itself known. However in the case of ATTAC Germany it is not clear that it was the financial issues that were important in this, rather than the organization skillfully making use of media interest in large multi-issue protests, and Muro's (2003: 161) account highlights the difficulty of bringing the technical detail together with the activist aspect: "it has not managed to become a single transnational community. It remains unclear whether this transformation would be possible within such an informal network." The tax itself has not moved much closer to implementation, largely due to the opposition of the US government.

In general civil society critics of global finance have focused on public driven arrangements rather than on private driven arrangements or particular firms, although drawings of bankers, piles of money, or dollar signs have occasionally been used to make the operations of global finance more concrete.[5] The public driven arrangements that have been targeted are traditional ones that are associated with conventional public-sector actors, such as the formal intergovernmental organizations of the IMF, World Bank, or the Organization for Economic Cooperation and Development (OECD), and from which civil society organizations are traditionally barred, or governments themselves, and very little attention has been devoted to the newer informal public driven or hybrid arrangements in which international financial standards and codes are developed. As noted below, these latter arrangements are where the most important efforts to regulate international private-sector financial flows take place. In recent years these private-sector flows have greatly exceeded cross-border public-sector flows. It is noticeable that most critics of global finance have moved laterally into this issue area from other issue areas such as the environment, economic development, or trade (see for instance Brown and Fox 2001: 46–7).

Three factors affecting the capacity of civil society to supply countervailing power stand out. First, problems associated with global finance do not lend themselves well to the type of framing that allows civil society actors to mobilize support. Often the problems are abstract and systemic and are not likely to easily lead to the type of local testimonial knowledge that creates an emotional reaction. Negative effects can be experienced at great distances from their source, reinforcing their impersonal character. This is reinforced by the tendency to frame problems as the responsibility of the individual – as associated with individual risks willingly taken on. There are some exceptions to this, including the success in the *Jubilee 2000 campaign* in having their call for debt relief resonate with the original biblical reference to wiping debts away and freeing slaves every fifty years (Collins *et al.* 2001; Grenier 2003). The campaign began as a small informal effort in the early 1990s to a broad-based coalition with organizations in 69 countries, mobilizing millions of people in 166 countries and collecting 24.2 million signatures on its petition (Grenier 2003: 86), only a few years later. Its politicization of a biblical idea contributed to its ability to work through both political and church networks, although concrete features of its mobilizing structure, such as its skilful use of the internet and the support it received from organized UK participants, were also important. The *Jubilee 2000 campaign* was an important factor in the agreement of developed countries to mitigate the negative effects of their market-oriented approaches through the Highly Indebted Poor Country (HIPC) debt relief and Poverty Reduction Strategy Paper processes. The linking of financing for power generation projects to the destruction of ancestral lands of indigenous peoples is another example of effective framing (Brown and Fox 2001: 47).

Second, many problems in global finance, while severely negative for the average citizen, can appear to be primarily the ones affecting wealthy elites, undermining the sense of unfairness that allows civil society groups to mobilize countervailing power. For instance hedge funds like Long-Term Capital Management can do a great deal of harm to the average citizen by speculating against currencies or creating systemic instability, but traditionally they have been seen as risky vehicles for high net worth individuals who do not deserve any assistance.

Third, most of the activities in global finance that might lend themselves to the generation of revenue streams for civil society organizations are problematic because of the high level of knowledge needed to engage in them, or because they would implicate civil society organizations in the problems and reduce their support among the general public. In other issue areas than finance, by contrast, when consumer groups receive a stream of revenue for fostering a sustainable and humane production process, such as with the selling of fair trade coffee, or the provision of specialized knowledge, such as reporting on environmental matters, or the delivery of aid in famines, they enhance their own financial sustainability while also contributing to the solution of the problem. A partial exception is microfinancing, in which civil society organizations and other actors provide very small loans to poor individual borrowers, especially women. While much microfinancing substitutes social networks for traditional forms of security to assure repayment, it is not as much a source of countervailing power to traditional banking as a complement that serves populations that would otherwise be overlooked by banks.

The mediating role of public-sector institutions and political opportunity structures

Over the past quarter century in global finance there has been a progressive strengthening of public driven arrangements designed to help manage systemic risk, but these arrangements take the form of decentralized and overlapping public policy networks that are often not recognized even by observers with considerable familiarity with finance. A full account of these institutions goes beyond the scope of this chapter (see Porter 2005), but they include groupings based at the Bank for International Settlements (BIS) in Basel, Switzerland, such as the Basel Committee on Banking Supervision (BCBS), the Financial Stability Forum (FSF), the International Association of Insurance Supervisors (IAIS), the Committee on Payment and Settlement Systems (CPSS), and the Committee on the Global Financial System (CGFS). They also include more traditional formal institutions such as the International Organization of Securities Commissions (IOSCO), some of which, like the World Bank (IBRD), the International Monetary Fund (IMF), and the Organization for Economic Cooperation and Development (OECD), have other responsibilities than contributing to the regulation of global finance, including in the cases of the Bank and the IMF, economic development and the management of exchange rates. The G7 and the G20, informal groupings which operate at the level of finance ministers, the G10 which includes central bank governors and the G8, which brings heads of governments together, are also important.

These traditional arrangements are important for global public policy both for what they do and what they do not do. They contribute to the regulation of global finance by setting technical standards, which are implemented and monitored at the national level or by market actors. These technical standards can have a positive impact on the stability and efficiency of global finance. However these arrangements do not go very far in addressing the concerns of civil society organizations about the negative impacts of global finance on the living conditions of those affected by financial crises, of financially driven economic restructuring, and of the growing inequality that financial liberalization can bring. Moreover, the decentralized and informal character of these arrangements is a political opportunity structure that makes it difficult for civil society organizations to press for the implementation of policies that would more effectively address their concerns. There is some overall coordination, such as through the FSF, which includes representatives from most of the other bodies and which monitors the standards and codes that these other bodies create, through the G7, which takes high level political initiatives such as its creation of the FSF in 1999, and through the World Bank and IMF, which incorporate observance of standards and codes into loan conditionality processes. However in general these institutions operate by bringing experts together in highly technical discussions about best practices and standards.

While these regulatory and policy networks are the most important public-sector institutions concerned with the regulation of cross-border private-sector financial flows, the IMF and the multilateral development banks, such as the World Bank, which are hierarchical and bureaucratic rather than decentralized and informal, continue to play an important role in the organization of market-friendly public-sector loans, grants, and policy advice. The IMF has remained much more impervious to its critics than the World Bank, in part because of it being more closely linked to monetary issues and the World Bank to development issues (O'Brien *et al.* 2000; Edwards and Gaventa 2001: part 2). Central bankers and other monetary officials are traditionally secretive, conservative, and highly committed to rigorous economic modeling. By contrast, and in large part in response to civil society critics, the World Bank has become more eclectic in integrating individuals and social science methodologies that are more attuned to the non-economic factors that may be important to development even if they can be at odds with business interests. This process can be dated back to the NGO-World Bank Working Group, established in 1981. This institutionalization of NGO participation in the activities of the World Bank corresponds to what Ronit, in Chapter 1, identifies as a new public driven policy.

The *50 Years is Enough* campaign, targeting the Bretton Woods institutions, which brought together a wide variety of civil society organizations on the occasion of their fiftieth anniversary, is one of the more prominent interactions between civil society and the IMF and World Bank. Two examples of the influence of civil society organizations are the IMF's Poverty Reduction Strategy Papers, a process that requires governments to consult with civil society if they are to obtain IMF funding, and the UN Financing for Development process, which brought the IMF and World Bank together with the UN for the first time. The UN historically has had closer relations with civil society organizations than the IMF or World Bank, and this process involved a significant effort to foster dialog between civil society and these public-sector institutions, even if many civil society critics felt that their concerns were still not adequately heard.

There are a number of ways in which civil society organizations see the IMF and the World Bank as biased toward the interests of business and against the interests of their constituencies. Both organizations have a weighted voting system that gives wealthy countries a much bigger say than the developing countries that are most affected by the IMF and World Bank policies. Large financial firms are headquartered in these wealthy countries, and they can lobby their national governments to get the IMF and World Bank to pursue business-friendly policies. The IMF and World Bank are overwhelmingly staffed by economists who have been trained in US universities. US academic economists tend to focus on the benefits of markets and individual utility maximization, and many civil society organizations have seen this as promoting business values at the expense of other values. This was especially the case for the Washington Consensus, an aggressively market-oriented set of macroeconomic policies that became dominant in the IMF and World Bank through the 1980s and 1990s. IMF and World Bank policies often rely on the activities of financial market actors (such as policies designed to stimulate flows of investment into developing countries) and thus there is an inherent tendency to listen to and cater to the needs of these actors.

Private driven arrangements are important in global finance, but they generally remain off the radar screen of civil society actors, and business actors see no reason to invite these actors to participate. These arrangements include lobby groups, the most influential of which is the Institute of International Finance (IIF). The IIF was formed in the 1980s by the largest international commercial banks, and it has become the main business group that interacts with public driven arrangements, such as the IMF or the international regulatory groups listed earlier. Private driven arrangements also include clearing houses and exchanges that facilitate cross-border transfer of money, stocks, and other financial instruments, and associations of financial professionals that set standards for their profession. Many of these private driven arrangements make rules, the most impressive example being the International Accounting Standards Board (IASB), mentioned earlier.

Private-sector actors have also become much more directly involved in public driven arrangements as they have developed. For instance a major 2004 revision of the Basel Committee on Banking Supervision's 1988 capital adequacy standards was striking for the high level of consultation between the public-sector regulators and the IIF as well as for the incorporation of private-sector risk models and credit rating, none of which had been present in the earlier standards. Civil society actors are absent from these types of public–private consultations and regulatory innovations, even though the changes can involve issues that in other settings have been of concern to civil society.

For instance the financial press and officials from developing countries have expressed concerns that the 2004 revisions may favour firms from developed countries that have experience with private-sector risk models and credit rating, especially those from the US, and disadvantage developing country actors. Concerns have also been expressed that the new standards as a whole may exacerbate economic cycles as the risk models and credit ratings respond to economic downturns by requiring banks to be more conservative in their lending. In short, the 2004 revisions could create the type of damage to vulnerable actors that in other contexts civil society actors have criticized.

The overall picture that emerges of the mediating role of public-sector institutions and political opportunity structures is one that is much more positive for business than for civil society, and that makes it difficult for civil society organizations to countervail the power of business. The most important policy arrangements are public driven, and there is some involvement of civil society organizations in these, or in response to these. However many of these public driven arrangements are linked to private driven arrangements or particular business actors in a way that tends to make them more attentive to the needs of business. There are also private driven arrangements that are involved in rule-making, and civil society organizations play no significant role in countervailing these, in part because these private driven arrangements engage in more technical work that appears obscure to non-experts, and in part because civil society organizations do not have the resources to play this role. While much of the work of these private driven arrangements is indeed technical and peripheral to the concerns of civil society organizations, this technical work can also play an important role in establishing the practices upon which public driven arrangements build their policies. The particular character of these private driven arrangements can be seen as an element of industry opportunity structure that is distinctive to finance.

It is possible that this relatively inhospitable character of the public driven and private driven policy and regulatory arrangements will be offset if civil society develops the type of technical capacity that it would require to effectively intervene in the discussions that take place in these arrangements. In contrast to trade and other traditional negotiations, agreement in these arrangements is based to a much greater degree on logical and empirical arguments than on the exercise of power or bargaining over an exchange of resources. A well-formulated and well-supported critical argument might therefore receive more consideration than in traditional negotiations. However unfortunately many of the analytical models used in these networks are closely tied to individualized rational actor approaches that are not especially amenable to the types of social concerns that many civil society actors might wish to raise.

Conclusions

In this conclusion we have an opportunity, based on the discussion to this point, to consider both the potential for civil society actors to provide a countervailing power to business power in global finance, and the significance of the answer we give to this first question for our understanding more generally of the relationship between business and civil society at the global level.

The first section of this chapter set out the contribution that social movement theory can make to our understanding of the potential for civil society organizations to provide a countervailing power to business at the global level. Social movement theory analyzes both formal civil society organizations and more informal activities such as coalitions or networks, and it sees these organizational forms as related to one another, for instance when formal organizations produce detailed policy analysis and informal coalitions produce street protests that provide an incentive for authorities and the media to pay attention to civil society concerns.

The chapter discussed three factors identified by social movement theory as important in the development of an actively engaged civil society – political opportunity structures, mobilizing structures, and strategic framing – and it considered how these factors are affected when we shift our analysis from the national to the international level. The section then discussed the idea that industries differ from one another and from public-sector institutions in the degree to which they stimulate and are amenable to the countervailing initiatives of civil society actors, a factor that can be labelled "industry opportunity structure." The section then distinguished between a demand and supply dimension of the four factors with regard to the propensity of civil society actors to provide solutions to problems, including the construction of countervailing power. The discussion of the case of global finance in the chapter's next section examined demand factors, supply factors, and the mediating role of public-sector institutions and political opportunity structures.

With regard to demand factors, the chapter pointed to negative externalities in which financial markets impose unexpected costs on citizens that are not part of market exchanges, including the costs of financial crises and fraud. It also pointed to the social inequality that accompanies the globalization of finance, and the elevation of financial and market values at the expense of other values. All these are the type of negative effects that have led to the emergence of a countervailing power of civil society in other industries or issue areas.

With regard to supply factors, the chapter pointed to three difficulties that civil society organizations face in responding to this demand. These include the difficulty of framing issues in global finance, although the success of *Jubilee 2000* in linking debt to a biblical reference shows that these are not insurmountable. They also include the way in which many financial risks and costs appear to be of more concern for wealthy investors than for the average citizen, even if they can also seriously hurt the average citizen in different ways, making it harder to clearly target the usual constituencies of civil society organizations. The difficulty for civil society organizations of developing steady streams of revenues is also a challenge. Nevertheless there are examples where civil society organizations have been quite successful in mobilizing supporters, including ATTAC's building of support for international financial transactions taxes.

With regard to the mediating role of public-sector institutions and political opportunity structures, the reliance of governance arrangements in global finance on informal international groupings of public and private regulators, along with the traditional secrecy or impermeability of central banks and the International Monetary Fund have been negative for the capacity of social movements to develop countervailing power. Civil society actors have tended to focus on the IMF and World Bank, which, as very visible public-sector institutions, are more accessible than informal policy networks, and the World Bank has become more open, in part in response to the countervailing power of civil society. However the most important initiatives in global finance have increasingly involved cross-border private-sector financial flows rather than the official lending that is the primary focus of the IMF and World Bank, and the less visible character of governance in this area poses a challenge to civil society organizations. This challenge is also due to the industry opportunity structure: finance is complex, dispersed, mobile, and often operates in elite settings that are difficult to monitor.

The case of finance also highlights a tension for civil society organizations that is related to, but different from, a set of other tensions that have already been identified in the social movements literature. This is the tension between the importance of understanding the abstract systemic dimension of many contemporary problems and the need to communicate the meaning of this dimension in a way the constituencies of civil society organizations can understand and care about, but also act effectively to influence. This is related to the professionalization/extra-institutional tensions that were noted earlier in the chapter. Understanding "supply" and "demand" variation across industries and issue areas, a task to which this chapter has sought to contribute, should be useful in working with these tensions, by making visible the concrete instances of negative financial effects that can and should be a priority to address through the counter-vailing power of civil society.

Notes

1 On the variation in responses to global regulatory problems see Braithwaite and Drahos (2000).
2 Bandy and Smith (2005: 235) make a passing reference to the openness of corporations to change, which is suggestive of the idea of a corporate or industry opportunity structure, but the implication is not developed. McAdam (1996: 25) has identified four "facilitative conditions": (1) The dramatization of a glaring contradiction between a highly salient cultural value and conventional social practices, (2) "Suddenly imposed grievances," (3) Dramatizations of a system's vulnerability or illegitimacy, (4) The availability of an innovative "master frame" within which subsequent challengers can map their own grievances and demands," and while these could be linked to variations in industry characteristics this is not a line of inquiry that has been pursued.
3 In moving beyond social movement theory I will use the label "civil society organizations" to include both formal organizations and other forms of organization, such as networks or coalitions, consistent with the use of this label elsewhere in this book.
4 The somewhat puzzling neglect in social movement theory of what I have called variations in "demand" may be due to the assumption that there is always an underlying systemwide need for social change, and lack of social movement activity is due to what I have called the "supply" dimension of the factors listed earlier. The use of the word "opportunity" reinforces this conjecture: the need for change is invariant, and it is the opportunities for bringing about this change that vary. However, it is important to understand the "demand" dimension, both theoretically and for social movements that wish to allocate their limited energy and resources effectively.
5 For instance School of Americas Watch North East has entwined IMF, SOA and WB in a dollar sign that sits above a silhouette of protesters and the phrase "Trickle Down Oppression" (School of Americas Watch North East, 2005). Rather than money, ATTAC International's website uses an image of a Universal Product Code that turns into a world map in order to illustrate the excessive commercialization of the world (ATTAC 2005).

References

ATTAC (2005) Available http://www.attac.org (accessed May 27, 2005).
Bandy, J. and Smith, J. (eds) (2005) *Coalitions Across Borders: Transnational Protest in a Neoliberal Era*, Lanham, MD: Rowman & Littlefield.
Bennett, W. L. (2005) "Social movements beyond borders: understanding two eras of transnational activism," in D. della Porta and S. Tarrow (eds) *Transnational Protest and Global Activism*, Lanham, MD: Rowman & Littlefield.
Braithwaite, J. and Drahos, P. (2000) *Global Business Regulation*, Cambridge: Cambridge University Press.

Brown, L. D. and Fox, J. (2001) "Transnational civil society coalitions and the World Bank: lessons from project and policy influence campaigns," in M. Edwards and J. Gaventa (eds) *Global Citizen Action*, Boulder, CO: Lynne Rienner.

Clark, J. D. (2003) *Globalizing Civic Engagement: Civil Society and Transnational Action*, London and Sterling: Earthscan.

Collins, C. J. L., Gariyo, Z., and Burdon, T. (2001) "Jubilee 2000: citizen action across the north-south divide," in M. Edwards and J. Gaventa (eds) *Global Citizen Action*, Boulder, CO: Lynne Rienner.

Cutler, A. C., Haufler, V., and Porter, T. (1999) *Private Authority and International Affairs*, Albany, NY: State University of New York Press.

della Porta, D. and Tarrow, S. (eds) (2005) *Transnational Protest and Global Activism*, Lanham, MD: Rowman & Littlefield.

Edwards, M. and Gaventa, G. (eds) (2001) *Global Citizen Action*, Boulder, CO: Lynne Rienner.

Galbraith, J. K. (1952) *American Capitalism: The Concept of Countervailing Power*, Boston, MA: Houghton Mifflin.

Grenier, P. (2003) "Jubilee 2000: laying the foundation for a social movement," in J. D. Clark (ed.) *Globalizing Civic Engagement: Civil Society and Transnational Action*, London and Sterling: Earthscan.

Hall, R. B. and Biersteker, T. J. (eds) (2002) *The Emergence of Private Authority in Global Governance*, Cambridge: Cambridge University Press.

Hoggarth, G., Reis, R., and Saporta, V. (2001)"Cost of banking system instability: some empirical evidence," *Bank of England Working Paper* No. 144. Available htttp://www.bankofengland.co.uk/publications/workingpapers/wp144.pdf

International Monetary Fund (1998) *World Economic Outlook: Financial Turbulence and the World Economy*, October, Washington, DC: IMF.

Keck, M. and Sikkink, K. (1998) *Activists Beyond Borders*, Ithaca, NY: Cornell University Press.

Kellow, A. (2006) "Privilege and underprivilege: countervailing groups, policy and the mining industry at the global level," in K. Ronit (ed.) *Global Public Policy: Business and the Countervailing Powers of Civil Society*, London and New York: Routledge.

Khagram, S., Riker, J. V., and Sikkink, K. (eds) (2002) *Restructuring World Politics: Transnational Movements, Networks and Norms*, Minneapolis, MN: University of Minnesota Press.

Kolb, F. (2005) "The impact of transnational protest on social movement organizations: mass media and the making of ATTAC Germany," in D. della Porta and S. Tarrow (eds) *Transnational Protest and Global Activism*, Lanham, MN: Rowman and Littlefield.

Kriesi, H. P. (1996) "The organizational structure of new social movements in a political context," in D. McAdam, J. D. McCarthy, and M. N. Zald (eds) *Comparative Perspectives on Social Movements: Political Opportunities, Mobilizing Structures, and Cultural Framings*, New York: Cambridge University Press.

McAdam, D. (1996) "Conceptual origins, current problems, future directions," in D. McAdam, J. D. McCarthy and M. N. Zald (eds) *Comparative Perspectives on Social Movements: Political Opportunities, Mobilizing Structures, and Cultural Framings*, New York: Cambridge University Press.

McCarthy, J. D. (1996) "Mobilizing structures: constraints and opportunities in adopting, adapting and inventing," in D. McAdam, J. D. McCarthy, and

M. N. Zald (eds) *Comparative Perspectives on Social Movements: Political Opportunities, Mobilizing Structures, and Cultural Framings*, New York: Cambridge University Press.

Muro, D. (2003) "Campaign for a 'Robin Hood Tax' for foreign exchange markets," in J. D. Clark (ed.) *Globalizing Civic Engagement: Civil Society and Transnational Action*, London and Sterling: Earthscan.

O'Brien, R., Goetz, A. M., Scholte, J. A., and Williams, M. (2000) *Contesting Global Governance: Multilateral Economic Institutions and Global Social Movements*, Cambridge: Cambridge University Press.

Porter, T. (2002) *Technology, Governance and Political Conflict in International Industries*, London: Routledge.

Porter, T. (2005) *Globalization and Finance*, Cambridge: Polity.

Reinicke, W. and Deng, F. (2000) *Critical Choices: The United Nations, Networks, and the Future of Global Governance*, Ottawa: IRDC.

Ronit, K. (2006) "Introduction: Global public policy – the new policy arrangements of business and countervailing groups," in K. Ronit (ed.) *Global Public Policy: Business and the Countervailing Powers of Civil Society*, London and New York: Routledge.

Ronit, K. and Schneider, V. (eds) (2000) *Private Organizations in Global Politics*, London and New York: Routledge.

Scholte, J. A. and Schnabel, A. (eds) (2002) *Civil Society and Global Finance*, London: Routledge.

School of Americas Watch North East (2005) http://soawne.org/a16pix.html (accessed May 27, 2005).

Sikkink, K. (2005) "Patterns of dynamic multilevel governance and the insider-outsider coalition," in D. della Porta and S. Tarrow (eds) *Transnational Protest and Global Activism*, Lanham, MD: Rowman and Littlefield.

Slaughter, A. M. (2004) *A New World Order*, Princeton, NJ and Oxford: Princeton University Press.

Smith, J. (2006) *Changing the World: Social Movements in a Global System* (manuscript in preparation).

Smythe, E. (1998) "The multilateral agreement on investment: a charter of rights for global investors or just another agreement?," in F. O. Hampson and M. Molot (eds) *Canada Among Nations 1998: Leadership and Dialogue*, Toronto: Oxford University Press.

Streeck, W. and Schmitter, P. C. (eds) (1985) *Private Interest Government. Beyond Market and State*, London, Beverly Hills and New Delhi: Sage.

Tarrow, S. and della Porta, D. (2005) "Conclusion: 'Globalization', complex internationalism, and transnational contention," in D. della Porta and S. Tarrow (eds) *Transnational Protest and Global Activism*, Lanham, MD: Rowman & Littlefield.

Tarrow, S. and McAdam, D. (2005) "Scale shift in transnational contention," in D. della Porta and S. Tarrow (eds) *Transnational Protest and Global Activism*, Lanham, MD: Rowman & Littlefield.

Ul Haq, M., Kaul, I., and Grunberg, I. (eds) (1996) *The Tobin Tax: Coping with Financial Volatility*, Oxford: Oxford University Press.

Zald, M. N. (1996) "Culture, ideology and strategic framing," in D. McAdam, J. D. McCarthy, and M. N. Zald (eds) *Comparative Perspectives on Social Movements: Political Opportunities, Mobilizing Structures, and Cultural Framings*, New York: Cambridge University Press.

5 Privilege and underprivilege

Countervailing groups, policy and the mining industry at the global level

Aynsley Kellow

Introduction

This chapter focuses on the role of the mining and metals industry and various countervailing powers, especially environmental groups, seeking to develop and influence public policy at the global level. It describes the belated engagement by this industrial sector with the global policy environment and its belated formation of a substantial industry association at this level. A comprehensive international non-governmental organization to represent the mining and metals industry was not formed until 2001. Named the International Council on Mining and Metals (ICMM), this organization was limited in scope but succeeded in bringing together all the key participants in the global non-ferrous metals industry, and is playing an active role in policy development at the global level. The formation of ICMM came as part of the Global Mining Initiative (GMI), a private global policy initiative.

This chapter will note that international business representation is problematic because 'the privileged position of business' (in Lindblom's 1977 terms) does not always translate to the international and global levels, so a key question is what factors provide an industrial sector with sufficient reasons to associate and participate in the formation of public policy. It will examine the role of countervailing groups in helping provide an impetus for establishing an international mining and metals group, arguing that, while the activities of 'underprivileged' civil society organizations on environment and development issues superficially appear to have been important, many of the significant activities of these groups have represented a continuation by other means of more traditional struggles over issues like industrial relations. This will be illustrated by reference to campaigns against Rio Tinto, which then became a leading company in the formation of ICMM.

The conclusion will be drawn that the formation of ICMM was primarily attributable to factors other than the campaign against Rio Tinto, or other activities by countervailing groups. While its Chairman played a very prominent role in the events that led to the formation of ICMM, he was essentially drafted for this by the leaders of two other businesses. The GMI, one element of which was the formation of ICMM, was a response to the developing international public policy agenda, rather than to countervailing groups *per se*. The GMI and the formation of ICMM, however, represented an attempt to both engage countervailing groups and to facilitate a more active role for the sector in the development of global policy.

This chapter will first examine the emergence of countervailing groups in a global campaign against Rio Tinto, before examining factors in the industry itself and the industrial relations context in Australia, the location of the largest share of its assets. These aspects are woven into the analysis to suggest that the emergence of a global policy agenda stimulated the formation of a global mining industry association and its role in the development of global public policy affecting this sector.

Rio Tinto and countervailing groups

The link between the global campaign against Rio Tinto and the formation of ICMM, on the face of it, appeared quite direct. In February 1998 a visiting group of Dyak people attended a stopwork meeting of Construction, Forestry and Energy Union (CFMEU) miners in the Hunter Valley in Australia to seek support for their grievances about the impact of Rio Tinto's mining operations on their environment and their traditional lifestyle. Their translator put their case, and the Australian workers followed the presentation with a thunderous chant of 'the workers united, will never be defeated'. The Dyaks initially recoiled, intimidated by this chant, but – according to the *Newcastle Herald* (3 February 1998) – eventually they seemed to understand its meaning and began raising their fists in defiance, bringing further cheers from the crowd.

This unlikely clash of cultures was one of the first public manifestations of the global campaign against Rio Tinto over its environmental performance and treatment of indigenous people. It came after a meeting in November 1997 between the CFMEU and Vic Thorpe, general secretary of the International Federation of Chemical, Energy, Mine and General Workers Unions (ICEM), where it was agreed to attempt to devise a strategy to attack Rio Tinto. The Australian union and its international counterpart considered a range of environmental, consumer and land rights issues they believed had the potential to embarrass Rio Tinto. A further planning meeting was held in Johannesburg in January 1998.

Later in 1998, during Metals Week, an annual gathering and dinner every October associated with the London Metal Exchange,[1] ten of the world's largest mining companies established the Global Mining Initiative (GMI) to explore how the industry could engage with the sustainable development agenda. Within a year, these companies and 20 others, commissioned the International Institute for Environment and Development (IIED) in London, through the World Business Council for Sustainable Development (WBCSD), to conduct what was named the Mining, Minerals and Sustainable

Development (MMSD) project. This was an independent two-year project which sought to involve relevant stakeholders to try to develop an understanding of how the sector could make a transition to sustainability – a privately driven global policy arrangement.

There was limited success in engaging countervailing groups. The industry was essentially attempting to engage with its critics to develop policy in anticipation of global developments. A parallel process in the GMI saw a review of industry associations, culminating in the establishment in October 2001 of the first broad-based sector organization at the global level, the International Council on Mining and Metals, which would be charged with developing an industry response to the issues of sustainable development.

To what extent, if any, were these developments linked? Was the GMI a response to the campaign against Rio? Certainly, Rio Chairman Sir Robert Wilson was identified in playing a prominent role not just in these events, but also in responding to blunt developments at the Johannesburg planning meeting in 1998 and in playing a leading role in the industry response, and Rio Tinto seemed to be the prominent target of this and similar campaigns. Rio Tinto's Kelian gold mine in Kalimantan had twice been shut by blockades by protestors, which trimmed returns by $6m. It also had a 14 per cent stake in Freeport Indonesia, the operator of Grasberg, the world's largest gold mine, and a 40 per cent stake in some of its lucrative expansion activities, including Kucing Liar (*Weekend Australian*, 27–28 May 2000). Freeport had been the target of international campaigns and became intertwined with the separatist politics of the Free Papua Movement (OPM). The Rainforest Action Network and Project Underground ran a global campaign against Freeport-McMoRan (Rio Tinto's partner in Grasberg) from 1995 which Manheim (2000: 342) suggests might have been related to the Rio Tinto campaign.[2]

But campaigns initiated by unions had also been conducted against the US companies Phelps Dodge (1983, 1998–) and Kaiser Aluminium (1998–), as well as ENI the mining subsidiary of the Italian oil company Agip (1988–1989). So Rio Tinto was not alone, but it was one of the global mining giants. As this analysis will show, as with these other campaigns, the campaign against Rio Tinto had more to do with industrial relations than with environment and development, and while Sir Robert Wilson was an important player, others were as, if not more, instrumental in initiating and driving the new GMI.

Further, the GMI had as much to do with issues of improving industry financial performance as with sustainable development. The debate over sustainable development therefore was not solely about reconciling development in the Third World with environmental concerns, but also served as a medium through which other agendas were addressed, by both labour and capital, rather than an issue solely of concern on its own merits.

The CFMEU is notable in Australia for being relatively hostile to the environment, but it formed an alliance of convenience with interests which were basically anti-mining and therefore opposed to the basic interests of those employed in the industry. The union was strongly in favour of further mining activity, since this provided benefits for its members (though they wanted better wages), but the groups with which it formed the alliance were generally opposed to mining.

For the unions in Australia, sustainable development provided a means whereby their weakness in the industrial relations arena could be remedied by a campaign which was not just socialized, but globalized. It was an extension of Schattschneider's dictum that the loser in any conflict will socialize the conflict to draw in other participants to change the balance of power to the global stage (Schattschneider 1960). For the industry, sustainable development was an agenda which was important for its continued financial performance (which had been historically poor) and its continued 'licence to operate'. This is not to say that there was not concern on both sides for the issues of environment and development (especially as they related to indigenous peoples) which come together under the rubric of sustainable development. Rather, the point is that sustainable development also meant other things to each side, and there was at best a somewhat incidental connection through sustainable development which gave the illusion that the GMI was first and foremost a response to the union campaign against Rio Tinto and (to a lesser extent) others.

The extent to which the GMI (and the related formation of ICMM) was a response to countervailing groups was less immediate than might appear from the fact that the GMI was commenced shortly after the initiation of the global campaign against Rio Tinto. The more concerted attempt to create an industry association at the global level (which ICMM represented) was really a response to both the emergence of a series of international agendas with which it needed to engage, including chapter 19 of Agenda 21 coming out of UNCED in Rio de Janeiro and the amendment to the Basel Convention which banned trade in hazardous waste for recycling and recovery (see Kellow 1999, 1999a). To be sure, these developments reflected the activities of countervailing groups – both environment and industry groups – but they were more significant than the Rio Tinto campaign, despite the impressive organization of the latter. In particular, the looming World Summit on Sustainable Development in Johannesburg in 2002 served as a focus for the industry, which was keen to avoid a repetition of what were seen as unfavourable outcomes from the United Nations Conference on Environment and Development in Rio de Janiero in 1992, and the mining industry (and business as a whole) certainly engaged much more effectively in Johannesburg.

In summary, then, Rio Tinto came under concerted attack in an international campaign against its activities, particularly over issues relating to environmental performance and treatment of indigenous peoples. These issues were to be the drivers for the GMI and thus the Mining Minerals and Sustainable Development project and the formation of the ICMM.

At first sight, this represents a significant achievement for groups broadly representative of 'new politics' at the international level, often referred to as 'new social movements' because they target changes in society or in corporate policy and behaviour rather than seeking to influence policy development by governments or intergovernmental organizations.

But was all as it seemed? I will argue that the environment-development issue, often described in the shorthand of 'sustainable development', was in fact used by the labour movement as a means of enhancing its bargaining power at a time when, especially in Australia, its influence was under serious challenge. But the initiation of the GMI had less to do with the campaign against Rio Tinto itself, and more to do with the thrust of the global sustainable development agenda. Furthermore, the response of Rio Tinto and the global mining industry also reflected other aspects of globalization and brought benefits for the large corporations which dominate the global industry, not just in allowing them to address the issues of corporate social responsibility, such as securing and maintaining their 'licence to operate', but also benefits of a more straightforward economic nature associated with regulation.

We shall now turn to these less obvious factors. These events occurred within contexts which must be understood if the links between them are to be appreciated. Most significant are the context of the global mining industry and the industrial relations context within Australia. Each of these are now examined before returning to look at the details of the campaign against Rio Tinto and the trajectory of the GMI. Then, it will be concluded that the GMI and the belated formation of the International Council on Mining and Metals owed more to factors other than the globalized industrial relations conflict that underlay the campaign against Rio Tinto.

The mining industry context

The mining and minerals industry came under increased pressure in the 1990s to improve its social and environmental performance. These challenges were described in the report of the MMSD project (MMSD 2002). The challenges were many faceted. Rio Tinto's Bougainville copper mine, then owned by its subsidiary Conzinc Rio Tinto of Australia (CRA), became caught at the centre of a separatist movement seeking independence from Papua New Guinea, motivated at least in part by a desire for better returns for Bougainville from the mine, which ironically closed – perhaps never to reopen – as a result of the conflict.

The Papua New Guinea government, pressured especially by the loss of taxation revenues and foreign exchange earnings, was caught in a poacher–gamekeeper dilemma over its equity holding in the Ok Tedi mine, majority-owned by BHP where an early attempt to build a tailings dam failed and operations proceeded with massive tailings contamination of the

Fly River. This resulted in legal action by landholders in Australian courts and ultimately in BHP quitting its interest in the mine (which continues to operate) and establishing a trust fund to compensate landholders.

Similar problems were apparent elsewhere, especially but not exclusively in the developing world. Gold mining, which almost universally relies on the use of cyanide in ore treatment, was especially problematic, with tailings dams failing at Omai in Guyana and the Esmeralda mine in Romania causing widespread biological kills. Esmeralda, a small Australian-owned company, went into liquidation when faced with the clean-up costs from the disaster, which killed fish downstream in Hungary.

Other corporate sectors also came under pressure to improve their 'corporate social responsibility', but in the mining and metals sector, companies were also coming under increasing pressure over their poor financial performance. In short, the sector was failing to earn the real cost of its capital, meaning that investors would have earned higher returns had they invested in bonds. Rio Tinto CEO Leigh Clifford stated in 2002 that while average annual returns earned by business globally were 7.35 per cent and slightly higher in the oil and gas sector, mining was at the bottom with only 4.67 per cent (Gottliebsen 2002).

Globalization had exacerbated the predicament of the mining sector. Not only did an end to the Cold War result in substantial privatization of assets (such as Zambia Consolidated Copper Mines in Zambia, tin producer Comibol in Bolivia, copper producer Tintaya in Peru and Karaganda Steelworks in Kazakhstan) and the opening up of new areas for exploration, but the competition between the large global players for access to these new exploration and development opportunities brought into sharper focus the important role played by reputation in the granting by governments of a 'licence to operate'. Increasing pressures surrounding existing operations on social and environmental issues meant that the 'licence to operate' could no longer be taken for granted in any jurisdiction, but a good corporate reputation came to be seen as an almost 'bankable' asset in securing access to new prospects and projects.

Transnational ownership of the largest global players not only accentuated the willingness of civil society organizations to criticize corporate behaviour, but it also helped drive pressures for a 'race to the top'. The large global players had global reputations to worry about – in the manner described by Leonard (1988) – whereas the smaller players frequently had only one or two mines and were immune from the damage that criticism of their operations might mean for government approvals in other jurisdictions. Clark (1995) has discussed some of these factors in relation to the mining sector.

The problem was that many mining operations could be commenced by smaller players, particularly in the gold sector, where operations could start and stop according to gold price movements. The Esmeralda disaster seemed to typify the problem, because this small undercapitalized operation did serious harm to the reputation of the sector as a whole, which was also dependent on the use of cyanide extraction methods. In an industry which is fundamentally a price taker, this ability for small players to either continue with less than 'best practice' approaches to environmental or indigenous people's issues, or to enter the market with minimal standards was a serious problem as it limited the ability of any players to bring external diseconomies within their cost structure. It also threatened to undermine any pressures for a race to the top among the larger global players, since they were vulnerable to reputational damage at the sectoral level as a result of the practices of the smaller players.

These industry characteristics are important. Most mining occurs outside Europe, in countries such as Canada, South Africa, Russia (and other former Soviet states), Chile, Brazil and the United States. One of its challenges was that it had little presence in Europe where many civil society organizations were active and where many global policy initiatives had their origins in arenas such as the European Union and the OECD. It could not rely on structural power within European nations to influence global policy agendas. But the political influence which might come with economic importance was also limited elsewhere.

Considered in a global context, the minerals industry is relatively small, despite the appearance that they are large players in countries such as Australia, Canada and South Africa. The top 150 international minerals companies had a combined market capitalization of only US$224 billion at the end of September 2001. This was less than the capitalization of single companies in other sectors, such as General Electric ($469 billion), ExxonMobil ($289 billion) and Wal-Mart ($241 billion). The top 10 mining companies had a combined capitalization of $92 billion, with Alcoa valued at $26 billion, BHP-Billiton at $25 billion, Anglo-American $17.5 billion and Norsk Hydro at $10 billion.

There are about 30–40 large multinational corporations which explore, mine, smelt, refine and sell metal concentrates and metals on world markets. Low commodity prices and poor returns among the big players produced greater concentration in the late 1990s. A number of mergers occurred, including BHP and Billiton, Cominco and Teck and the acquisition of Asarco by Grupo Mexico, CRA and North Ltd by Rio Tinto.

While there has been considerable privatization over the past 20 years there are still many state-owned companies, though they are concentrated in a few countries, such as China, although in Chile, the large copper–molybdenum producer Codelco is state-owned, and the state takes a minority share in mining activities in a number of countries, such as Papua New Guinea, Botswana and Namibia.

India still has huge state-owned companies coal producer CIL, steel producer Sail, Hindustan Copper, Hindustan Zinc and aluminium company Nalco. Many of these are small by global standards, have few reputational concerns (especially as they operate in a single jurisdiction) and enjoy a privileged position in relation to the state which, as owner, is caught in a classic poacher–gamekeeper problem.

The degree of concentration varies significantly across producers metals and minerals. Steel has a relatively dispersed structure, with the ten largest firms producing less than 30 per cent of global output, but the ten largest producers of aluminium account for more than 90 per cent of global output. There is little vertical integration in iron and steel and of the top five iron ore producers, only Rio Tinto is active in as many as three countries. In aluminium, the industry is highly vertically integrated, but this is atypical. Co-products are often significant. For example, firms producing nickel from sulphide ores (such as Inco, Norilsk and Falconbridge) derive significant by-product revenues from copper, cobalt and precious metals. This means that there is significant trade in non-ferrous metal concentrates and residues, many of which are potentially classifiable as hazardous wastes, which is why the industry became concerned over the proposal to adopt a trade ban under the Basel Convention. There are thus also numerous small traders, fabricators and recyclers, although there are some exceptions, such as the fully integrated copper producer Phelps Dodge, which is involved in all stages of copper production from mining to wire making.

The large multinational companies are highly visible and thus relatively well-focused on the need for a licence to operate. Many have developed company codes of practice, business plans and reporting procedures in response to environmental and social concerns, and they were at the forefront of efforts to improve performance at the sectoral level, such as the development of a Code for Environmental Management in 1996 by the Minerals Council of Australia. Many of these activities involved attempts at engagement with countervailing groups, either seeking direct input into their preparation or through representation on various advisory committees, at the firm level and on a sectoral basis at the national level. For example, the Minerals Council of Australia established an independent External Environmental Advisory Group (EEAG) in July 2000 to provide advice to its Environment Committee on environmental and social matters of concern to the community. Membership of the EEAG included prominent scientists and indigenous leaders, as well as government environment officials and a representative from WWF.

Multinational corporations are more likely to make a substantial effort to assess, minimize and mitigate many of the environmental and social impacts of a new mine development, to develop an effective closure plan, and to seek to engage with the local community. This is driven by their concern with global reputation, and while they can more readily afford to meet the costs of such improved behaviour, they are vulnerable to competition from those not globally focused.

This includes intermediate companies operating several small to medium-sized (typically gold or base metal) mines in one or a few countries selling concentrates to a trader or custom smelter, but also companies known as 'juniors', which might be involved exclusively in mineral exploration, negotiating agreements with larger players for the development of an ore body they have discovered, or perhaps trying to exploit the ore body themselves. Canada has more than 1000 junior companies (compared with about only 100 in the United States), and they are also active in Latin America, Australia, the Pacific Rim, Europe and Africa.

While some intermediate and junior companies meet the highest environmental and social standards, they are in a minority, and many consider sustainable development to be a 'big company game' that has little relevance to them, as they have less financial capacity to meet higher standards and fewer reputational reasons to want to do so. Regulation, be it state-imposed or self-regulation through an industry code of practice, is likely to raise the costs of their doing business, and disadvantage them relative to the global players. The larger transnational players, which are susceptible to both reputational harm and international regulation, have an interest in spreading any regulation to the smaller players. This both includes those for whom reputation is less important and applies to self-regulation, such as the industry codes which were to be developed by ICMM. We shall return to this point later.

This fragmentation of the industry plus the absence of any governance-related reason to organize made for low associability at the global level (Kellow 2002), with the key issues of concern to the industry traditionally being access to land for exploration and mining. Its products had rarely excited regulatory concern as toxic chemicals, and when they began to do so (first with lead, cadmium, arsenic and so on), it was usually on a single metal basis which tended to divide the industry, rather than provide a basis for association. The emergence and strengthening of an international policy agenda was to provide a firmer basis for association. The GMI process led to the formation for the first time of a comprehensive mining and metals group at the international level, replacing a much more limited predecessor. Prior to this, the mining industry had simply not organized effectively at the international level. This was partly because of the complex industry structure described earlier, but also because what Lindblom referred to as the 'privileged position of business' does not always translate well to the international level (Lindblom 1977).

We shall return to this point later, but we can note that the national or (in federal systems) subnational levels of governance were much more significant for the industry, because its primary point of contact with governments was in the granting of licences to prospect or mine for minerals. New agendas relating to environment and indigenous peoples began to emerge in the last quarter of the twentieth century, but these, too, tended to impact at the national level or below. As an industrial sector, it had much less experience with product regulation than industries such as chemical manufacturing, and therefore no interest in harmonizing global regulatory regimes to ensure market access. Also unlike chemicals, it had little historical concern for tariff protection, a traditional concern for chemicals associations, though one which drove national associability until the globalization of corporate ownership gave more relevance to trade liberalization and the International Council of Chemicals Associations became more active in seeking trade liberalization and regulatory harmonization.

The industrial relations context

The campaign against Rio Tinto gave prominence to its corporate behaviour in the Third World, but these were in reality concerns added to the issues of industrial relations which were of greater concern to the trade union movement.

The extent to which the concern about Rio Tinto's performance in the Third World was secondary to the issues of industrial relations can be seen by asking just how serious the threat Rio Tinto posed to the Third World was. And, similarly, by asking how serious the threat of a campaign based on Third World concerns was to Rio Tinto. It is easy to overestimate the importance of both, as Rio Tinto had relatively little exposure to developing countries. Rio Tinto's assets were located 45 per cent in Australia, 40 per cent in North America and 3 per cent in Europe – 88 per cent in old (First and Second World) politically stable areas. Only 3 per cent were in Africa and 5 per cent in South America (Gottliebsen 2002). Although there was good prospectivity outside its traditional areas of investment, Australia was the location of the largest share of its assets, and industrial relations there was a much more significant factor.

Rio Tinto had gained a reputation for aggressive industrial relations at its iron ore mines in the Pilbara region of Western Australia. The rewards for the company were significant: Rio Tinto had improved vastly the productivity of its Hamersley Iron subsidiary in the Pilbara, with tonnes per employee rising four-and-a-half-fold over 20 years (Gottliebsen 2002). A key to this had been the introduction of individual employment contracts under the government's industrial relations policy, which effectively shut unions out of the mines.

The election of a Liberal-National coalition government and the defeat of the Australian Labor Party (ALP) nationally in 1996 heralded a new era in industrial relations in Australia, which seemed to provide Rio Tinto with an opportunity to bring its industrial relations practices from its iron ore mines in the West to its coal mines in the East. This was largely because the new legislation (*Workplace Relations Act 1996*) prohibited the so-called secondary boycotts on the threat of substantial penalties and the possibility of damages being awarded against unions. Secondary boycotts had previously limited attempts at industrial relations reform in the coal industry because, in the event of an industrial dispute involving the coal mining union (the Construction, Forestry, Mining and Energy Union, or CFMEU), the waterfronts would likely be closed down under secondary boycotts by the maritime unions, inflicting heavy costs on the substantially export-oriented industry. (Australia is the world's leading coal exporter.) Ironically, the first major test of the 1996 legislation involved the dockworkers of the Maritime Union of Australia (MUA), breaking restrictive work practices which resulted in poor 'lift rates' in container cargo terminals in a bitter dispute.

The MUA set a precedent for the CFMEU campaign against Rio Tinto in the 1997 waterfront dispute when it recruited support from the International Transport Workers Federation (ITWF) to threaten an international ban on shipping (*The Australian*, 27 February 1998). The ICEM was later briefed by the ITWF on the strategy of international campaigns. The resort by the MUA to international support in itself indicated the new realities, because its power to close ports in the days before the *Workplace Relations Act* usually would have sufficed. The new industrial laws on secondary boycotts meant the MUA was forced to pursue an international campaign.

The international campaign against Rio Tinto followed immediately from the failure of the CFMEU to get Rio Tinto to change its industrial relations policies at the Hunter Valley No. 1 mine. The CFMEU was forced to take the fight offshore because it could not win the battle on the ground or in the Industrial Relations Commission, after a full bench verdict overturning a decision to arbitrate the dispute at the Hunter Valley No. 1 Mine. The CFMEU attempted to portray Rio Tinto internationally as a pariah because it was seeking reform of work practices while attempting to sideline the CFMEU.

In countering the proposed extension of individual work contracts from the Pilbara to the coal mines of the Hunter Valley the CFMEU was seriously weakened by the secondary boycotts provisions of the *Workplace Relations Act*. The eventual gains for the company were even more spectacular than they had been in the Pilbara, achieving similar gains to iron ore in coal mine productivity over only a decade, with productivity increasing three-and-a-half-fold over only five years at the Blair Athol and Mt Thorley mines (Gottliebsen 2002). Individual work contracts, however, posed a threat not so much to workers' incomes as to the union itself, since the company was seeking better productivity by weakening restrictive work practices rather than wage cuts, and individual contracts between the company and workers rather sidelined the CFMEU.

Restrictive work practices included restrictions on freedom to use contractors, part-time, temporary or casual labour on any work as required; on the right to allocate overtime at management's discretion, rather than through a union seniority list; and the right to hire and fire on merit as decided by the company in place of recruitment from a union list of retrenched miners and retrenchment on a 'last on, first off' basis. The company offered substantial inducements to anyone accepting an individual contract, but all but seven of the 430 workers refused the contracts, insisting instead on a collective agreement, triggering a five week strike at the Mt Thorley mine.

This occurred in a context where the labour movement in Australia was already in some trouble, in both its political and industrial wings. The poor electoral performance of the Australian Labor Party over the past decade is well-enough known, and its membership was also in decline. Just as important was the decline in membership of the trade union movement, with whom it was formally affiliated (on an individual union basis). Trade union membership in the private sector had dropped to below 20 per cent, and even with membership approaching 50 per cent among public sector employees, only one in four men and one in five women were trade union members. Organized labour was losing power, and the Rio Tinto campaign was an attempt to respond to that loss by socializing the conflict, moving it into other arenas (environment and indigenous people) and onto the global stage.

Ultimately, however, the coal disputes were settled with union representation continuing in the Hunter Valley, but with sweeping reform of work practices which yielded Rio Tinto the productivity gains it sought. One observer remarked that there was now less of an ideological emphasis on industrial relations in Rio Tinto than there had been in the past, and a much greater focus on outcomes beneficial for shareholders. Since then, the global campaign has subsided, although the election of an ALP government in Western Australia saw some rolling back of individual contracts there, and Rio Tinto warned publicly during the 2004 national election campaign about the consequences of an ALP victory nationally.

The Rio Tinto campaign and the GMI

Journalist Robert Gottliebsen (2000) identified Rio Tinto's chairman Sir Robert Wilson as leading the renewed emphasis in the industry on profits and the movement to set guidelines for sustainable development in mining projects that formed the core of the GMI. The question therefore arises as to whether the GMI was a response by the industry to the campaign initiated by the CFMEU and extended to include environment and development NGOs. The Rio Tinto campaign certainly commenced just before the GMI was initiated and Wilson certainly played a prominent role in the GMI process, so it appeared on the face of it that there is a strong prima facie case that the GMI and thus the formation of the ICMM were responses to the activities of countervailing groups in the environmental field. There is, however, a more complex explanation for the development of the GMI and formation of ICMM, and the activities of countervailing groups at the international level were of only minor direct significance, with the global policy environment being more significant.

The origins of the GMI and thus the ICMM go much deeper than the international campaign against Rio Tinto. Far more significant, even for

Rio Tinto alone, were the issues related to the industry's 'licence to operate' and the need to improve its performance on issues, such as environment and indigenous people. Rio Tinto (initially as CRA) was undoubtedly a leader in this process, adopting a much more progressive approach to indigenous issues in Australia under CEO Leon Davis, and chastened by its experience with Bougainville Copper, after the loss of which it set itself the ambitious goal of only ever operating with the consent of the local people. Just how seriously it took this soon became apparent when it abandoned its Century Zinc project (sold to Pasminco, now renamed Zinifex) after activist Murrandoo Yanner threatened action over the slurry pipeline to ship concentrates. Similarly, it abandoned the Jabiluka uranium mine development it had acquired with its takeover of North Ltd following the same principle, though it must be said this decision probably came easier as uranium was not as close to core business as had been zinc. Rio Tinto had decided as an individual corporation that the costs of the negative impact on its global 'licence to operate' outweighed any advantages of influencing any government authority to impose outcomes against the wishes of traditional owners.

The appearance of the lead role being played by Rio Tinto – and thus that the GMI came in response to the international union campaign – was enhanced by the fact that an important role in facilitating the GMI was played by George Littlewood, a former Rio Tinto executive who was working out of the Melbourne company Allens Consulting. In fact, Littlewood's engagement came from a less likely source, as he was hired by the Australian miner WMC Resources. In addition, while the GMI was administered out of Rio's head office in St James's Square in London, it was run by Anita Roper, on secondment from WMC (and later to be deputy at ICMM, running it for much of its early life when the CEO fell ill). The surprise was in the fact that WMC was headed by Hugh Morgan, who had a reputation in Australia for being not just a laggard on environmental and indigenous issues, but also a combative critic of both these movements and their agendas. But WMC under Morgan began to change its performance, behind probably only CRA and BHP in Australia, and Morgan then led the move to establish the GMI.

Morgan played a role few who know his reputation would credit. The stimulus for the change was a very public ticking-off of Morgan by his chairman, Sir Arvi Parbo in the early 1990s which led to a transformation within WMC throughout the 1990s, with commitments to improved performance on environmental and indigenous issues, with the instigation of reporting on both these issues under the oversight of external reference groups – like the Rio policy on operation only with consent, a proactive private policy response aimed not just at pre-empting government regulation but at enhancing the reputation of the corporation. Atypical in an industry where mining engineers tend to dominate, Morgan was a lawyer, and he transformed WMC through the mid-1990s.

Morgan, together with Gerry Ellis, then CEO of BHP, had played a key role in the establishment of the predecessor of ICMM, the International Council on Mining and the Environment, but ICME had a narrow remit and was seen by the Australians and South Africans as too close to the US and the Canadians. Secretary-General of ICME, Gary Nash, was seen as resisting a broader role and a location closer to significant intergovernmental organizations than Ottawa. Nash saw advantages in an Ottawa location because of the access to information his contacts gave him.

Rio Tinto Chairman Sir Robert Wilson did play an important role in the initiation of the GMI, but essentially at the invitation of Hugh Morgan and Doug Yearley, CEO of Phelps Dodge, who together took the initiative, but recognized that they needed Rio Tinto on board and recruited Wilson. (Littlewood also contributed to the initiative). The three issued a joint invitation to 12 mining CEOs to the October meeting in London, emphasizing their view that they were destroying shareholder value by not engaging proactively with the issues of market contraction due to the regulation of toxic substances and the difficulties they were facing in getting access to new land for exploration, especially in developing countries. The GMI therefore came about as an attempt to influence global policy through the concerted effort of the global industry leaders, both by developing codes of practice and other private policy initiatives and organizing in order to exert a greater influence over global policy processes.

The former concern had emerged around what were widely considered as losses for the industry: chapter 19 of Agenda 21 coming out of Rio de Janeiro and the ban amendment to the Basel Convention. While Agenda 21, a plan of action to guide future global policy-making, was merely 'noted' by governments at Rio de Janeiro, rather than adopted as a binding commitment, it had assumed some epistemic hegemony and chapter 19 included the aim of phasing out chemicals which were 'toxic, persistent and bioaccumulative' – a description which fitted almost all metals under some circumstances. Moves, led particularly by the Nordic nations, in the OECD and European Union to put this plan into effect were seen by the metals industry as a significant threat to its markets.

Rather than responding to countervailing groups, the move to establish a new global industry association reflected moves towards global regulation of the industry's products by intergovernmental organizations and an increasing regulation of access to land by domestic governments. Global chemicals regulation after Rio de Janeiro saw the establishment of an Intergovernmental Forum on Chemical Safety and the negotiation of the (Rotterdam) Convention on Prior Informed Consent and the (Stockholm) Convention on Persistent Organic Pollutants. Threats to lead in the OECD (Kellow 1999) and copper and zinc in the European Union (Kellow and Zito 2002), together with potential threats to the international trade in metal concentrates, residues, ashes and scrap through the amendment to the Basel Convention focused the attention of the industry on the international level like never before. The campaign against Rio Tinto was motivated by concerns over industrial relations, and the sustainable development agenda was used by the protagonists to socialize that conflict, which in turn was resolved once the industrial relations issues were settled. The campaign against Rio Tinto, therefore, was only tangentially related to the GMI, which was the industry's response to the emergence of joint challenges of global regulation and increasing difficulty at the national level of getting access to mineral deposits because of industry-wide reputational issues.

CEOs from eight companies (Anglo-American, BHP, Billiton, Noranda, Phelps Dodge, Placer Dome, Rio Tinto, WMC) attended the founding London meeting, which was jointly chaired by Morgan and Yearley. There was a shared recognition that the industry was facing a 'trust deficit' and that the existing industry associations were ineffective. There was recognition that the industry had been too passive for too long. One insider put it that whenever CEOs would meet at the London Metal Exchange, they would constantly swap 'war stories', with the industry always on the wrong side of issues that were difficult to defend, and bemoan the ineffectiveness of industry associations. The Sustainable Development agenda covered all the major issues, so they decided to make it the focus and established a 'Group of 8' (modelled on the G-8 process), influenced by Tom Burke from Friends of the Earth, who had previously advised the Conservative government in the United Kingdom and was now advising Rio Tinto.[3] The sustainable development issue was chosen carefully to provide a basis for associability. The CEOs agreed that Sustainable Development had become the context for IGOs, civil society organizations and increasingly companies, but it was also recognized that Sustainable Development was essentially both a non-competitive issue for potential members *and* that companies could not engage with it alone. Individual companies could only go so far on Sustainable Development without being held back by the performance of the industry as a whole. There were still competitive factors such as the desire to differentiate the leaders from the rest and individual companies from the pack: Rio Tinto, for example, aimed to be seen as the 'preferred developer'. Individual companies were beginning to act as pioneers in developing initiatives that could be turned into privately driven policy arrangements. There were also competitive pressures between sectors which had metals that were substitutes, especially between aluminium and steel, where there was a higher degree of vertical integration than which existed in the non-ferrous metals, which was a potential problem. The GMI (and thus the MMSD exercise) also deliberatively excluded the climate change issue on the grounds that it was a potentially competitive issue, with different impacts on coal and uranium producers and metals such as aluminium which were more energy-intensive in their production processes.

The GMI then proceeded down three tracks, agreed to at a meeting of CEOs at Davos in January 1999 at the World Economic Forum: a review of industry associations, the MMSD process and the conference held in Toronto in May 2002, all with the intention of playing a positive and more effective role at World Summit on Sustainable Development at Johannesburg in 2002. This agenda was progressed using 'Sherpas' – personal representatives of the CEO, who held four meetings each year, and CEOs would meet again at the London Metal Exchange week in 1999, 2000 and 2001, these meetings then being replaced by the formation of ICMM. The International Institute for Environment and Development was engaged through the auspices of the World Business Council for Sustainable Development, for which it had conducted a similar study for the paper industry, to conduct the MMSD process. (Several of the leading companies were WBCSD members.) At the 2000 meeting the industry association restructure was agreed to, and in 2001 plans for the Toronto Conference in May 2002 were finalized and ICMM established. ICMM faces a number of challenges, and has already seen some member resignations, but it has also developed a private policy arrangement: a code of practice has been agreed to in association with the World Conservation Union (WCU, formerly IUCN) which has seen members foreswear future mining in national parks. In another example of an attempt at global self-regulation, ICMM has also focused on mine safety, an issue of competitive concern especially for global coal producers, because the rate of mine fatalities in China, 100 times that in the US and elsewhere, threatens to undermine the global competitiveness of those producers which must face higher standards (and costs). This has involved ICMM in association with ICEM, the ILO and Chinese government agencies.

The GMI has thus been a significant development in both industry behaviour and association. It was commenced after the emergence of the global campaign against Rio Tinto, but it cannot be held to have occurred simply because of it. The emergence of a global policy agenda and the advantages of developing privately driven policy arrangements at that level have been far more significant drivers of change.

The environment and development civil society organizations were able, with union funding, to produce better publications and to enhance their visibility, but the coalition of the unions with environment and indigenous groups was an alliance of convenience, not one based on fundamentals, and was therefore vulnerable to countermeasures. Some civil society organizations were fundamentally anti-mining whereas ICEM was fundamentally committed to mining. Rio Tinto engaged with the union movement at the highest level, and talked with ICEM about the possibility of a global agreement. The ICEM leadership had no beef with Rio Tinto and it played a role in MMSD, with Reg Green representing it on the MMSD Assurance Group. The ICEM view was that unions had a stake in the mining industry and this differentiated his stance from the civil society organizations. At the level of the Australian union movement, the CFMEU's John Maitland continued to be disgruntled, but Rio Tinto wanted outcomes, so yielded on the question of union agreements to achieve the productivity improvements it wanted. Rio Tinto resolved the industrial relations issues by negotiation within the new legal framework; it had a strong incentive to do so, but had lower incentives to yield as much to environment and development groups.

Rio Tinto also responded to the campaign against it as an individual company. In a move to divide the union and environment alliance at the domestic level, it committed $1.4m over four years to WWF to fund a frog conservation programme (*Mining Monitor* 2000). This provoked an angry response from John Maitland, who wrote to WWF Australian CEO Dr David Butcher, pointing out that Rio Tinto was currently the focus of an international campaign on its human rights, environmental record and occupational health and safety performance and arguing that it was 'stunning' that WWF could associate itself with the company and allow its PR machine to assert how wonderful the company was because it had a partnership with WWF (Moody 2001).

So the international campaign against Rio Tinto changed little on the ground. It helped focus attention within Rio Tinto on outcomes rather than on ending union representation and thus moved some ideologues in Rio Tinto. It also encouraged Rio to engage more actively with the investment community, moving it to take a more proactive role in response to the shareholder proxy battle the union movement used as one of its tactics. But the GMI was driven by a number of companies, not just Rio Tinto, and as we have seen, WMC and Phelps Dodge were in the vanguard with Rio Tinto, if not slightly ahead of Rio. The GMI was fundamentally a response to 'the licence to operate' issue. The industry was being driven out of markets and off land because of perceptions about its behaviour, and the timeline was dictated by the Johannesburg summit.

At best, the campaign against Rio was a catalyst, helping accelerate the move to openness and recognition of the need to engage with stakeholders, but it did so by focusing on the key stakeholders – unions and communities, more so than environment and development civil society organizations – engaging with them separately and leaving the more extreme groups on one side, selecting from numerous countervailing groups partners with which to engage, groups to effectively marginalize, and so on. But these developments were well under way within Rio Tinto well before the union campaign commenced in 1998; Rio had been at the vanguard of improving performance on the social dimension, and with its relative lack of investment in developing countries, it would have made a strange choice as a target were it not for the industrial relations issue.

The threats to the licence to operate was greatest for the global players, because they had global reputation to defend. It was not the campaign by unions and its allies against the industry in the form of an international social movement that was important in driving the GMI response, but concerns over access to ground for prospecting and mining development (matters within the competence of national and subnational governments) by companies with global reputations, together with the emergence of an international regulatory agenda.

The reputational factor was in essence competitive for the global companies in one sense, bringing benefits at the level of the individual firm. But there was an emerging international regulatory agenda, seen in policy measures such as the Basel Convention, the OECD Risk Reduction Program, and the possible regulation of cyanide use in gold extraction which posed threats to the sector – or in some senses to the larger global players. In short, some firms are embraced by and produce global public policy more readily than others. Because the products of mining are undifferentiated, and producers are price-takers, the efforts of the larger players to earn better reputations through improved performance on sustainability issues are constantly at risk through the lack of commitment to this agenda by the smaller players which need only deal with a single regulatory government. The risk included both being hit in terms of prices, with lower cost producers clipping the peaks off commodity cycles (just at the time when denationalization was making the bottom more shallow), as well as the risk to whole sectors, such as cyanide to gold or toxics regulation to individual metals (such as lead or copper). Similar factors exist in other policy domains, such as health and safety. As with mortality rates in Chinese coal mining, for example, global regulation – even weak self-regulation – helps limit the damage to those regulated by either governance structures or reputation from those hitherto free from regulatory costs. Such factors have the potential to impact on regulation at several levels (Eisner 2004).

Conclusions

The GMI and the related MMSD project and formation of ICMM came after the global campaign against Rio Tinto, but not because of it. The Rio campaign had its origins in industrial relations in Australia, where a dispute in a changed industrial law context saw the mining union form a tactical alliance with civil society organizations that were essentially opposed to mining, and an attempt to globalize this conflict. When the industrial relations issues were settled, the global campaign evaporated (assisted by the companies gesture in funding a WWF conservation programme). The GMI, on the other hand, had its origins in the conjunction of a number of factors internal to the sector and an emerging policy agenda at the international level which made better organization and policy engagement at the international level imperative.

These factors have provided an improved basis for association for the mining industry at the global level, where associability was previously weak. As we have seen, the establishment of the Global Mining Initiative and the related formation of the International Council on Mining and Metals were not responses to the global campaign against Rio Tinto in any direct sense. These developments can only be understood within the contexts of the nature of the global industry at the time and significant developments in industrial relations within Australia, where the Rio campaign had its origins.

To understand why a greater level of engagement and association occurred, we need to focus on the reasons why associability was previously problematic for the sector. Put simply, intergovernmental organizations are not as structurally dependent on business as are national governments because they do not depend (directly at least) upon the profitability of business for revenue. Being global in nature, most multilateral organizations are indifferent to the risks of capital movements between nations. As national governments, rather than intergovernmental organizations, are responsible for policy implementation, these organizations are less dependent upon the cooperation of business for the provision of practical knowledge (much to the cost of policy effectiveness). While there is a need for business organizations to gather at a global level information valued by intergovernmental organizations in formulating global policy responses, this 'access good' is not without cost to associations and cannot be taken for granted. Business often enjoys greater access and the influence it brings at the national level, and it will often (though not necessarily always) concentrate its investment in political organization at that level.

At the early stages of international policy development, creative ambiguity is preferable to the detail where the devil of potentially divisive interests lies. Iterative functionalism is often the order of the day, with detail and more meaningful commitments being added only in successive visits to the policy arena. If global policy arrangements develop sufficiently that they get down to detail, business will find a more comfortable niche – either for individual firms or relevant industry associations, although association and participation are costly.

As a result of these factors, which make the international level less propitious for business, sometimes it tends to invest less at the international level than at the national level, so its greater ability to mobilize resources relative to non-business groups is less relevant (see Kellow 2002).

These differences between association and participation can have consequences for policy, and the relative lack of engagement of a sector internationally compared with its (perhaps considerable) domestic influence can produce what Hanf and Underdal (1998) have referred to as a 'vertical disintegration of policy' as powerful interests bloc implementation at the national level of global policy. The GMI and the related formation ICMM therefore reflect a heightened relevance at the international level for the mining industry, a maturing of the regulatory domain at that level for a sector which is not just wishing to adopt private responses at the level of the individual firm, nor just responses to global public policy being developed by intergovernmental organizations, but to undertake private policy responses at a global level.

What has been the role of countervailing groups in the formation of a more well-organized mining industry group at the international level?

This question is important, not just because environment civil society organizations can be more influential relative to business at that level than they are at the domestic level, but because their influence was amplified by the use of the Sustainable Development agenda by the trade union movement internationally in response to changes in the Australian industrial relations context, which encouraged the unions to socialize their conflict by going global and making linkages with environment and development groups.

Both these factors reflected to some extent the activities of civil society organizations, but the main driver was the changing nature of governmental and intergovernmental policy rather than the need to respond directly to the competition of civil society organizations as participants in social movements, supporting a top-down rather than bottom-up view of the factors driving interest group formation and the efforts of the industry to take a more active role in the formulation of global policies, through intergovernmental organizations and through coherent business initiatives. It would appear that (in this case at least), it was less the direct threat of the campaign by countervailing groups against individual companies that stimulated the formation of a new international industry group and the development of more sophisticated policy approaches (including self-regulation).

The campaign against Rio as a single company was met with an individual response by that company, both on the industrial relations issues that provoked it, and in attempting to split the tactical alliance between unions and civil society organizations. If the aim of these groups had been to attack the mining industry on indigenous issues and general performance in the Third World, Rio Tinto made a poor target, since its activities in such countries were limited and its conduct on issues such as land rights was at the leading edge of enlightenment in the industry. Rio became a target only because of the industrial relations context, and the campaign against it subsided once the industrial relations issues were settled. Further, while Rio was prominent in initiating the GMI, it was at best first among equals, or probably slightly behind WMC and Phelps Dodge in the vanguard.

Rather, it was through their success in pushing the development of international policy to the extent that countervailing groups were significant in stimulating organizational and policy initiatives at the global level. It was the need to respond to the global policy agenda of Sustainable Development that provided the stimulus for action. That new organization is now engaging with civil society organizations such as WWF in developing its policy responses. And ironically, just as the CFMEU used the Sustainable Development agenda as the basis for globalizing its campaign because of threats to its organization, the industry quite selectively chose Sustainable Development as its organizing focus because it would maximize associability, carefully avoiding those issues which might have divided the industry. Having been prompted to form ICMM by the emerging global policy agenda, the mining industry is now engaging in further global policy development using this new organization.

Acknowledgement

Research for this paper was supported by the Australian Research Council through Grant No. A00001222.

Notes

1 The London Metal Exchange (LME) is a market in which refined copper, aluminium, nickel, lead, zinc, tin and silver are bought and sold, for delivery either immediately or at fixed dates in the future. LME prices are used world-wide as the basis price for transactions in these metals (with the exception of silver), and for products upstream (such as ores and concentrates) and for downstream products, and even scrap prices. Most LME contracts are hedging transactions and only an estimated 5 per cent of the metals produced annually are physically traded through the LME, with most metal normally sold directly or through merchants.

2 In addition to environment and indigenous issues, the most common basis for such global campaigns appears to be human rights (see Rodman 1998).

3 Many former civil society organisation office-holders continue to exert influence (and find careers) via the route of consulting. Former Greenpeace UK head Lord Melchett and Greenpeace International CEO Paul Gilding are two prominent examples, besides Burke.

References

Anon. (1998) 'Dispossessed Dayaks Slam Rio Tinto Mining Methods at Stopwork Meeting', *Newcastle Herald*, 3 February, p. 4.

Anon. (1998) 'Global union campaign claims Rio Tinto abuses', *Australian Financial Review*, 25 May, p. 4.

Anon. (1998) 'Unions use offshore big guns to battle Rio Tinto on home turf', *The Australian*, 27 February, p. 40.

Clark, G. (1995) 'Global competition and environmental regulation: is the "race to the bottom" inevitable?', in R. Eckersley (ed.) *Markets, the State and the Environment: Towards Integration*, South Melbourne: Macmillan Education Australia.

Eisner, M. A. (2004) 'Corporate environmentalism, regulatory reform, and industry self-regulation: toward genuine regulatory reinvention in the United States', *Governance*, 17 (2): 145–67.

Gottliebsen, R. (2000) 'Oresome prospects', *Weekend Australian*, 3–4 June, p. 52.

Gottliebsen, R. (2002) 'Master of mine games', *Weekend Australian*, 5–6 October, p. 46.

Hanf, K. and Underdal, A. (1998) 'Domesticating international commitments: linking national and international decision-making', in A. Underdal (ed.) *The Politics of International Environmental Management*, Dordrecht: Kluwer.

Henderson, I. (2000) 'Reith sets up shop in Beazley's yard', *Weekend Australian*, 3–4 June, p. 32.

Kellow, A. (1999) *International Toxic Risk Management: Ideals, Interests and Implementation*, Cambridge: Cambridge University Press.

Kellow, A. (1999a) 'Baptists and bootleggers? The Basel Convention and the metals recycling trade', *Agenda*, 6 (1): 29–38.

Kellow, A. (2002) 'Comparing business and public interest associability at the international level', *International Political Science Review*, 23 (2): 175–86.

Kellow, A. and Zito, A. R. (2002) 'Steering through complexity: EU environmental regulations in the international context', *Political Studies*, 50 (1): 43–60.

Leonard, H. J. (1988) *Pollution and the Struggle for World Product: Multinational Corporations, Environment, and International Comparative Advantage*, Cambridge: Cambridge University Press.

Lindblom, C. E. (1977) *Politics and Markets*, New York: Basic Books.

Manheim, J. B. (2001) *The Death of a Thousand Cuts: Corporate Campaigns and the Attack on the Corporation*. Mahwah, NJ: Lawrence Earlbaum.

Mining, Minerals and Sustainable Development (2002) *Breaking New Ground: The Report of the MMSD Project*, London: Earthscan for IIED and WBCSD.

Mining Monitor (2000) 'WWF signs $1.2M partnership with Rio Tinto', *Mining Monitor*, 5 (1), March. Available http://www.mpi.org.au/mm/editions/mining_monitor_vol5no1.pdf

Moody, R. (2001) 'Sleepwalking with the enemy – or waking the truth', Mines & Communities. Available http://www.minesandcommunities.org/Charter/sleepwalk2.htm

Rodman, K. A. (1998) ' "Think globally, punish locally": nonstate actors, multinational corporations, and human rights sanctions', *Ethics and International Affairs*, 12 (1): 19–41.

Schattschneider, E. E. (1960) *The Semisovereign People*, Hinsdale, Ill: Dryden Press.

Uren, D. (2000) 'Unions hit campaign trail', *Weekend Australian*, 27–28 May.

6 Two worlds apart?
Davos' World Economic Forum and Porto Alegre's World Social Forum

Michelle Beyeler

Introduction

"Porto Alegre and Davos in an annoying dialogue of the deaf" was the headline of an article published in the Bolivian newspaper *El Diario* (January 29, 2001) on the occasion of a video-conference between representatives of the World Economic Forum (WEF) and the World Social Forum (WSF) in 2001. The two gatherings, Davos with its neoliberal jargon, and Porto Alegre with its anti-capitalist Esperanto, more than any other site represent two opposing poles of the discourse on global governance. Even if there are attempts to establish contacts between the two sites, the framing of global issues and problems prevailing at the two meetings is so different that a real dialog and exchange seem to be impossible.

Nevertheless, the two summits connect people from different cultural, social and geographical backgrounds and encourage a debate on the pressing problems of an interdependent world. The fact that mainstream newspapers all over the world, even those located in peripheral regions of the world such as the Bolivian *El Diario*, report on the two summits, is telling with regard to the standing they have in the "global public sphere." Business elites and the countervailing powers of civil society not only establish their own conferences with a worldwide reach; they also succeed in attracting attention by the media and the wider public.

What is the role of the two forums for global governance and international public policy formulation? Are the meetings merely large cocktail parties or youth festivals which get standing in the media mainly because of the celebrities that participate? Or, are these the sites where an important part of the global political agenda is formed? Is it those summits where relevant private driven policy arrangements (Ronit 2006) are or at least could be discussed, initiated and administered? This chapter addresses these questions by giving some insights into the origins, the structure and the functioning of the World Economic Forum and the World Social Forum.

The aims of describing the special features and characteristics of the two private summits are twofold. On the one hand, the interest is in identifying their capacity of playing a relevant political role, including their possibilities of contributing to the development of policy arrangements. On the other hand, it shall be evaluated whether the forums foster interaction between business and civil society, and whether and how these interactions may lead to arrangements that involve actors from the two opposing poles in global governance. The next section provides insight into the difference between the World Economic Forum and the World Social Forum on the one hand, and general UN-centered world summits on the other. The origins, structures and goals of the two private summits are described in sections three and four. Section five points out to the roles Porto Alegre and Davos may play in global governance. It mainly presents a discussion of the possibilities the two conferences as well as the participants have in developing policy arrangements. Section six assesses the prospects of the conferences to engage the business and civil society organizations in cooperative interactions.

World summits: the specific features of Davos and Porto Alegre

The World Economic Forum originated from a management symposium arranged in the early 1970s to bring together managers from Europe and the United States. Over the years, parallel to growing international economic interconnectedness, the annual meeting became the most illustrious private gathering of the world's business and political elites.

The World Social Forum, first held in 2001, was originally established to be a counter-event to the World Economic Forum. Deliberatively, the initiators chose a name that should reflect this counter-idea and staged the event on the same date, albeit at a geographically distinct area (Cassen 2003a). The venue of the World Economic Forum, the Swiss ski resort of Davos, contrasts sharply to Porto Alegre, a city with over one million inhabitants in southern Brazil. The World Social Forum emancipated itself quickly from being an anti-WEF-conference to being an independent entity connecting movement organizations and individuals that take a critical stance toward globalization and neoliberal political thoughts.

Although the two World Forums are different in many ways they are also characterized by important commonalities compared with the rest of the world summits which are commonly arranged by international organizations and based on intergovernmental cooperation. Examples for the latter are the UN-centered world summits, such as the climate conferences dealt with in Chapter 7 or the ministerial conference of the World Trade Organization (WTO).

Unlike these other conferences, the two world summits are not concentrated on one specific issue or policy field and it is private actors who organize them. The organizers specify their own rules about who is allowed to participate and how the program is set up. The topics under discussion are broad, including, for instance, issues like poverty, development, peace, environment, human rights, management, health, social security, arts, technology and many more. The lack of focus on a specific policy field inhibits the two forums as such from becoming part of an international policy network. Nevertheless, as shown in the next sections, a number of specific policy initiatives are discussed, shaped and initiated in the context of the two summits. They can thus be regarded as arenas (or discussion forums) where policy exchange is possible in two ways: between actors belonging to certain policy networks and also among actors from different policy networks.

The aim of the intergovernmental conferences is to negotiate agreements for international cooperation in a specific policy field. A central part of the work at each conference and the preparatory meetings is the creation of a final conference document which has to be approved by the participating governments. In case, the goal is to set up new international regulations, the formal decision-making body often consists exclusively of state representatives who negotiate an agreement which then has to be ratified by national parliaments.[1] At the conference diplomats and other state representatives are therefore the main actors while representatives of business and non-profit organizations are given some limited time and space to address government delegations (Smith 2004: 322).

The presence of nongovernmental organizations, however, is often welcomed by the international agencies and sometimes even promoted, for instance by organizing parallel conferences with a separate agenda for non-governmental organizations (NGOs). Such parallel NGO forums have been a feature of most UN conferences and their preparatory meetings since the 1972 Stockholm Conference on the Environment (Clark *et al.* 1998: 8). The UN conferences thus offer opportunities for issue-specific influence as well as for building up networks between activists from various geographical origins.

The fact that international agencies welcome and even facilitate the participation of civil society groups may be explained by two functions that the latter perform. First, these groups may contribute to ensure state compliance with international treaties. International organizations often lack the formal and de facto power to enforce a government's commitment. Particularly in the fields of human rights or the environment, many civil society organizations collect information and bring attention on violations of international norms. This strategy has proven a powerful way to increase state compliance as they attempt to evade such international blaming (Keck and Sikkink 1998; Ball 2000). Second, civil society groups help to link the public with international organizations, which may improve the legitimacy of the democratic foundations of global governance (Charnovitz 2003: 77).

While at the intergovernmental conferences interest groups primarily participate to shape the agenda of the conference according to their interests, and – so to say as a by-product – use the opportunity of the meetings for networking, in the two World Forums building and intensifying connections as well as arranging new initiatives and business contracts is often the first reason for participation. Probably because the priority of the World Forums lies in networking, both are also accompanied by a large number of cultural and social events that not only entertain the participants but also contribute to connect them on a more personal level.

In the case of the WEF this focus on networking is reflected by the attempts of building a club atmosphere by selecting a venue that keeps the participants together and focused on the event. The remote, small Alpine town of Davos offers an ideal place in this respect. Unlike the intergovernmental conferences, which are hosted by a member country and are therefore organized in rotating locations, the World Forums rather prefer continuity with regard to the location. There have also been attempts, however, to switch the venue, for instance the World Economic Forum 2002 was held in New York and the World Social Forum 2004 in Bombay.[2]

At the intergovernmental conferences the goal is to set up institutions which support international cooperation in different policy fields; at the World Forums networking, the initiation and continuation of business contacts or political and social action initiatives are in the fore. Still, the ambitions of the organizers go beyond providing just an entertaining and stimulating meeting space for individuals or groups. As shown in the next two sections, both forums ultimately have political goals on a global scale. The WEF Foundation, the organizer of the annual meeting, is a not-for-profit organization that claims to sensitize its members for a number of global problems and to incite them to develop solutions for such problems.

The World Social Forum, having a much less formalized organizational structure than the WEF, in its charter even more explicitly emphasizes the political nature of its meetings: although, the organizers refuse to formulate specific political programs, only those participants are welcomed who are inclined to a certain political agenda. The following two sections will discuss in more detail the aims and means of the two arenas in order to assess to what degree these two conferences are able to play such a political role.

The World Economic Forum – exclusiveness with selective inclusion

In 1971, managers, high profile European industrialists as well as some well-known representatives of American business schools convened at Davos. The occasion for the first *European Management Symposium* was the twenty-fifth anniversary of the Centre d'Etudes Industrielles (CEI) in Geneva – at the time one of the most prestigious management schools in Europe. Klaus Schwab, a junior faculty member of the CEI, had the idea of celebrating the anniversary by a large conference. Although Schwab built on the reputation and the resources of the school to attract illustrious guests, he managed to formally detach the conference from the CEI

(Graz 2003: 328). He founded a company owning all rights and being fully responsible of the realization of the Symposium.[3]

During the first symposium Schwab created the non-profit Foundation of the European Management Forum (FEMF) which continued to organize annual conferences at Davos. At these conferences, management experts – mainly from the USA – were paid for offering their knowledge to European business leaders. While the demand for such a knowledge-transfer initially was quite large, during the 1980s increasingly firms started to train their junior managers directly in the United States. Schwab therefore decided to redirect the objectives of the Management Forum (Neue Zürcher Zeitung January 27, 1997).

In 1987, the foundation was renamed to World Economic Forum, the internal organization was professionalized and the Foundation Board, which had been made up of low profile associates of Klaus Schwab until then, was changed to include chief executive officers from the major multinational corporations such as Nestlé, Dell, Coca-Cola, ABB and Enron. The cornerstone for today's most illustrious meeting of the business elite was set.

According to Schwab, the conception of the new World Economic Forum was sensitizing the foremost business leaders to the political, social, economic and technical environment (Neue Zürcher Zeitung January 27, 1997). He therefore increasingly extended the spectrum of participants to academics from different disciplines, political leaders and high profile diplomats (Graz 2003: 330). The redirection in the objectives of the foundation proved to be successful. In the following years, the World Economic Forum's prestige, as well as the number, geographical and sectoral origins of the participants augmented strongly. Being part of the club became an asset for which the world's largest multinational corporations are willing to pay considerable sums.[4]

Today the World Economic Forum is an organization with about 180 employees recruited from approximately forty different countries. The Forum's headquarters are located at Colony, a small town near Geneva in Switzerland. The overall responsibility and the strategic decisions are taken by the Foundation Board which is chaired by Klaus Schwab. The International Business Council (IBC),[5] made up of one hundred chief executives from different industries serves as an advisory board. Klaus Schwab is also the Executive Chairman of the Management Board, which additionally consists of seven management directors who take care of the executive and operational tasks of the foundation.

The headquarters are organized in a hierarchical and professional manner. The possibilities for control and co-determination of the WEF agenda by the members are rather small. The WEF management, although it attempts to satisfy the demand of its members, does not consider itself to be their interest organization. As World Economic Forum director André Schneider claims: "We rather see ourselves as intellectual precursors" (Interview March 8, 2004).

The WEF management declares to provide a collaborative framework for the world's leaders to address global issues and to engage its corporate members in global citizenship (World Economic Forum, 2005). These goals are approached through different tools. A first set of activities consists of establishing direct contact between those who are considered to be the world's leaders, and to initiate them to discuss management issues as well as broader global economic, political and social problems.

To facilitate face-to-face contacts, the World Economic Forum arranges a number of meetings in different parts of the world and, most importantly, its famous annual meeting at Davos. At the annual meeting, business leaders from the member firms cover about half of the over 2000 participants. The second largest group of participants is journalists (about 10 percent), followed by academics (6–7 percent), representatives of national governments (4 percent) as well as some heads of civil society organizations, together with cultural, religious and union leaders (2 percent).

To disseminate knowledge and to encourage debates and discussions, the official program of the annual meeting schedules around 200 sessions. The World Economic Forum is very keen on offering topical themes to be debated at the panels. A team of staff members, in consultation with a variety of experts, tries to identify the important issues and those which may become important in the future. Management and business, as well as economic and technology issues still take a central place in the agenda. The sessions also cover topics presented under the headline of "Art and Culture," "Environment," "Peace and Security" or "Globalization" (World Economic Forum 2005a).

The largest part of the sessions is parallel sessions, there are, however, also a number of plenums where highly prominent people – mostly current or former heads of state – hold speeches. Most of the sessions take the form of discussion panels and speeches, allowing for some limited interaction between the speakers and the audience. Recently the organizers have also put some efforts in the introduction of new, more participative formats, such as workshops, assemblies or round tables (Davis 2004). For instance, in 2005 the so-called *Global Town Hall*, an interactive plenary session to collectively discuss the most pressing global problems, was set up. Politicians and diplomats often use the setting of the annual meeting to address the assembled business elite. An example of how high level international diplomats introduce their ideas is the United Nations Global Compact: in 1999, the United Nations Secretary-General Kofi Annan held a plenary speech where he challenged business leaders to join an international initiative that brings companies together with UN agencies, labor and civil society to support a number of principles in the areas of human rights, labor, the environment and anti-corruption (UN 2005).

While the panels and the plenary sessions are open for the news media, the WEF offers its participants also the possibility to discuss and negotiate their affairs in smaller circles behind closed doors. These sessions outnumber the sessions included in the official program. Occasionally, such smaller circles are also encouraged to bring together antagonist parties in political conflicts.

Besides the meeting space, some activities of the foundation also aim at establishing more institutionalized processes, by setting up arenas for continuous activity and interaction. One approach is to support the formation of communities such as the Young Global Leaders, a group of over 1000 people from business, science or civil society organizations aged under forty, and the Technology Pioneers, comprising about thirty companies in the fields of biotechnology, energy and information technology. The Foundation encourages these communities to be active year-round.

A second measure is to involve the member firms in concrete projects addressing specific economic, social and ecological problems. The Forum has created a subdivision – the Global Institute for Partnership and Governance (GIPG) – that administers a number of programs. These initiatives have names like Corporate Citizenship, Partnering against Corruption, Greenhouse Gas Register or Global Health.

The approach of the World Economic Forum regarding these programs can be illustrated by the example of the Water Initiative, launched at the annual meeting 2004. The goal of this initiative is to encourage, as the initiators claim, "public–private partnerships" in addressing sustainable water resources management. To get there, the WEF invites proposals for specific projects from civil society actors, scientists or public agencies. It then uses its influence and network to find private companies which support these projects with financial and other resources (World Economic Forum 2005b). A last field of activities of the foundation consists in providing services for its member firms in areas like crisis management, global competitiveness and motivational techniques.

Overall, the approach taken by the World Economic Forum is a "top-down" one. The addressees are elites. By confronting them with global problems and inciting them to think of solutions, the organization tries to realize its goal, which it claims to be: "to improving the state of the world." Participation in the annual meeting, therefore, is highly exclusive and contained to persons who are considered to belong to an elite, it being economical, political, cultural, religious or social.

This selective top-down approach and the large presence of multinational corporations made the WEF a target of a critical campaign by the global social justice movement (Smith 2001; Andretta *et al.* 2003). This movement consists of diverse loosely connected groups (Bennett 2004), ranging from anarchist groups, newly established global social justice organizations such as The Association for the Taxation of Financial Transactions for the Aid of Citizens (ATTAC), as far as to professionally operating civil society organizations, trade unions and political parties (della Porta 2004: 184). These groups rely on diverse patterns of action such as peaceful vigils, counter-conferences, discussion forums, street theaters, dance parades, legal and illegal demonstrations which sometimes have escalated into street fights, blockades and even sabotage acts.

The activists argue that the business elite meeting at Davos is responsible for the exploitation of workers in the South and for labor market liberalization in the North. The Forum itself is criticized for providing an arena that allows business leaders and politicians to engage in agreements without public transparency and democratic legitimacy. The club-structures promoted by the World Economic Forum, such as the Young Global Leaders or the World Media Leaders are rejected for contributing to generate loyalty patterns across market, state and civil society actors that make a critical dialog difficult (Erklärung von Bern 2005).

The forum is also considered a leading player in the construction of ideology and in the implementation of a neoliberal agenda. Partially, the mainstream newspaper supported these arguments. For instance, a journalist of the liberal Swiss newspaper *Neue Zürcher Zeitung* (February 5, 2002) wrote that the World Economic Forum arrogates decision-making power without any legitimacy. Given the positive self-image the World Economic Forum has about itself, the anti-WEF campaign took the organizers by surprise:

> The critique is incomprehensible. A look at our history shows that we have always dealt critically with globalization. We tried to support solutions. Certainly, we have to admit that those solutions sometimes took a long time and that they did not always bring what they were meant to bring. But suddenly we were considered hyper-globalizers. That was very astonishing for the World Economic Forum.
>
> (Interview March 8, 2004)

Nevertheless, the World Economic Forum needed to react, in particular because the protests initially had a disastrous impact on its public image. The media, which for long have hardly taken notice of the event, suddenly covered the World Economic Forum extensively and also rather critically. The Swiss public became hostile, as it made the WEF responsible for the costs that the state had to bear to secure the conference, as well as for the large damages caused by violent street protests. For some time it was not clear whether the Swiss Economic Forum could continue to meet at Davos. The WEF mainly reacted by changing its communication strategy and by a selective opening of the conference toward the public.

Among other measures, the World Economic Forum together with a number of selected civil society organizations, like the Max Havelaar Foundation, Terre des Hommes (TDH) and Bread for All (BFA), organized a number of discussion panels that are open to the public – the so-called Open Forum. The organizers put an effort in choosing well-known panelists for the Open Forum. The attending public is invited to ask questions to the Nestle CEO Brabeck or the President of the Swiss confederation.

Moreover, the WEF management also started to pay more attention to civil society groups, by inviting representatives from third world, human rights, and environmental organizations. Since 2002 the WEF has considerably increased the number of representatives of civil society organizations dealing with environment, human rights and development issues. In 2003, 61 groups participated and the WEF organized a session at the beginning of the conference to bring them together as well as a feedback session at the end of the conference (Franklin and Ries 2003: 25).

The World Social Forum – inclusiveness with selective exclusion

The World Social Forum initially was meant to be a counter-event to the Davos meeting. The idea emerged from a collaboration of French and Brazilian activists. During the World Economic Forum 2000, Oded Grajew, a former toy manufacturer and businessman in Brazil as well as supporter of the workers party, had the idea to launch a counter-forum (Grajew 2005). He discussed this idea during a meeting in Paris with Bernard Cassen, French journalist, director general of the *Monde Diplomatique* and at the time president of ATTAC, and Chico Whitaker, another social cause activist from Brazil and later international secretary of the World Social Forum. Cassen, in favor of such a project, suggested organizing the forum in Porto Alegre, because so far attempts to organize a transnational counter-summit at Davos, following the model of the Seattle counter-summit to the ministerial conference of the World Trade Organization (Smith 2001), had failed. Not only had the authorities prohibited demonstrations, Cassen also considered the site and locality of the Swiss Alpine ski resort to be suboptimal for staging a large and effective alternative forum.

By choosing a country from the geopolitical South, the initiators of the World Economic Forum wanted to mark not only a geographical, but also symbolic break with Davos. Porto Alegre was considered an ideal site also because both, the city of Porto Alegre as well as the state of Rio Grande do Sul, were governed by the Brazilian Workers Party and therefore were in the hands of "political friends" of the World Social Forum initiators (Cassen 2003a: 21–22).

Once this decision had been taken, the initiators set up an organizing committee in Brazil. The plan was to have a first meeting exactly at the same date as the annual meeting of the World Economic Forum in 2001. In order to launch the project publicly, they used the opportunity provided by the UN Social Summit in Geneva that had attracted many civil society organizations. At this occasion the vice-governor of Rio Grande do Sul promoted the idea of the World Social Forum and "provoked an enthusiastic response" (Cassen 2003a: 49). The central catchphrase "Another World is Possible" was adopted from ATTAC France, which had organized an international meeting in Paris under this title. Due to the short time horizon, the WSF remained in the beginning basically a Brazilian–French initiative.

Although at the first forum the geographical range of the participants was rather limited, in terms of international publicity Porto Alegre immediately was a big success. Its standing in the media benefited from the coincidence with Davos (Cassen 2003b). In addition, the World Social Forum received considerable political backing. Besides the ideal, material and organizational support by the Brazilian Workers Party also the French government seems to have quickly acknowledged the World Social Forum as a relevant site. At least it took some efforts to send equally important - delegations to both summits, the WEF and the WSF (Le Monde January 24, 2003).

The formal organizational structure of the World Social Forum is very limited. The "highest" body is the international council, which is responsible for the formulation of its strategy. This council, which has neither mechanism for disputing representation nor for voting, was formed as a permanent body only after the first Social Forum. The central idea is that the members of the council are representing the diverse regional, geographical and sectoral (trade unions, grassroot movements, civil society organizations, etc.) origins of the WSF participants.[6]

The international council formulated and adopted the *Charter* which specifies the central principles of the event. Besides the international council and the organizing committee, which consists of organizations from the country where the forum takes place, the WSF now has a secretariat in charge of coordinating the process, whose main office is located in Sao Paulo.[7] The organizers of the World Social Forum claim that it is not merely an event but rather a process which includes activities all year-round. Besides regional Forums such as the European, Pan-Amazonian and Americas Social Forums, these activities include thematic conferences, for example on democracy, human rights or war, which follow the methodology and political criteria set by the *Charter*. Porto Alegre has also inspired many other local, regional or thematic events.

The World Social Forum considers itself as an open meeting space where groups and movements of civil society opposed to neoliberalism and capitalism come together to debate ideas, to share experiences, to formulate proposals and to build action-networks. In contrast to Davos, Porto Alegre is based on a very inclusive and participatory approach. The threshold for participation is very low and those that can afford to travel to Porto Alegre can participate for a small registration fee.[8] The organizers, however, insist that those taking part accept the commitment of the *World Social Forum Charter of Principles* and that they neither represent a specific political party nor a military organization. Whatever alternatives are discussed and debated, they must...

...stand in opposition to a process of globalization commanded by the large multinational corporations and by the governments and international institutions at the service of those corporations' interests, with the complicity of national governments. They are designed to ensure that globalization in solidarity will prevail as a new stage in world history.

(Article 4)

Government leaders and members of legislatures who accept the commitments of the charter may participate but only on a personal capacity. At several occasions, the organizers refused admittance to politicians and representatives of intergovernmental organizations. For instance in 2002, IMF- and World Bank officials, as well as the Belgian Prime Minister Guy Verhofstadt, were not allowed to participate because the organizers claimed that they represent and defend the neoliberal policy against which the World Social Forum is fighting (Neue Zürcher Zeitung February 1, 2002).

Although selectively people have been excluded, the overall threshold for participation is very low. Starting with 20,000 participants in 2001, the World Social Forum quickly became a mega-event with 155,000 participants from 135 countries in 2005. Although the participants have very diverse origins, the largest part of the participants came from Brazil, Argentina, France, the United States and Uruguay. Given the huge size of the forum and the diversity of the participants with regard to cultural, language and educational backgrounds, the organizers face many logistical problems. The World Social Forum relies on a large number of volunteers to build up an infrastructure capable of hosting the different workshops and other activities. To illustrate the dimensions: in 2005, over 1000 volunteered only for language translation tasks.

Since the first Forum, held in 2001, the organizers have constantly worked on developing a methodology for setting up the conference-program in a way that is consistent with the promoted inclusive and pluralist approach. While in the beginning, the organizing committee took the leading role in proposing and selecting issues and speakers, in the subsequent summits, the program was specified in a more participatory way. Already in 2002, over 600 participating groups organized their own workshops and seminars. In the two following years the organizers of the World Social Forum still increased the share of self-organized activities in relation to centrally organized events. However, it became clear very quickly that the self-organized events were problematic insofar as the coordination or even aggregation of workshops with similar topics is difficult without central coordination. To address this issue, the organizers set up an internet-based coordination system to bring together groups and organizations with similar goals.

The international council insists on the "non-political" principles of Porto Alegre. The charter states that the World Social Forum "does not constitute a locus of power to be disputed by the participants in its meetings" and no one will be "authorized, on behalf of (...) the Forum, to express positions claiming to be those of all its participants. The participants (...) shall not be called on to take decisions as a body, whether by vote or acclamation" (Article 6). Nonetheless, "organizations or groups of organizations that participate in the Forums meetings are assured the right (...) to deliberate on declarations or actions they may decide on," which the coordinators of the forum will disseminate widely (Article 7). In contrast to the WEF, where the management of the event itself engages in setting up initiatives, the WSF coordinators only facilitate the connection of people from different countries and different organizations to set up plans for action and they support those groups in terms of distributing information, but they generally do not themselves become coordinators of such activities.

The activities set up by the participating groups are diverse including calls for mobilization and other conferences, projects aiming at gathering information with regard to a specific policy issue, concrete political initiatives, for instance the promotion of the Tobin tax, but also concrete projects within different policy fields, and initiatives to build up networks in specific issue-areas or among different stakeholders such as science and civil society.

Many of the civil society groups going to Porto Alegre are not themselves organized transnationally but try to use the platform of the WSF to set up transnational networks with regard to specific political demands, campaigns and joint projects within specific policy fields. Thereby, national civil society groups can use the setting of the WSF to increase the leverage of their policy demands, for example by not only addressing national governments but also intergovernmental organizations or many national governments at the same time. Peter Niggli, participant at the WSF representing Alliance Sud, a coalition of Swiss development organizations, states:

> We tried to convince the government to lobby for a water convention at the UN. But we were not heard. Therefore we tried to find other groups at the World Social Forum to help us to directly lobby at the UN for such a convention.
>
> (Interview April 30, 2005)

Another priority of Alliance Sud also is the fight against tax evasion, an issue that is difficult to bring on the agenda in Switzerland. Therefore, together with a German partner it decided to found the International Tax Justice Network (TJN) whose central strategies would be to lobby at the OECD and at the UN to use tax justice as a new tool for economic development. The network was launched shortly after Porto Alegre 2003. In comparison to the WEF, where joint action with regard to a specific issue is fostered by the organizers in the context of their initiatives, at the WSF the building of political alliances is a goal of the participating groups which find Porto Alegre a helpful arena for this task.

In order to bring in civil society organizations from all over the world, the initiators organized workshops at the European Social Forum in Florence (2002) and at the WSF. Another example of how the arena of the WSF is used to increase leverage are the huge demonstrations against the Iraqi war on February 15, 2003, which mobilized millions all around the world. European peace activists used the settings of Florence and Porto Alegre to launch the idea for such a coordinated demonstration and to find supporters for this idea from many different countries. Sometimes new ideas and project may emerge from the discussions at the forum, but often they are not developed at the forum itself. As Niggli holds:

> It is rather unlikely that new ideas emerge at the World Social Forum. Rather, existing ideas are brought in and the WSF offers an open arena for discussing them and the opportunity to get to know new people that are prepared to support it.
>
> (Interview April 30, 2005)

The main challenges and debates about the self-image, the position and the functioning of the World Social Forum are not coming from the direct adversaries, that is those that promote market-liberal capitalism, but from those adhering to the anti-capitalist critique. The internal critique concerns the organization of the forum, its social structure, its transparency and its democratic processes. Moreover, there is disagreement on its means and status in the mobilization of a new political program. Partially, the struggles were carried out in quite a confrontational manner.

At the occasion of the first World Social Forum, activists associated with the anti-capitalist sector of the anti-globalization movement demonstrated against the World Social Forum. In 2002 the situation partially escalated, as the local authorities had deployed 5000 security forces against radical activists (New York Times February 1, 2002). In 2004, part of the critical groups, mostly stemming from the far-left sector of the movement organized an alternative social forum, Mumbai Resistencia 2004, across the road from the official one (Vanaik 2004: 61). The organizations participating in this "counter-conference" criticized the World Social Forum for its lack of effective organization, its refusal to formulate a specific program, for its rejection of the more militant organizations, and for taking funds from agencies, such as the Ford Foundation or Oxfam, which according to these groups have a vested interest in preserving the capitalist system (see Mumbai 2005).

The internal struggle often also relates to the difficult relationship between those groups which are formally organized and those grassroots movements relying on horizontal network-structures without leadership (Tarrow 2005). While the latter group is probably larger in terms of forum participants, the activities of the former group are more visible, since this sector of the movement has leaders who speak at the occasion of the bigger sessions and get media attention (Hardt 2002).

For instance, a Brazilian activist claims that the Brazilian old left and international NGOs co-opt the other parts of the movement: "to present their part of the movement as the whole of it and so, in a way, to channel all our novelty and energy into hierarchical and bureaucratized forms of politics."[9] Another critique is the unbalanced representation of the world's civil society. The misbalance, on the one hand, concerns the geographical origin of the participants, especially the African continent, but also Asia and Eastern Europe are only marginally represented at Porto Alegre. On the other hand, also delegations of the different countries lack a balanced inclusion of people representing the lower classes (Cassen 2003a: 139) or different racial groups (Hardt 2002: 112).

The role of Davos and Porto Alegre in global public policy

What role can the world forums play in global public policy? To answer this question, it is important to distinguish among the conferences themselves, the organizations administrating and coordinating the conferences and the participants. The conferences are arenas where politically relevant issues are debated and discussed. Both, the WEF and the WSF are not set up in a way that would allow taking concrete decisions over a specific political issue and therefore they should not be considered as strategic political actors.

Their political relevance, however, should not been ruled out from the onset: the interactions among the participants may lead them to adopt a shared understanding of how the world works, to build up common frames of references regarding different political issues, and maybe even to develop a sort of "class consciousness" (Graz 2003). If the conferences are able to exert political power, it is however mainly indirectly by influencing the political agenda of the participants.

The organizers shape the conferences and therefore also to some extent the discussions that take place, they do not, however, have any power or legitimacy to speak in the name of the participants. There are important differences between the WEF foundation and the organizational structures behind the WSF, which affect their respective capacities to become relevant players in the setting up of policy arrangements. The World Economic Forum is an organization with clearly defined, quite transparent hierarchies, disposing of highly skilled, professional staff.

The long history and the well-trained staff contribute to the accumulation of a high level of experience and competence in its domains and activities. Due to the diligence applied in building up connections to prominent and powerful individuals, the organization is embedded into an outstanding network that further increases its possibilities to influence policies. The network includes financially powerful business leaders, which by paying their membership fees and partnership contributions make the highly professional structure of the organization possible, as well as high level government officials with direct access to political decision-making.

The socio-organizational and material resources on which the World Economic Forum builds are clearly related to the membership of the largest and wealthiest companies. The WEF Foundation is therefore able to play a relevant role in the setting up and coordination of private policy arrangements. It does so by designing and promoting initiatives in a number of policy fields. Moreover, because the WEF management also chooses to a great extent the topics of the panels, the organization also has considerable power over the agenda and thereby might use the arena for promoting certain political ideas.

However, the single-sided membership structure also constrains the moral resources of the organization. The fact that the material and organizational resources of the World Economic Forum are to an overwhelming part provided by big companies feeds the arguments of the critics, that the strategies developed in the forum are likely to reflect the interest of business more than those of the general public. The participation of government representatives and the partially closed-door meetings further nourish arguments about an undemocratic and illegitimate use of power of the World Economic Forum.

The critical campaign initiated by the global-justice movement has greatly increased media and public attention toward the World Economic Forum. Together with the shift in the own communication strategy, this new attention has improved the possibilities of outside actors to monitor the strategies it developed. Since the public and civil society actors are much more aware of the existence of this forum, public surveillance of its activities has greatly increased.

On the one hand, this has a positive effect for the public distribution of the ideas that are developed in the context of the forum. On the other hand, the alertness of the public and the dissemination of contentious views by the critics reduce the capability to promote political projects. As Graz (2003: 336) puts it: "the bigger the suggested influence of transnational elite clubs, the greater the problems to legitimize its informal power." Once the activities and ideas debated in the forum are questioned from the outside, it becomes also more difficult to reach a consensus among the very diverse participants in the inside, as the participants increasingly become aware of diverging arguments.

In contrast to the highly formalized, hierarchical and professional organization which sets up the Davos meeting, the World Social Forum lacks a clear organizational basis. The attempts of the organizers to depoliticize and decentralize the forums structures as well as the continuing internal disaccords about the procedures and the role of the organizing committee and the international council severely restrict the possibilities for strategic action. The main contributions of the WSF with regard to the formulation of concrete policy proposals therefore are to provide a meeting space, physical and virtual, which then can contribute to the initiation of more concrete ideas and projects.

However, the organizers of the World Social Forum have, in contrast to the WEF Foundation, no possibilities to monitor those projects, to ensure continuity and effectiveness, neither to set priorities. Although the World Social Forum lacks many of the material and organizational assets the World Economic Forum has at its disposal, it nevertheless has access to important resources. In particular, the World Social Forum has considerably less problems concerning its public image.

Legitimacy, on the one hand, stems from the participatory approach whereby ideas are discussed from below by involving large numbers of people representing a considerable wider share of the world's population: while at Davos middle-aged white men are highly overrepresented, Porto Alegre hosts a much younger, female and colored crowd. The enthusiasm and motivation of the activists, as well as the absence of any material self-interest concerning their participation and contribution to the forums activities, further contribute to the Social Forums credibility. While the WSF does not dispose the money to hire a large pool of professional staff, its human resources are nevertheless very high. Not only are there many highly committed volunteers who support the Forum according to their skills and expertise, also many participants contribute to the organization of the forum by organizing the largest part of the activities themselves.

On the other hand, because the WSF brings together people with a similar political ideology and because it even excludes participants who are considered to represent the wrong values, it cannot create a true arena for conflictive political discussions. Unlike the WEF-management, the WSF organizers explicitly make clear that they consider themselves as promoters of a certain political position. Although they refuse to create a sort of party-structure, the internal debates over the direction one should go in a way do show parallels to the struggles between different camps of a political party.

Despite these internal quarrels one might argue that the political capacity of the WSF consists in the possibility of socializing and training of activists and thereby giving the dispersed and very diverse global-justice movement a common face and contributing to its relevance as a political actor – an actor that does not only protest against globalization but also seeks to develop ideas and solutions for the problems related to the growing interconnectedness.

The participants in the two forums represent actors who may play political roles at the national or the international level – such as corporate or collective actors (e.g. interest groups, parties, churches, trade unions, human rights or other civil society groups) or state actors (representatives of government, diplomats, central bankers etc.). A participant may relate to another participant in a variety of ways. She might be interested in concrete cooperation, she might be willing to learn from him or simply persuade him about her positions, she might also take a conflictive or even hostile stance, and finally, she also might simply ignore him.

Whatever the interactions may be, the different participants at the private conference relate to each other in a horizontal way and in principle no participant can force another one to support a political campaign or to contribute to a project. If the participants have a specific mandate or obligation, it stems from the group or firm they represent. Although, as we have seen, internal struggles about the structure and the aims of the WSF are common, the likeliness that participants have fundamentally different positions over concrete policy issues is much higher in the WEF arena, since representatives with different political views are allowed to participate.

The fact that openly debated internal struggles mainly occur within the WSF reflects the stronger personal engagement in political issues of the participants. While participating at the elite club of the WEF is not necessarily connected to political goals (many representatives of corporations participate primarily to set up business connections), participation in the WSF is. As a result, contest over political issues and strategies are part of the program. As della Porta (2005) shows, participants of the Social Fora aim at consensual decisions, they consider, however, controversial discussions as a necessary basis to reach an agreement.

At both meetings, participants may see a need for and develop strategies for private driven policy arrangements and also get involved in these. In the case of the WEF this involvement is encouraged through the initiatives administered by the management. According to World Economic Forum director Schneider, the member firms are increasingly willing to participate in such initiatives:

> About twenty percent of the companies are highly engaged and another fifty percent are increasingly open to such initiatives. The rest is not yet ready – but they are confronted with these possibilities over and over again in the context of the World Economic Forum.
>
> (Interview March 6, 2004)

At the WSF the participants themselves foster initiatives to address public policy issues. The prospects for interactions between participants from both forums are discussed in the next section.

Interactions: dialogue or confrontation?

Both forums claim to make the world a better place. The identified sources of the problems as well as the proposed solutions, however, are so different most of the time that collaboration between Davos and Porto Alegre in achieving such goals seems possible only in a very limited way.

One of the controversial points is the issue of self-regulatory regimes that involve only the corporations. While the WEF member firms generally favor solutions to the problems of globalization that do not involve state regulation, a large part of the activists at the WSF and in the global social justice movement are fundamentally skeptical about such regulatory systems. It seems that the market–state nexus characterizing the national struggles between left and right wing political forces is transferred to the transnational level. When, for instance, Kofi Annan launched the Global Compact at the WEF 2001, as a tool to improve corporate governance on a voluntary basis, many civil society organizations refused to support this project (Le Monde January 23, 2001), as they considered it a tool for multinational companies to evade state regulation.

Similarly, civil society groups also criticize the initiatives promoted by the WEF as unbalanced in terms of involvement of civil society actors and the state. According to an activist, the political goal of the WEF is "to promote voluntary arrangements instead of public regulations. We want the politicians to remain at the wheel and set political regulations" (Interview March 23, 2004). The more radical groups only consider private arrangements acceptable if civil society organizations are involved in the setting up of the rules as well as in their surveillance.

Besides the political differences, an important obstacle for cooperation between the two World Forums is Porto Alegre's social movement character. The capacity of protest groups to mobilize depends on the involvement of people who are highly committed to the ideological goals of the movement. To achieve such an ideological commitment, social movements use simplifications as well as a reduction of the message to strong images and symbols. They develop collective action frames which stress injustice on the one hand and attribute blame to concrete actors (Snow and Benford 1992). Because the protest groups framed the World Economic Forum as a symbol for neoliberal globalization, it is practically ruled out for members and sympathizers of the movement to becoming involved in activities with the World Economic Forum.

In the eyes of many supporters of the movement such an involvement means collaborating with the enemy and therefore they consider it to go against the basic principles of the movement. For instance, when in 2003 Luis Lula da Silva, the newly elected Brazilian president and a symbol of the movements' hopes for "another world," traveled directly from Porto Alegre to Davos, many movement actors openly criticized his presence at the Davos meeting as a betrayal. Lula nevertheless used his speech at Davos to deliver a global-justice message to the transnational business and political elites.

The resistance of the radical movement sector does not completely impede more pragmatic civil society organizations to collaborate with Davos, for example by taking part in the initiatives, or by participation in the World Economic Forum. More participation of civil society actors at the WEF was one of the goals pursued by critical groups. As the coordinator of the counter-conference *Public Eye on Davos*, Mathias Herfeldt, states: "We wanted more NGO, more critical voices. It can't be that they discuss issues of public interest and set the track for certain political ideas without involving actors being critical towards neoliberalism" (Interview March 23, 2004).

Since Schwab has accommodated this demand quite quickly, the more radical groups have changed their strategy, however. The main reason for this turn was that activists feared to be instrumentalized for public relation campaigns by the WEF. According to Herfeldt The Public Eye on Davos therefore seized to address concrete demands at the WEF and changed its goal to mainly inform and sensitize a larger public about the issues and problems related to globalization. This does not mean that the organization he represents, the Swiss Third World organization Erklärung von Bern, is not interested in direct contacts with the business world. However, such contacts are, as the activist claims, established directly between the critical groups and the firms. As an example for a policy arrangement that emerged through such direct contacts, he names the Clean Clothes Campaign. The idea of this campaign is that firms sign a social codex whose implementation is then surveyed by internationally operating civil society organizations.

Some of the more pragmatic civil society organizations do not refuse to collaborate with the WEF, they send representatives to the meetings or use the arena of the Open Forum to distribute their message. Sometimes they do this at the risk of becoming targets of radical sectors of the protest movement themselves. For instance, the headquarters of a section of the aid organization Red Cross was attacked with paint because of their engagement in the Open Forum (Neue Zürcher Zeitung January 16, 2003).

Despite this threat representatives of these civil society organizations consider it useful to participate at the WEF. For instance, Andrea Durbin, representing Friends of the Earth (FOE), argues that having both, civil society groups inside the WEF and protests in the street, is needed in order to build enough pressure for change (New York Times January 30, 2000). Still, also those organizations that participate at the WEF remain skeptical about the impact this may have, as the following statement from Amnesty International (AI) representative Pierre Sané illustrates: "It seems like business and NGOs come from two different planets, our problems and issues are not really taken for serious. Because we are not heard, denunciation and violence seem to be the only alternative" (Le Monde January 3, 2001). Thilo Bode, participating at the WEF as a representative of Greenpeace, considers the dialog between civil society and business to be useful. He, nevertheless, complains that the business representatives "not really understand our concerns" (Le Monde January 3, 2001).

These public statements by activists that have access to the WEF nicely illustrate the dilemma of being radical and able to threaten and pressurize the business world on the one hand, while on the other hand also being accepted as a partner in the realization of concrete projects. It seems, however, that the double strategy of putting pressure for change from the inside as well as from the streets improves the bargaining power of the critical groups.

Because of the street protests and the refusal of dialog by the more radical movement sector, other civil society groups get more access to the discussions in the WEF arena. As already mentioned, the WEF management quickly responded to the demands for more inclusion of civil society groups. According to Sarah Saffar, the community manager of the WEF responsible for the NGOs, most of the member firms welcome the greater participation of these groups. Still, the WEF employee points to the fact that the business representatives generally pursue other priorities at Davos than exchange with those groups. Many firms would consider direct contacts with critical groups to be more fruitful and therefore do not need the WEF as a facilitator in this respect.[10]

Overall, the prospects for a constructive, public dialog between the two World Forums are low. The critical groups have little other means to put pressure on business actors than to inform the public about negative implications of firm behavior. The fear that the image of the firm may be damaged or the prospects to improve public image can certainly be considered important incentives for profit-seeking corporate actors to engage in the supply of public goods, such as environmental protection or social welfare.

The critical actors, however, can only uphold the attention of the media and the public if they continue to produce newsworthy events. This is only possible if they use more extreme frames and tactics. Nevertheless, behind the public rhetoric and outside of the big media rooms, actors from both sides show will to engage in collaborative frameworks.

Acknowledgments

The empirical material used in this chapter was collected in the context of a larger research project which analyses the impact of the global social justice movement in political processes in general and in the public political debates in particular. The Swiss National Science Foundation generously supported this research (Grant No. 1214–066967).

Notes

1 An exception is the International Labour Organization (ILO), which is based on a tripartite representation. The formal delegation of each participating country consists of two state representatives, one representative of the countries labor organizations and one delegate of the employer's organizations.
2 While the World Economic Forum is likely to continue its meetings in Switzerland, the World Social Forum is still struggling with finding a formula that fits the ambitions of being a truly global event. In 2006, therefore, the organizers experimented with a decentralized conference that is spread out over different continents.
3 The details on the legal deals previous to the 1971 conference are presented in Graz (2003: 328–330). Graz criticizes that Klaus Schwab today presents himself

152   *Michelle Beyeler*

as the initiator who took the full financial responsibility, thereby obscuring the
institutional context in which he was able to set up such an undertaking.
4 The member firms represent the world's 1000 leading companies. They pay a
membership fee of 30,000 Swiss Francs each (about 25,000 US$). Besides the
ordinary member firms, the World Economic Forum also encourages the wealthiest corporations to become strategic partners. In this case the fee is substantially
higher.
5 The IBC was established in 2001 to replace the Council of the World Economic
Forum.
6 At the time of writing the international council is formed by 129 organizations (see
World Social Forum 2005). Available http://www.forumsocialmundial.org.br.
Accessed February 4, 2005.
7 The eight organizations that started the organization of the first WSF –
Associaçao Brasileira de Organizaçoes Nao Governamentais (Abong), ATTAC,
Commissao Brasileira Justiça e Paz (CBJP), Associaçao Brasileira de
Empresários pela Cidadenia (Cives), Central Única dos Trabalhadores (CUT),
Instituto Brasileiro de Análises Sociais e Economicas (Ibase), Movimento
dosTrabalhadores Rurais Sem Terra (MST) and Rede Social de Justiça e Direitos
Humanos – form this secretariat.
8 For the 2005 forum, participants from the North paid about 115 US$ per orga-
nization and about 12US$ per individual. Participants from the South paid half
of this fee.
9 For this activist comment: Available http://www.nycsocialforum.org/articles/
critique.5html
10 Interview with WEF community manager Sarah Staffar, cited in Franklin and
Ries (2003: 26).

References

Andretta, M., della Porta, D., Mosca, L. and Reiter, H. (2003) *No global – new
global. Identität und Strategien der Antiglobalisierungsbewegung*, Frankfurt/
Main & New York: Campus.
Ball, P. (2000) "State terror, constitutional traditions, and national human rights
movements: a cross-national quantitative comparison," in J. A. Guidry,
M. D. Kennedy and M. N. Zald (eds) *Globalizations and Social Movements:
Culture, Power, and the Transnational Public Sphere*, Ann Arbor, MI: University
of Michigan Press.
Bennett, W. L. (2004) "Social movements beyond borders: understanding two eras
of transnational activism," in D. della Porta and S. Tarrow (eds) *Transnational
Protest & Global Activism*, Lanham, MD: Rowman & Littlefield.
della Porta, D. (2004) "Multiple belongings, tolerant identities, and the construction of 'another politics:' between the European Social Forum and the local social
fora," in D. della Porta and S. Tarrow (eds) *Transnational Protest & Global
Activism*, Lanham, MD: Rowman & Littlefield.
della Porta, D. (2005) "Making the polis: social forums and democracy in the global
justice movement," *Mobilization,* 10 (1): 73–94.
Cassen, B. (2003a) "On the attack," *New Left Review,* 19 (Jan/Feb): 41–60.
Cassen, B. (2003b) *Tout a commencé à Porto Alegre... Mille forums sociaux!* Mille
et une nuits.
Charnovitz, S. (2003) "The emergence of democratic participation in global
governance (Paris, 1919)," *Indiana Journal of Global Legal Studies,* 10 (45): 45–77.

Clark, A. M., Friedman, E. J. and Hochstetler, K. (1998) "The sovereign limits of global civil society: a comparison of NGO participation in UN world conferences on the environment, human rights, and women," *World Politics*, 51 (1): 1–35.

Davis. G. (2004) *GBN Interview with Ged Davis, Global Business Network (GBN)*, March 2004. Available http://www.gbn.com, global business network, 2004.

Erklärung von Bern (2005) Available http://www.evb.ch/index.cfm?page_id = 1697&archive = none (accessed January 20, 2005).

Franklin, C. and Ries, A. (2003) Analyse, Dialog und Dialogformen zwischen NGO und Wirtschaft im Rahmen des WEF 2003 und Entwicklung eines vertrauens-bildenden Dialogframeworks," report for the foundation "In the Spirit of Davos" approved May 30, 2003.

Grajew, O. (2005) Available http://www.inmotionmagazine.com/global/og World Social Forum_int.html (accessed February 4, 2005).

Graz, J. C. (2003) "How powerful are transnational elite clubs? The social myth of the World Economic Forum," *New Political Economy*, 8 (3): 321–40.

Hardt, M. (2002) "Today's Bandung?," *New Left Review*, 14 (Mar/Apr): 112–18.

Keck, M. E. and Sikkink, K. (1998) *Activists Beyond Borders: Advocacy Networks in International Politics*, Ithaca, NY and London: Cornell University Press.

Mumbai (2005) Available http://www.mumbairesistance.org (accessed March 15, 2005).

Ronit, K. (2006) "Introduction: Global public policy – the new policy arrangements of business and countervailing groups," in K. Ronit (ed.) *Global Public Policy: Business and the Countervailing Powers of Civil Society*, Routledge: London and New York.

Smith, J. (2001) "Globalizing resistance: the battle of Seattle and the future of social movements," *Mobilization*, 6 (1): 1–20.

Smith, J. (2004) "Transnational processes and movements," in D. A. Snow, S. A. Soule and H. P. Kriesi (eds) *Blackwell Companion to Social Movements*, Oxford: Blackwell.

Snow, D. A. and Benford, R. D. (1992) "Master frames and cycles of protest," in A. D. Morris and C. M. Mueller (eds) *Frontiers in Social Movement Theory*, London and New Haven, CT: Yale University Press.

Tarrow, S. (2005) "The dualities of transnational contention: 'two activists soli-tudes' or a New World Altogether," *Mobilization*, 10 (1): 53–72.

UN (2005) Available http://www.unglobalcompact.org (accessed March 5, 2005).

Vanaik, A. (2004) "Rendevous at Mumbai," *New Left Review*, 26 (Mar/Apr): 53–65.

World Economic Forum (2005) Available http://www.weforum.org (accessed March 5, 2005).

World Economic Forum (2005a) Available http://www.weforum.org/ KnowledgeNavigator (accessed March 5, 2005).

World Economic Forum (2005b) Available http://www.weforum.org/water (accessed March 5, 2005).

World Social Forum (2005) Available http://www.forumsocialmundial.org.br. (accessed February 4, 2005).

7 The evolution of climate policy

Business and environmental organizations between alliance building and entrenchment

Shannon K. Orr

Introduction

The negotiation for the United Nations Framework Convention on Climate Change (UNFCCC), the Kyoto protocol and related agreements involved a broad range of interest groups engaged in a wide variety of activities. Their participation leads to the question, what is the role of business and countervailing interests in the climate change policy formation process? This chapter will analyze the participation of interest groups within the context of the United Nations negotiations. Following a review of the general role of business and civil society NGOs in the United Nations and background information on the UNFCCC and the scientific context of climate change, this chapter will discuss the interests of NGO participants and their reasons for participating in the global arena. This will be followed with an analysis of how these NGOs engage in conflict and collaboration as they try to influence global public policy, and how the UN facilitates contacts between NGOs as they attempt to gain access to government delegates.

It will be argued that interest groups participate in United Nations negotiations not just to influence global public policy as is commonly assumed, but also to fulfil their own separate self-interests through parallel activities such as negotiating business contracts, raising the profile of their organizations, participating in protests, monitoring governments, disseminating research, networking and establishing their expertise in the area. These activities may of course have future implications on the policy activities of these organizations. For example, networking now in order to build coalitions in the future, or establishing expertise in the short term so as to assume a more influential role in global public policy making in the long term. These short-term activities as a result may have far reaching implications for the policy process.

NGOs and the United Nations

The study of organized interests[1] within the United Nations (UN) begins with Article 71 of the UN Charter, which empowers the Economic and Social Council (ECOSOC) to "make suitable arrangements for consultation with nongovernmental organizations which are concerned with matters within its competence." Over 1500 NGOs, both civil society organizations and business interest associations, have consultative status with ECOSOC, enabling them to send observers to public meetings of the Council and subsidiary bodies, submit relevant written statements and consult with the UN Secretariat (United Nations 2003).

Over time, opportunities for NGOs to participate in United Nations activities and global policy-making have increased significantly. In the 1940s and 1950s, organized interests participated in UN affairs as consultants or observers through ECOSOC, the UN Department of Public Information, and UN agencies such as the United Nations Children's Fund (UNICEF), the United Nations Educational, Scientific and Cultural Organization (UNESCO) and the World Health Organization (WHO). Over time however, the expansion of the UN opened up new opportunities for NGOs, most notably in the area of human rights in the 1960s (Princen 1994; Spiro 1995; Arts 1998; Keck and Sikkink 1998; Smith *et al.* 1998; United Nations 2003). In the mid-1980s and early 1990s, organized interests received formal access to more UN bodies. Significant changes were implemented in 1995 with the revival of an Inter-Departmental Working Group on NGOs in 1995, followed by a 1997 directive from the UN Secretary-General to all departments to appoint an NGO liaison officer (Reimann 2002). Participation has continued to expand rapidly since that time. In particular, organized interests are now participating in international treaty negotiations UN Conferences in unprecedented numbers.

While the UN has expressed an interest in further expanding participation, many questions have yet to be answered about the actual role and activities of these organizations within negotiations and the global policy process as a whole. The granting of participatory rights has become an important aspect of most of these meetings, and NGOs continue to organize for increased access in order to influence the formation of global public policy.

Since the 1972 United Nations Conference on the Human Environment in Stockholm,[2] the United Nations has been increasingly recognized as an effective arena for the deliberation of global environmental policy (Chasek 2001). Environmental issues such as climate change, biodiversity and ozone depletion are impervious to geopolitical boundaries and as such are best served by international deliberation and decision-making. The process of negotiating environmental agreements involves significant and unique challenges due to scientific uncertainty, political controversies, economic stakes and often-distant time lines. The negotiations themselves are both complex and time-consuming from the initial scientific fact-finding to the debate on solutions and costs involved, to the discussion of how to enforce final agreements. The conference venue is also ideally suited to the complex environmental issues because it provides an arena in which different organized interests with expertise in the policy domain have the opportunity to participate.

The 1992 United Nations Framework Convention on Climate Change was signed by 154 states (plus the European Union) at Rio de Janeiro during the Earth Summit. The UNFCCC sets out a framework for action to control and reduce greenhouse gas emissions. The objective of the convention is "to achieve... stabilization of greenhouse gas concentrations in the atmosphere at a level that would prevent dangerous anthropogenic interference with the climate system... [and] to enable economic development to proceed in a sustainable manner" (United Nations Framework Convention on Climate Change 2002).

The UNFCCC came into force in 1994 after being ratified by 50 countries. The Convention holds developed countries and those with economies in transition to nonbinding commitments to try to reduce their greenhouse gas emissions back down to 1990 levels by 2010 (United Nations Framework Convention on Climate Change 2005). A Protocol to the Convention was adopted in 1997 in Kyoto, Japan. The Kyoto Protocol commits industrialized countries to achieve quantified targets for decreasing their emissions of greenhouse gases (United Nations Framework Convention on Climate Change 2005).

The Conference of the Parties (COP) to the UNFCCC, is the highest decision-making body for global climate change, and comprises all the countries that are Parties to the UNFCCC. Government delegations may involve multiple ministries representing different, and often conflicting, constituencies and interests. Delegations usually include representatives from the executive branches of government as well as representatives from ministries such as foreign affairs, transport, trade, environment, science and technology, industry, foreign aid, finance, energy and agriculture (Newell 2000). Meetings are held annually to negotiate further details.

Accredited observers to the negotiations include a diverse set of organized interests representing both business interests and countervailing powers of civil society. In order to be accredited as observers, organizations must be legally constituted entities with "not for profit" status, and competent in the areas related to the Convention. Accredited organizations do not have voting rights, but they may, by special invitation from the chair of the negotiations, address the COP and subsidiary bodies in plenary meetings. These opportunities are rare however, and are usually only offered to observers who agree to represent a larger constituency such as environmental or business groups that are in attendance (United Nations Framework Convention on Climate Change 2005).

Scientific context

Central to understanding the role of organized interests in global climate change policy is the scientific context of the debate. The scientific community has had a significant role to play within the climate change regime. The Intergovernmental Panel on Climate Change (IPCC) is a UN sponsored international group of climate change scientists which has been at the forefront of the debate. As well, universities and think tanks make up a significant number of the NGOs at the negotiations. The universities and think tanks in many ways create a link between the science concerns of climate change, and the politics inherent in the policy arena.

The issue of climate change has evoked a passionate political debate concerning the validity of scientific data, appropriate policy responses, culpability and responsibility. Scientists continue to argue over competing interpretations of scientific data and climate models (Hoffman 1998). The climate change controversy is characterized by scientific uncertainty and conflict between economic and environmental interests.[3] It is generally accepted by all parties involved in the debate that human activities such as energy production, transportation and agriculture have increased the quantity of these greenhouse gases in the atmosphere, in particular carbon dioxide (Jacoby *et al.* 1998; Morgan 1998; Lomborg 2001).

Greenhouse gases are emitted as a result of human activities such as energy production, industry and vehicle exhaust. Without emissions-control policies, it is anticipated that atmospheric concentrations of carbon dioxide will rise from 367 parts per million in 2002, to 490–1260 parts per million by the year 2100. This would represent an increase of 75–350 percent since the year 1750. Climate models predict that the global temperature will continue to rise by 1.4–5.8°C by the year 2100. While historically the global temperature has fluctuated naturally, this change would be significantly greater than any climate change in the last 10,000 years. These projections are based on a series of assumptions about greenhouse gas emissions such as population growth and technological change based on present emission trends but do not include any consideration of efforts to reduce or control emissions due to concerns about climate change.

In the opinion of the UNFCCC and the Intergovernmental Panel on Climate Change, climate change is likely to have a significant effect on the global environment. The mean sea level is expected to rise which would cause flooding in low-lying regions of the world. Other possible effects could include an increase in precipitation, and increased severity and frequency of extreme weather events. Physical infrastructure could be vulnerable to rising sea levels and severe weather events (United Nations Framework Convention on Climate Change 2005).

The competing viewpoint as espoused by climate change skeptics focuses on a number of different areas: proof that climate change is happening, evidence that human activities are the cause and substantiation that there will in fact be negative consequences associated with climate change if it does happen. Climate change skeptics themselves represent a diversity of views. One skeptic argument is that increased concentrations of carbon dioxide would actually be beneficial for plant life and food sources on earth. Carbon dioxide, as the basic raw material for photosynthesis, is involved in the conversion of solar energy into food and other biomass. As carbon dioxide concentrations increase, plants will grow faster and larger due to more efficient photosynthesis. Plants will also develop better resistance to temperature extremes and pollutants, and the soil will be richer in nutrients as a result (Committee for a Constructive Tomorrow 2004).

Another viewpoint is that throughout the earth's history the concentration of carbon dioxide has actually been in the thousands of parts per million, and that present levels are actually a low aberration. Other arguments suggest that global cooling, not warming, is occurring and that polar ice sheets are growing, and that temperature measures are inaccurate because they fail to take into account the increases in temperature at airport weather stations due to the "urban heat island" effect whereby blacktop and construction materials trap heat and cause a rise in local temperature.

It is a mistake to broadly generalize business and civil society organizations as competitors in the debate, or to argue that one sector represents a particular viewpoint.

A common misconception is that business interests are those promoting the skeptic viewpoint. In fact, many business interests such as those in alternative energy fields are committed to the UNFCCC process and are staking their business on climate change science. Many of the business interests support the UN position on climate change science; however, they are concerned about the effects on their operations. This is very different from being a climate change skeptic. In fact, most skeptic NGOs are activist organizations with no business ties.

In his highly publicized book *The Skeptical Environmentalist*, Lomborg makes a nuanced argument that bridges the two sides of the debate. Lomborg accepts the presence of human-caused global warming but advocates extreme caution in the development of responses. He argues that

> we should not spend vast amounts of money to cut a tiny slice of the global temperature increase when this constitutes a poor use of resources and when we could probably use these funds far more effectively in the developing world.
>
> (Lomborg 2001: 322)

Climate change models are not yet sophisticated enough to include all of the competing variables, and so there is a great deal of uncertainty as to the effect of various policy proposals and the degree of warming that can be expected (Lomborg 2001). It is this uncertainty which has been exploited to great effect by both climate skeptics and business interests concerned about how climate change policies will affect them.

The controversy is summarized by UNFCCC:

> We must not expect a single, dramatic discovery to confirm 'global warming' once and for all. If we wait for that discovery we will wait for a long time – until well after it is too late to do much about it. There is no climatic counterpart to the Antarctic ozone hole.
>
> (United Nations Framework Convention on
> Climate Change 2005)

Business and countervailing groups

Many questions remain about how global public policy is shaped by the interactions of organizations at UN conferences. These conferences bring together diverse interests and policy goals in an environment of self-contained, time restricted negotiations. In order to study the role of interest groups in global climate change policy, a web-based survey was conducted of 286 organizations from 50 countries that have attended at least one Conference of the Parties of the United Nations Framework Convention on Climate Change since 1997, the year the Kyoto Protocol was drafted.[4] The final response rate was 52.4 percent. In addition field observations and interviews were done at the eighth COP in New Delhi, India in 2002.

While 21.3 percent of the survey respondents indicated that climate change was the primary focus of their organization, the rest of the participants indicated a diverse range of principal interests including: heritage protection, religion, alternative energy, gender, fire services, health, indigenous people, international law, manufacturing, construction, industry, waste management, sustainable development, standards development, transportation, biodiversity, forestry, ethics, unions, publishing and defense contracting. This suggests that the participants represent a great range of interests, bringing unique perspectives to the negotiations. Climate change policy is highly complex, intersecting with many other policy areas such as sustainable development and the economy; and affecting many sectors from manufacturing to public transportation. In part this is why the policy formation process is so contentious, competing and conflicting interests further complicate the development of global public policy.

The breakdown of interests also indicates that business interests are not necessarily working towards the same goals. Alternative energy interests do not support the views of the oil and gas industries. Even within the same industries such as manufacturing, interests do not necessarily agree and collaborate. Many of the business interests interviewed indicated that the Kyoto Protocol in fact created a wealth of new business opportunities, and opportunities for companies to diversify. One North American business interest indicated that her company welcomed the opportunity to expand their business, and predicted only growth for their company once the Kyoto Protocol went into effect. While many business interests expressed great concern for how global climate change policy would affect their bottom line, this is by no means reflective of all the business interests active in the global climate change arena.

While we see a broad array of interests represented within the UNFCCC negotiations, similar to what has been identified in for example American domestic politics, one striking difference is that business interests do not dominate the population of organized interests, as they do in the United States (Baumgartner and Leech 1998). Less than a third of the participants were from business. Within domestic politics economic interests have come to dominate policymaking for a number of reasons. Most importantly, business interests may feel that their operations are at stake. A profit motive is a compelling reason for active involvement in the policy process. Business organizations may have a more stable membership that they can call on for support compared with civil society organizations which must compete amongst a great many similarly minded organizations for supporters (Olson 1965; Salisbury 1969; Heinz *et al.* 1993; Hula 1999).

So what accounts for the numerical underrepresentation of business interests in the UNFCCC negotiations? One possible reason is that economic groups may be more concerned with the interpretation of climate change policy at the domestic level, rather than the formation of broad international policy that takes place at the UN level. They maybe better served by concentrating their resources domestically; influencing the passage of the treaties through government, and trying to manipulate the country-specific details of implementation. The international venue may also be less important for American economic interests since the United States is pursuing its own climate change initiatives separate from the Kyoto Protocol. This also highlights the fact that businesses do not necessarily represent unified interests, but rather may be pursuing their own unique policy concerns within the global arena.

This may also be a case of the free rider problem as identified by Olson (1965). Free riders fail to take responsibility for their fair share of a resource or activity, instead taking advantage of the contributions of others. Economic interests may then be underrepresented because they are assuming that there is already sufficient representation in the international arena (Olson 1965). This is a possibility, however much more research would be needed to show this effect.

Another possibility is the fact that participation in the UN is limited to non-profit organizations that are officially accredited. A large portion of the interest group universe in many countries such as the United States is made up of individual economic interests (usually for profit) which participate directly in the policy process, rather than operating through industrial and trade associations as is the case in the UN (Browne 1998). Thus, in order for business to participate in the UN negotiations, they must do so through as part of delegations from non-profit industry or trade associations. Representatives from companies such as Shell Oil are not excluded from participating; however, they must attend under the umbrella of non-profit organizations. Thus, the UN restrictions on participation preclude the direct participation by those interests that are particularly active in, for example, US domestic politics.

When asked in the survey, "Why did your organization attend the Conference of Parties?," the answers were diverse. Organized interests attend for a variety of reasons. As expected a common reason for participating was to try to influence government policymakers as cited by 38 percent of the respondents. A US business group indicated that they decided to attend "to try to influence the delegates to employ an objective, science based approach to influencing the development of energy resources."[5] A European economic group attended "to ensure that [alternative energy's] role as a climate change solution is understood by decision makers." Representing specific interests was an often-repeated reason, as a South East Asian environmental organization suggested "to bring the voices of the indigenous communities who are the worst affected communities by climate change – flash floods, drought, cyclone, heavy rainfall and pollution." Much more simply, a North American economic organization attended because they wanted "to make a difference."

Of the organizations, 40.8 percent indicated that they attended in order to be involved in research activities such as disseminating research, information gathering or doing on-site research. A representative from a European think tank responded: "Even though we're here for research reasons, we are not about passive attendance at the plenary sessions. We are trying to engage all groups through our research." General information gathering was also cited as an important reason, in order to have direct access to the most up-to-date information on climate change activities.

A small number of organizations (4.8 percent) indicated that they decided to attend in order to learn about the negotiation process, or how the Conference of Parties operates. A North American think tank decided to attend in order to gather "information about the process and the practicality of participating." Or in the words of a European environmental organization "to see how the circus works." Other reasons for attending included being interested in the area of climate change (8.2 percent), observing the proceedings (8.2 percent), trying to raise the profile of the organization in the field of climate change (2 percent), and monitoring government behavior (2 percent). According to one North American think tank: "One reason why we're here is to monitor our government in key areas. If they do good work, we commend them; if they do bad work, we criticize."

Organizations also indicated that they attended the COP for reasons other than influencing policy directly. A European business organization indicated that "our organization attended to network with other organizations, we can influence policy by phone." Networking with other organizations was cited by 11.6 percent of the organizations. In an interview a think tank representative from Canada said that they attend "to hold side meetings with other groups. It is easier to organize meetings with other organizations because they are all here... we're not even meeting about climate change, this is a separate business meeting on sustainable development."

Some organized interests take advantage of the opportunity to meet with others and to create new opportunities for their organization. A North American think tank attended because "we're launching a new project here. We're here to make contacts and advertise what's going on. We're not actually here to participate in the climate change negotiations." Another economic organization from Africa stated in an interview "we are here to try to do business; we are trying to make business contacts."

Thus far it is clear that organized interests are attending for a wide array of reasons, many of them unexpected. While many are attending in order to try to influence government delegates as expected, they are also participating in order to influence the policy process in other ways, such as making professional contacts. While these are the stated reasons for deciding to participate in the global policy arena, as is discussed later, the actual activities that organizations engage in are similarly diverse.

When NGO activities are broken down, there are striking similarities between the activities of business and countervailing interests. Neither group was more likely to observe plenary sessions, network, work with the media, organize a side event (i.e. a research panel), distribute literature or do research. Activist organizations were more likely to prepare COP newsletters for distribution, serve on government delegations, to try to influence government delegations, and much more likely to participate in protests. These differences are striking as it suggests that business interests are much less active at these negotiations than are activist organizations, at least in the sense of engaging in fewer directly policy-related activities.

These findings are significant because they suggest that participation in the COP for all actors in business and civil society is about more than just influencing policy, although that is certainly an important part of the negotiations, but also about advancing organizational interests through activities such as networking. Organized interests are making the most of the opportunities created by bringing together international experts on the topic of climate change to hold parallel activities to the negotiations such as research forums and personal meetings. As such, the United Nations seems to be supportive of these activities; including them on the daily agenda and providing meeting space to accredited organizations. Thus, the UN, at least somewhat, facilitates the participation of interests in global public policy. Public driven policy arrangements such as these can provide unique opportunities for collaboration and networking, and organized interests are clearly prepared to take advantage of these occasions.

Like domestic interest group activities, these organizations are involved for the purpose of influencing policy, protecting an interest, or discovering whether they have an interest that might be affected by the proceedings. Organized interests were observed engaging in a wide range of activities. It appeared that many were participating for reasons other than influencing policy, and some actually had no interest in the negotiations themselves, but rather were exclusively engaged in other activities such as networking, presenting research or negotiating contracts. The earlier discussion of why organized interests attended hinted at this idea, and the survey data and interviews provide further support for this observation.

Conflict and collaboration

It is clear that both business and countervailing groups are highly involved in the climate change negotiations, particularly in trying to influence public policy both directly and indirectly. While often relationships between organizations that share policy goals and interests are based on collaboration that is not always the case here, as many organizations reported significant conflict during the negotiations.

In this context, findings by Salisbury, Hula and Berry on American interest groups are also relevant for the study of global public policy. According to Salisbury, the rise in the number of interest groups in the Unites States has meant less clout for each of them (Salisbury 1990). Given the increasing complexity and multifaceted demands facing policymakers, Hula found that in many cases policymakers preferred that groups assimilate their demands; this creates an incentive to join coalitions as the alternative may be that their interests are overlooked or ignored (Hula 1999). This is also relevant in climate politics because there is such a diversity in the interest group landscape.

One decision an organized interest must make is whether or not to collaborate with other organizations, and if so to what degree. The more issues that an organization is involved in, the more useful participation in coalitions may be. Organizationally, the more staff that an organization can devote to its activities, the better its capacity to seek political influence. One person acting on his or her own will be unable to contact as many government representatives as a team of people. However, organizations may be able to overcome these deficiencies by acting within a coalition (Berry 1989). The advantages of working within a coalition include pooling resources and diversified skills and expertise. "Working with others is a case of speaking from the same voice," reported an African activist, "we all meet to collaborate and develop strong positions" (African activist organization).

In terms of coordinated activities, the most frequently cited activity was organizing events, and coordinating COP activities. When the responses are collapsed, those choosing five or greater for each of the questions were as follows: organizing events together (54 percent), coordinating COP activities (46.5 percent), lobbying government together (40.9 percent) and applying for funding together (33.4 percent).[6]

Table 7.1 breaks down these coalition activities by group type for responses of five and higher.[7]

With respect to organizing events, experts from universities were more likely to collaborate (50 percent), followed by think tanks and then activist groups. Business organizations were least likely to organize events with other organizations. In terms of research, as expected universities again were most likely to collaborate with other organizations (78.6 percent), followed by think tanks (50.8 percent). Activist organizations representing some of the diverse interests of civil society were significantly more likely to collaborate on coordinating COP activities (54.8 percent) compared with other organizations. Collaborating on funding was low across all group types; perhaps a reflection of competition for limited support. In terms of lobbying activities, activist groups were significantly more likely to work with other organized interests (51.6 percent), which likely reflects the fact that most are part of the Climate Action Network umbrella group.

Table 7.1 Collaboration: organized interests and activities[a]

Activity	Business (N = 46)	Activist (N = 31)	Think tank (N = 59)	University (14)
Organizing events	26.1%	45.2%	45.8%	50.0%
Research	28.3%	25.8%	50.8%	78.6%
Coordinating COP activities	28.3%	54.8%	25.4%	21.4%
Funding	15.2%	12.9%	28.8%	35.7%
Lobbying	26.1%	51.6%	16.9%	14.3%

N = 150

Note

a Survey question: to what degree does your organization work with other organizations on climate change in the following areas (note: 1 means not at all, and 7 means frequently). Percentages indicate respondents choosing 5 or higher on the 7 point scale.

The Climate Action Network is a formal network of more than 300 environmental organizations that are committed to the UNFCCC and the Kyoto Protocol. They meet daily during the COP to strategize activities and discuss the proceedings.

   While it would be speculation to try to determine why certain organization types are more likely to collaborate than others, it is important to note that collaboration may be the result of formal agreements, or it may be more free-flowing:

> "we work with lots of groups, both formally and informally, sometimes we have a memorandum of understanding, other times we are much more loose. It partly depends on who it is we're working with, and what it is we're trying to do,"

said a South East Asian activist. While groups actively participate in coalitions, there is also a fair degree of tension and competition between organized interests, which may have repercussions for the policy process. In interviews, organizations reported withholding information from other coalition members because they felt that they had an advantage by being in possession of the information. An environmental group representative from the United States shared a story of climate change groups engaging in an argument over statistics and treaty text that resulted in physical violence. The repercussions of this argument are still continuing years later with members of these groups refusing to talk to one another:

> it was almost scary...people started yelling at each other about some statistics and what we should all do, and suddenly they're up on tables and chairs, and other people started joining in. Security came running just as fists started to fly...they still don't talk to each other and they used to work together all the time.

In a joint interview with two North American think tanks that work quite closely together, one representative refused to disclose his sources while the other person was present. Even groups with similar goals may compete within the global public policy arena.

There is also concern amongst organized interests about the activities of other organizations. According to one South East Asian think thank, "we are very concerned about NGOs that make a big stink and give other NGOs a bad name." In the words of one Asian activist organization "[NGOs] try to precipitate crises so that there are more conferences and more funding.". A North American activist organization commented, "as long as environmental organizations are winning, let's not try to promote our own egos."

It would appear that collaboration fulfils important purposes for organized interests, both at home and at the COP. By combining resources organized interests are able to lobby more government delegates based on a common purpose, and can vocalize their concerns more effectively.

However, both business and civil society organizations also exercise caution in their relationship and can be very competitive with other organizations. Just because organizations share common interests does not mean that they will necessarily collaborate and work together. Personal conflicts on more than one occasion have derailed collaborative activities. There may be a tendency to romanticize civil society organizations and their policy work at times, but the reality is in fact much more complex. Competition, personal differences and the desire to claim credit for achievements may all intervene and prevent organized interests from pooling resources and working together.

A common theme running throughout the supplemental interviews was the conflict that activist organizations in particular experience between wanting to foster collaboration and pool resources in order to bring the Kyoto Protocol into force, and yet also wanting to promote the organization and receive individual recognition for their work. A North American activist group commented that "we work together but we also compete. We all care about climate change, but the fact is we also care about making sure we get our name out there."

Although the survey was not sent to government delegates, interviews at the COP helped to shed some light on the government perspective on this relationship, and their view of the role of both business and civil society organizations in global policymaking. According to a government delegate from Asia "We talk to NGOs here. We get information from them; we get their contribution regarding environmental impacts. We work together." A government delegate from Africa commented:

> NGOs in my country are important – they sensitize the public, train government and provide information. On the downside, international NGOs have too high expectations. They want you to jump too fast. There is too much comparison with developed countries. The NGOs

here [at the COP], I don't see them doing anything. I'm unclear of what they're doing. I see publications lying around, but that's it. I think they are doing something. I think they are.

Other delegates expressed similar concern about some of the organized interests at the COP. A South East Asian government delegate commented: "The NGOs are too aggressive. Sometimes I think that they are only interested in preventing things from getting done so that their organizations have a reason for being." Comments such as this highlight the inherent diversity among organized interests, a common theme throughout this analysis. Organized interests can be members of government delegations, hostile adversaries of government policies or anything in between. Motivations and approaches vary wildly within the universe of organized interests, with some clearly focused on policy outcomes, and others pursuing tangential interests. The very nature of the UN arena supports this diversity by providing opportunities for organized interests to pursue their own interests whether it be negotiating business contacts or networking or doing research. In other words, through the participation of these varied organizations, the UN facilitates the cooperation between organizations, thereby supporting NGO input into global public policy.

While such conflict occurs, the UNFCCC is also a rare opportunity for business and activist organizations to meet, engage in dialog and share ideas. These informal exchanges, often taking place outside the strict confines of the meeting are an invaluable aspect of the global public policy arena, which is rarely replicated at the domestic level where meeting usually only occur between those with similar interests and viewpoints. The UN negotiations bring actors together in a confined setting where they have the opportunity to interact over meals, on shuttles to and from meetings, at organized social events and in the breaks between sessions. These opportunities can foster an environment of engagement and dialog if participants choose to take advantage of this unique setting.

Access to government

Some of the organizations that participated in the negotiations indicated that the Conference of Parties could be improved to better support NGOs. Some of the respondents indicated that they had no complaints with the way the COP operates. A representative from a European University stated: "It need not be improved. The COP consists of governments negotiating, not organizations: there is already enough high-quality input from organizations when governments prepare the negotiations." However, many offered critiques and recommendations. A common complaint was about lack of access to the negotiations: "improve the transparency of sessions," "more sessions should be open for observers," "more sessions where NGOs are allowed to participate, so many of them now are closed," "provide more space for plenary statements from civil society," "better access to sessions – too many meetings are closed for observers. The consequence is that we sometimes have to act on the basis of second hand sources."

Many of the actual negotiations and treaty writing sessions are held in closed door session to which organized interests are not invited. While much of the informal decision-making does take place in the hallways in between sessions, the closed door negotiations prevent organized interests from being fully integrated into the policy process. Of course this represents just a small facet of the policymaking process.

Government delegates in those situations can and certainly do leave these closed negotiations in order to consult with organized interests, for example, to obtain policy analysis. However those organizations are those which have long established relationships with government delegates. In other words, governments – to different degrees – contribute to the development of public driven policy arrangements at the global level. Having expertise and a trusting relationship with government delegates is invaluable for organizations that wish to have direct and regular access to government delegates.

Organizations that have access to both their own governments and are active within the context of the conferences appear to be the most influential. Large, international organizations such as Greenpeace International are usually umbrella organizations for domestic groups, which in turn develop their own unique relationships with domestic governments, as well as organizing to participate in the global arena.

At the COP, there appeared to be a fair degree of informal interaction between delegates and organized interests. This likely accounts for the discrepancy in numbers between those who said they interacted with delegates in the survey (78.5 percent) and those who indicated that they engaged in lobbying activities (44.3 percent domestic delegates, 45.6 percent foreign delegates). Informal interaction takes place in hotel lobbies, on the UN bus shuttles, on sightseeing excursions, in restaurants, over lunch, during side events where research is presented, during quiet periods between sessions, on airplanes etc... A European activist commented "It's not just about formal meetings; it really helps to get to know government delegates, and to do things like have breakfast every morning together." These interactions can be important to developing relationships and becoming known to delegates, and can be important for organized interests as a way to develop an inside track to other delegates. While much attention has been paid to formal interactions, the informal aspects of multi-day negotiations should not be ignored; "policy happens more at the clandestine meetings between Shell and government in the hallways than at the actual scheduled meetings," said the representative of one European business organization.

In order to engage in activities such as direct lobbying, organized interests must have access to government delegates. Depending on the goals and interests of an organization, access can mean the difference between success and failure at a COP. As the earlier discussion on why organized interests participate in the COP suggested, many organized interests are not interested in interacting with government delegates or in influencing policy. For some however, obtaining access is a significant challenge.

Organized interests can also play a supportive role for governments. According to a North American think tank "many of the parties lack the analytical capacity to negotiate effectively. The North has huge [government] delegations; the South needs the research capacity of NGOs to be on a fair footing." A European activist who had also served on her government delegation commented

> I want to lobby delegates, but in return I also deliver CAN [Climate Action Network] briefing papers, and do some translation of stuff from other NGOs here at the COP so they can stay up to date on what's going on.

Intergovernmental organizations and governments create arrangements where they can also draw on private resources. Public driven arrangements are not just created to allow for better participation but also to help public authority be more effective.

One of the key questions about state/organized interests relations is who initiates contact first. Table 7.2 examines this question through a frequency table. The survey questions ask about the frequency of contact with government officials at home specifically regarding climate change. It is clear that in fact there is only a minimal difference between who initiates contact with government, with a slightly higher mean, median and mode for contact initiated by the organization. States do not operate in isolation. This suggests that the relationship is characterized by a fair degree of interdependence.

According to a government delegate from Asia "We talk to NGOs here. We get information from them; we get their contribution regarding environmental impacts. We work together." Other delegates expressed similar concern about some of the organized interests at the COP, interestingly making no differentiation between business and civil society activist organizations. A South East Asian government delegate commented, "The problem

Table 7.2 Frequency table of government contact

	Contact with government initiated by organization	Contact with government initiated by government
N	138	137
Mean	4.75	4.21
Median	5.00	4.00
Mode	5	4
Std. deviation	1.580	1.695

with NGOs is that they are not accountable to anyone. They can say anything they want. I don't know who they should be accountable to, but it should be someone; maybe God." Another South East Asian delegate commented, "The NGOs are too aggressive. Sometimes I think that they are only interested in preventing things from getting done so that their organizations have a reason for being." These comments highlight the inherent diversity among organized interests, a common theme throughout this analysis.

Organized interests can be members of government delegations, hostile adversaries or anything in between. Motivations and approaches vary wildly within the universe of organized interests, with some clearly focused on policy outcomes, and others pursuing tangential interests. The very nature of the UN arena supports this diversity by providing opportunities for organized interests to pursue their own interests whether it be negotiating business contacts or networking or doing research.

It is clear that organized interests are not simply servants of state interests. Organized interests play an important role in disseminating information and policy analysis to government. Within the United Nations Climate Change negotiations, many of the smaller states in particular have depended on organized interests as part of their official state delegations to the climate change negotiations, and many states regardless of size rely heavily on think tanks to provide policy analysis. Perhaps this is a singly unique characteristic of scientific negotiations where government delegates may lack the technical sophistication necessary to fully contribute to the process at hand. Alternatively it may be that the high degree of scientific uncertainty that surrounds the issue opens the way for organizations to take a more proactive role in the debate,[8] as there may be more space for differently grounded perspectives.

One of the unique characteristics of this policymaking venue is that it occurs in a limited time span in a confined location. As a result, groups who may not otherwise have the connections to meet government delegates may have informal opportunities to develop such relationships while riding on UN shuttles, eating lunch in the cafeteria or standing in registration lines. Regular attendance at the COP seems to open the way for increased access to delegates, which is perhaps not just about becoming a familiar face but also becoming more familiar with the process and how to make the most of the limited time. In other words, the UN, apart from creating a forum for networking and the exchange of ideas for NGOs, also facilitates these contacts between individual government delegates and NGOs, thereby creating opportunities for NGOs to take a proactive role in policy formation.

Conclusions

The UNFCCC Conferences of Parties provides unique opportunities for organizations to engage in the policy process as well as pursue their own interests. Organized interests participating in UN policymaking conferences represent diverse interests, motives and expertise. With respect to the climate change negotiations there is a significant divide within the business interests between those that either represent or are dependent upon fossil fuels, and so are more generally against many of the provisions of the UNFCCC and Kyoto Protocol; and those that are more generally supportive such as the alternative energy industries. Similar divisions exist among other organizations, in particular the activist organizations. Under these circumstances privately driven arrangements involving certain business groups and civil society groups may emerge. These however are only in a nascent stage of development.

While climate change skeptics have received significant media attention in North America, the survey results did not reflect this controversy. With very few exceptions, the participating organized interests believe that climate change is a very serious problem and it is largely due to human activities. There was substantial consensus on the problem definition, both with respect to the severity of the problem (the vast majority claiming it is a very serious problem) and the possible causes (the vast majority claiming it is due to human activities rather than a natural phenomenon). Surprisingly only a few business interests supported the skeptic position, and almost 90 percent of all respondents indicated support for the Kyoto Protocol.

While business interests were slightly less likely than other organizations to indicate that climate change is a problem, there is also conflict on many of the finer points of the climate change issue. The technical complexities and scientific uncertainty inherent in many environmental negotiations limit the degree to which there are easily identifiable coalitions that consistently support each other across issue areas. For example, organizations may be united in their desire for the United States to ratify the Kyoto Protocol, but may conflict on other aspects such as whether the agreement should be voluntary or whether developing countries should be required to reduce their emissions or whether nuclear power should be promoted as an alternative energy source.

Organized interests are participating in the COPs for a wide array of reasons. In fact, many of the organizations attend with no intention of influencing policy and politics, but rather for other self-interested reasons such as research, business and networking; although of course in the long run these activities may have policy implications. One of the unique features of these negotiations is the mix of informal and formal opportunities for NGOs to fulfil their goals. These activities may be particularly important in fostering future cooperation for the organizations.

A theme running throughout the interviews was that organized interests were working together, yet also in a state of competition with one another. Whether it was competing for information or access to government delegates, organized interests seemed to be highly concerned about their own survival and making a name for themselves. Claiming credit is also an issue for individual organized interests, particularly when they are working within a coalition.

Government delegates also commented in interviews on this situation, recognizing it as a problem when it interferes with the work of the negotiations. Concerns were also raised that some organized interests may be more interested in ensuring that there are more meetings and COPs to attend, rather than actually working to resolve policy issues. Of course this does not apply to all participants, but rather to a select few who are able to draw negative attention to themselves and their activities.

The need to work together coupled with these mounting sources of tensions, results simultaneously in an environment of unity and conflict. Domestic politics is of course marked by similar competition between interests. When international policymaking occurs in an arena characterized by a condensed time frame and intimate setting, changes occur. Late nights, jet lag, pressures to draft international policy in a short amount of time raise emotions among participants. Perhaps it could be argued that this style of negotiation magnifies the relationships between organized interests, brining out both the best and the worst in the participants.

It also appears that there is a fair degree of interaction between government delegates and organized interests at the Conference of Parties, much of it facilitated by the UN. Many organized interests and government delegates have developed solid relationships through the long process of negotiating climate change policy. As such, organized interests can play an important role in providing information and support to government. Thus, intergovernmental organizations provide an important platform for policymaking at the global level. In this way patterns of publicly driven arrangements are stronger than privately driven arrangements.

These findings are reflective of a more pervasive pattern of unity and conflict between organized interests that was discussed earlier. In many respects the organized interests, both business and countervailing interests, exhibit a significant degree of unity, working together in coalitions, meeting regularly throughout the COP to discuss issues and strategies. At the same time however, these organizations exist in a state of tension and conflict – competing for scarce funding, jockeying for access to government delegates, protecting privileged information and competing for credit for their work.

Notes

1 This research uses the terms non-governmental organizations (NGOs), organized interests and interest groups interchangeably.
2 The United Nations Conference on the Human Environment was the first United Nations international conference on the environment.
3 The popular press tends to refer to climate change as "global warming"; however, the phrase has fallen out of use in the scientific literature in favour of "climate change" which takes into account a range of possible effects on weather and

climate as a result of increasing concentrations of greenhouse gases. Climate refers to the aggregated weather conditions over large regions and long periods of times (from seasons to millennia) (see Dotto 1999).

4 While there are 506 organizations that are accredited by the UNFCCC to participate in the Conference of Parties, only 302 organizations attended between 1997–2001. Of the 302 organizations, 10 were removed from the population because they have ceased to operate and their former employees could not be found. Another six organizations were removed because they have no full time employees and it would appear were created solely so that individuals could attend the Conference of Parties. The final survey population is 286 organizations. Details on the survey design and implementation can be found in Orr (2005). Full details of the study and data can be found Orr (2005a).

5 All quotations in this section are survey responses unless otherwise indicated.

6 Five or greater was chosen because it represents the responses above the median.

7 Universities are degree-granting institutions such as Oxford University. Research programmes and schools and institutes within universities were also included in this category. Non-university affiliated research oriented organizations were coded as think tanks. Examples in this category include the David Suzuki Foundation and the Wuppertal Institute for Climate, Environment and Energy. Activist organizations are those that engage primarily in non-research activities such as lobbying, media/information campaigns and event organizing. Activist organizations include Greenpeace, Birdlife International, and the Sierra Club of Canada. Business organizations represent industry or professional employment organizations. Examples include the Business Council of Australia, International Chamber of Commerce, and the International Association for Natural Gas Vehicles.

8 Despite general consensus on the problem definition, there still remains significant scientific uncertainty.

References

Arts, B. (1998) *The Political Influence of Global NGOs: Case Studies on the Climate and Biodiversity Conventions*, Utrecht: International Books.

Baumgartner, F. R. and Leech, B. L. (1998) *Basic Interests: The Importance of Groups in Politics and in Political Science*, New Jersey: Princeton University Press.

Berry, J. M. (1989) *The Interest Group Society*, 2nd edn, Glenview, IL: Schott, Foresman and Company.

Browne, W. P. (1998) *Groups, Interests, and U.S. Public Policy*, Washington, DC: Georgetown University Press.

Chasek, P. (2001) *Earth Negotiations: Analyzing Thirty Years of Environmental Diplomacy*, New York: United Nations University Press.

Committee for a Constructive Tomorrow (2004) *Global Warming: Melting Down the Facts*. Available http://www.cfact.org

Dotto, L. (1999) *Storm Warning: Gambling with the Climate of Our Planet*, Toronto: Doubleday Canada Ltd.

Heinz, J. P., Laumann, E. O., Nelson, R. L. and Salisbury, R. H. (1993) *The Hollow Core: Private Interests in National Policymaking*, Cambridge, MA: Harvard University Press.

Hoffman, A. J. (1998) "Introduction," in A. J. Hoffman (ed.) *Global Climate Change*, San Francisco, CA: New Lexington Press.

Hula, K. W. (1999) *Lobbying Together: Interest Group Coalitions in Legislative Politics*, Washington, DC: Georgetown University Press.

Jacoby, H. D., Prinn, R. D. and Schmalensee, R. (1998) "Kyoto's unfinished business," *Foreign Affairs*, 77 (4), 54–66.

Keck, M. E. and Sikkink, K. (1998) *Activists Beyond Borders*, Ithaca, NY: Cornell University Press.

Lomborg, B. (2001) *The Skeptical Environmentalist: Measuring the Real State of the World*, Cambridge: Cambridge University Press.

Morgan, M. G. (1998) "Policy analysis for decision making about climate change," in W. D. Nordhaus (ed.) *Economics and Policy Issues in Climate Change*, Washington, DC: Resources for the Future.

Newell, P. (2000) *Climate for Change: Non-State Actors and the Global Politics of the Greenhouse*, Cambridge: Cambridge University Press.

Olson, M. (1965) *The Logic of Collective Action: Public Good and the Theory of Groups*, Cambridge, MA: Harvard University Press.

Orr, S. K. (2005) "New technology and research: an analysis of internet survey methodology in political science," *PS: Political Science and Politics*, April 2005.

Orr, S. K. (2005a) *Organized Interests and International Climate Change Policy*, Wayne State University.

Princen, T. (1994) "NGOs: creating a niche in environmental diplomacy," in T. Princen and M. Finger (eds) *NGOs: Creating a Niche in Environmental Diplomacy*, New York: Routledge.

Reimann, K. (2002) "International politics, norms and the worldwide growth of NGOs," Paper presented at the Annual Meeting of the American Political Science Association, Boston, MA.

Salisbury, R. (1969) "An exchange theory of interest groups," *Midwest Journal of Political Science*, XII: 1–32.

Salisbury, R. (1990) "The paradox of interest groups in Washington: more groups, less clout," in A. King (ed.) *The New American Political System*, Washington, DC: American Enterprise Institute.

Smith, J., Pagnucco, R. and Lopez, G. (1998) "Globalizing human rights: the work of transnational human rights NGOs in the 1990s," *Human Rights Quarterly*, 120 (2): 379–412.

Spiro, P. (1995) "New global communities: nongovernmental organizations in international decision-making institutions," *The Washington Quarterly*, 18 (1): 45–56.

United Nations (2003) *The United Nations and Civil Society, 2003*. Available http://www.un.org/partners/civil_society/ngo/n-ecosoc.htm#charter (accessed October 22, 2003).

United Nations (2005) *United Nations Framework Convention on Climate Change*. Available http://www.unfccc.int.2005

8 Conclusions

The Predicaments of the new policy arrangements in global public policy

Karsten Ronit

Global public policy is today progressing in an increasing number of areas that in the past were either regulated primarily by public authority manifested by states, or surrendered to the market. Globalization typically has an uneven character, which means that not all continents are covered equally profoundly, and at the very same time, by public policy. No single and agreed-on goal characterizes these processes, and serious drawbacks occur; but seen in a wider historical perspective, globalization of policy has indeed a definite direction. However, if we recognize only the role of intergovernmental organizations and the inputs through states, we are merely scratching the surface of policy-making because global public policy is not formulated and implemented through states and intergovernmental organizations exclusively, but also through a variety of private actors in business and civil society.

At the global level, many economic issue areas involve various configurations of intergovernmental agencies, business, and civil society organizations. Much research concentrates on either business political action, the protests of civic groups, or the work of agencies as an expression of the interests of states, but these linkages are sidestepped and need to be studied. Consequently, many interesting forms of institutional innovation currently unfolding are ignored. To properly understand public policy, the fragmentation of research perspectives must be overcome and new approaches must be developed cogently accounting for the real life of global politics.

In this book we have identified two basic forms of policy-making: public driven and private driven policy arrangements. Under the auspices of intergovernmental organizations, business and civil society organizations are deliberately brought together to produce policy in ways that not only enhance the capacity of public authority but also offer private actors an opportunity to influence traditional forms of public regulation. In other words, policy in such cases is neither the output of states and autonomous agencies, nor the result of privileged access of business power; it is rather the coordinated efforts of a plethora of parties.

Furthermore, private actors produce policy outside the framework of these agencies. Business designs private rules to solve a range of problems in ways that tend to be functionally equivalent with public policy, and in some cases even dialog and formal cooperation are furnished between business and countervailing powers. This process provides arrangements with a quality other than purely industry-driven arrangements because the concerns of civil society are more easily included and respected and because business becomes accountable to civil society. Still, public authority can play a significant part by encouraging conflicting interests to leave confrontation aside and find mutually beneficial forms of compromise. Private driven policy arrangements are established to solve problems in the relations between business and civil society; public institutions, however, are not always passive and patient observers of private negotiations, but rather, are intervening parties casting a shadow over the arrangements by raising various procedural and substantial expectations or by imposing certain standards and demands on them whereby a variety of trilateral policy-making moves develop.

In the following, we present some of the major findings of this book and discuss how new policy arrangements take shape across major issue areas where labor and consumer interests are at stake in different industries in which a wide array of actors are politically active, and in arenas where strategies of the business community and civil society are formulated.

Key countervailing forces

Important elements in public policy are produced by intergovernmental organizations in fields affecting labor and consumers. As key countervailing forces, these two groups belong to the immediate environment of corporations. Yet, as seen in the chapters by Diceanu and O'Brien and Ronit, the role of these two countervailing groups in policy arrangements are in some ways also dissimilar.

In the case of labor rights, Diceanu and O'Brien demonstrate that much regulation is held within the context of national legislation and agreements; but that there is also, however, a global activity. Unlike for consumer policy, there is indeed one major regulatory agency, namely the ILO, one of the oldest of its kind. Its work is basically characterized by the participation of global labor organizations; a hallmark of its activities is the equal and balanced representation of labor and employers. This mandate is quite unique for an intergovernmental organization, and these principles have not been challenged.

However, labor rights is also an issue area, in which private driven policy arrangements usher in a new period of regulation. Many corporations and business groups actually have a strong preference for private and voluntary arrangements and seek to avoid public intervention at the global level. There has been a fervent corporate drive for privatization, and a strong business interest lies in market-based solutions in which business supremacy remains unchallenged. Private arrangements can be purely business driven, but cooperation with labor and other stakeholders between the two parties can also be found, although they do not enjoy the same degree of legitimacy as regulation instigated by public authorities.

Consumers are represented in some intergovernmental organizations, as shown by Ronit in his chapter, but they are not recognized by all those agencies that in one way or another resolve consumer issues. They are excluded from several organizations, but this does not necessarily suggest that business has easy, if any, access. Although a major breakthrough has not taken place, the participatory strategies of some agencies have been revamped in recent years so as to formally include an input from consumer groups as well as other civil society actors. Therefore, some policy processes now involve both consumers and representative business associations.

Consumer policy, however, is not a concern of only public authority with the assistance of relevant private organizations. Private driven policy arrangements have emerged in a number of areas, either sparked by international agencies or voluntarily initiated through business and civil society organizations with a consumer perspective. In such cases, groups with a broader focus than consumer affairs participate, and sometimes they play a more significant role than traditional consumer organizations. Many arrangements fulfil important functions but not all have a real public quality, because they include only elite corporations and because they are valuable to only particular consumer segments. Nevertheless, some arrangements pioneer new solutions, raise new agendas, and may eventually create or stimulate more encompassing arrangements.

To analyze the role of the key countervailing forces in labor rights and consumer policy, some historical contexts must be wheeled in to fully understand their engagement in a global perspective. The institutional history is different – there is one central intergovernmental organization covering labor issues, whereas no public authority at the global level specializes in consumer affairs. Policy fragmentation is a significant feature of consumer policy, whereas labor rights is, after all, more established as a policy field – although even here new issues arise and intersect with other policies and institutions.

As far as the private organizations are concerned, consumer organizations are not so well integrated as labor in global institutions of rule-making. In a historical perspective, consumers arrived relatively late on the global scene, and at a time when already established labor organizations covered many social issues. However, consumer organizations also were created relatively early – but not early enough to represent new issues properly, in particular environmental problems, which were occupied by new social movements. Squeezed in between older and modern countervailing organizations, consumer groups have been disadvantaged; but under the right circumstances, new alliances can enhance the countervailing power of civil society.

In both policy fields today, public driven as well as private driven policy arrangements contribute to the development of global public policy.

The relative weight of these arrangements is contested but recent changes have augmented the role of private arrangements. Especially in consumer-relevant areas we find some encouragement from intergovernmental organizations. This delegation of regulatory space to private actors is succinctly related to the global governance debate according to which various regulatory devices must be combined and resources from both public and private sources must be adequately integrated in problem-solving.

Similar encouragement is not found in the field of labor rights. Instead, business has been the major proponent of all kinds of privatization schemes, while labor has shown greater reluctance to join arrangements. Indeed, labor sees public regulation as an advantage. Under these circumstances labor can rely on public authority for the implementation and monitoring of rules, and is not left alone with business.

In consumer policy the picture is different because stronger proponents of private regulation can be found in business and among some consumer groups. Occasionally, single firms and associations are important advocates of private regulation that offers an opportunity to demonstrate social and environmental responsibility, also a key factor in competition. We have experienced a stronger willingness to run private arrangements in consumer policy, especially in some smaller expert- or activist-influenced initiatives, but there is much skepticism on the side of major consumer organizations. It seems that labor, after all, is a stronger countervailing force than consumers, and that more possibilities are tested to advance the consumer interest.

These complex strategies must be analyzed more closely in the context of the structural features of the two policy fields and the patchy landscape of countervailing forces. Thus, the national underpinnings of global countervailing organizations vary considerably, and there exists a longer and much more solid tradition of organizing labor that has a number of strongholds across the world. Consumers are more numerous and, from the viewpoint of collective action, are far more difficult to organize.

The field of labor rights is extremely varied but, compared with consumer policy, it is still less turbulent, is historically and currently better defined, and is more coherently managed at the level of intergovernmental organizations. The interpenetration with other policy fields is significant in the case of consumer affairs, and new and more specialized actors are continually drawn into private policy arrangements. These actors, however, are not constantly engaged in consumer issues; rather they occasionally take an interest in this field while they concentrate on environment, human rights, and other issues. These outfits tend to be more willing to engage in private policy-making, leading to cleavages between established and smaller activist groups in terms of their participatory strategies.

The domestic foundations of consumers have grown stronger, but consumers cannot rely to the same extent on existing organizational structures when building relevant global organizations. Both in the fields of labor rights and consumer affairs, some leading and encompassing organizations are recognized as the key organizations of the two interest categories they organize. Indeed, these organizations – some would see them as conservative, others would emphasize their solid experience – are also mostly in favor of public driven policy arrangements in which they are already recognized players.

Linked to these strategies is, of course, the quality of the different arrangements in which the two countervailing forces are engaged. Although public driven policy arrangements are characterized by different degrees of free-riding, inefficient implementation, and weak monitoring, they are generally preferred by the larger and established civil society organizations. In other words, such instances of suboptimal problem-solving do not necessarily speak for the introduction of alternative private arrangements. However, in cases where private regulation is wheeled in to compensate for a lack of traditional public regulation, private rule-making is not always highly controversial; indeed some private arrangements are quite stable and are backed by strong business associations and energetic movements. Conflicts arise mainly if they are instantly fragile or if they challenge established public regulation.

Sectors and policy fields

Labor and consumers are key actors in the environment of corporations. They engage in general and horizontal issues, but they also take action in relation to specific industrial sectors and policy fields. Together with industry associations, civil society organizations are involved in both public driven and private driven policy arrangements. This book draws on evidence from the financial sector and related industries and from mining. Each chapter demonstrates in its own way that global public policy is emerging and, focusing on different forms of policy-making, attributes different roles to business, civil society, and public authority.

Kellow shows that in several dimensions mining is not an extremely globalized industry. Traditional public regulation at the global level has so far not been significant, and the industry is mainly regulated through national legislation. In domestic contexts business often enjoys a privileged position, and Kellow demonstrates that this is to a large extent also the case in mining, a problematic industry struggling for a "license to operate." He entertains the argument, however, that this situation is not replicated at the global level, where associability has been slow to develop. Mining is a fragmented industry in the sense that it is concerned with a range of minerals and metals in an industry driven by many small and medium players, only some of whom have real international experience, and in the sense that ownership is both private and public.

Here it has been relatively easy for civil society organizations to build alliances to counterbalance the influence of business. Most interestingly, however, it is not environmental movements that have been most effective in changing the course of the mining industry. Unions have been able to tackle environmental issues relating to mining and have built linkages with other civil society organization. Civil society is not represented through a single actor: alliances with relevant stakeholders are essential to developing countervailing power; however, coordination is complicated when different interests and approaches must find common ground. Following this development, the industry has been forced to organize more coherently in a global framework, but significant internal developments within the industry, unrelated to countervailing actions and the role of intergovernmental agencies, have been even more important. Indeed, this has also propelled some new private policy arrangements. Countervailing forces, therefore, have not become major partners in these arrangements, but they have played a role in reformulating corporate strategy in the mining industry.

Unlike in mining, where domestic problems occasioned initiatives with global repercussions, the development of new policy arrangements in finance is discussed in broader terms. Porter sees the emergence of arrangements as being rooted in the behavior of business as well as in civil society. Drawing on insights from social movement theory and applied to the global level, the chapter identifies political opportunity structures, mobilizing structures, and strategic framing on behalf of civil society as important parameters in mounting countervailing forces.

Using the label of "industry opportunity structure," Porter recognizes the part played by business in provoking and responding to civil society action. In finance, business activity has a strong impact on the economy and spills over to those citizens not directly involved in exchanges with the financial industry. In other words, citizen interests are affected at a very general level, making large-scale collective action in civil society problematic.

The inclusion of civil society organizations into the decision-making structures of public sector institutions in global finance could stimulate countervailing action, but most institutions have adopted a restrictive practice. However, in some cases civic groups have been invited to participate in public policy arrangements and steps toward dialog have been taken, whereas the many private arrangements are almost all without civil society organizations. Instead, a strong tradition of effective industry regulation prevails.

The two policy fields and sectors discussed in this book do not provide a comprehensive overview of the evolving relationship between business and countervailing forces. Doing so would require the coverage of many more industries. Nevertheless, it is possible to point to some interesting features on the basis of the two chapters.

In the study on mining, chains of historical events fostered changes in corporate behavior and gave social forces opportunities to develop countervailing strategies. In finance, no such pattern can be identified. Here some kind of stalemate persists, with relatively little movement toward new policy arrangements; public institutions and the financial industry are better able to control political processes. Changes in mining were more accidental, arising in an *ad hoc* fashion impossible for any of the relevant parties to steer, and such processes are associated with a higher degree of uncertainty.

Private arrangements, involving either some kind of dialog or the direct participation of civil society organizations, do not address a broader selection of regulatory problems. They have been tailored to fit concrete environmental challenges, a uniqueness that seems to be typical of many private driven policy arrangements and shows the difficulty of building general models across different policy fields and sectors. These cases provide valuable insights into both planned and spontaneous forms of many private arrangements; further research is needed, however, to treat this interesting dichotomy in timing arrangements.

Changes leading to new global rule-making can also be treated from the perspective of territory. Thus, we have traced different territorial paths in the making of global public policy. Whereas the financial industries, and the policy fields surrounding them, have solid and mature institutional structures at public and private levels, such a framework is only now being constructed for the mining sector. These global underpinnings do not, however, determine the political process in a straightforward manner, and, in mining, local developments in Australia were crucial. This fact does not suggest that public policy will necessarily travel from national to global levels – many paths are open and many situational factors are at work.

Public policy at the global level is more likely to emerge in finance, with its strong global institutions. Given the many global features in the organization and regulation of the industry, such a development is also likely to affect other sectors characterized by the same kind of institutional maturity. This variation is quite demanding for both business and civil society organizations because we have no single and celebrated model, and, consequently, a high degree of strategic and institutional adaptability is required.

Collective action is essential to both business and civil society, and establishing associations or other outfits and keeping them running is a great challenge. Especially in relation to finance, it has been almost impossible to create relevant countervailing initiatives and organizations, even though finance produces many externalities, which, in principle, could be a key driver for collective action in civil society. The contrary is the case, because mobilizing such large groups is an immense task.

In relation to mining, much more specialized issues have attracted the attention of civil society, an aspect facilitating collective action. However, the type of countervailing activity that has unfolded is not a very coherent one. As mentioned earlier, collective action is to a large extent manifested through a number of new initiatives and new alliances, and the somewhat uncoordinated campaigning by and participation of civil society groups correspond with the specific circumstances in the policy processes.

In addition, business is confronted with collective action problems, a condition emphasized by Kellow, who challenges the assumption that business is always the privileged part in global politics. Although firm conclusions on business associability cannot be drawn from our cases, a pattern is observable, although not a pattern that applies uncritically to the role of group size. The financial industries – with a significant number of service providers and producers – are well organized and enjoy a high degree of associability, whereas the mining sector was until recently weakly organized. However, there are relatively few players in mining, a fact that should help lubricate concerted action by the companies, but many corporations are operating at a local level and are not highly experienced in a global context, and these factors have complicated concerted efforts. However, large corporations with global interests will pioneer or facilitate collective action, and set standards that will be followed by other and smaller players. A variety of circumstances must therefore be considered when analyzing this variation in business political behavior.

Financial services are produced by industries with global operations and identities, two factors prompting global coordination of interests. Also crucial is that the industry is surrounded by important intergovernmental organizations and is characterized by much global regulation. The role of public authority is therefore essential in explaining business collective action. Consequently, the impetus given to organizing interests is also important for the emergence of public driven policy arrangements in which private organizations are granted formal status by various intergovernmental bodies; in addition, initiatives of capacitated business actors are essential to the formation of new private driven policy arrangements.

Arenas

Today a range of conferences, forums, and meetings bring many categories of people and organizations together to solve global problems. In the context of this book, it has been interesting to analyze whether these arenas in one way or another foster the cooperation between business and civil society. As with the policy fields and sectors discussed earlier, it is not possible to cover all the sprawling life of these arenas, but two important nodes stand out: in the public domain, negotiations on climate policy in the context of the UN; in the private domain, the civil-society-run Porto Alegre meetings and the activities of the business-based World Economic Forum in Davos.

Investigating the climate policy process and the ecological issues debated, Orr sees the conference activity itself as a public driven policy arrangement. The rules governing the whole infrastructure of these conferences are made by states and intergovernmental organizations involved in the policy field, and various interests have been granted participatory rights irrespective of their origin in business or in civil society. In many contexts both civil society and business routinely participate in policy-making, and reforms are today directed at bringing to conference proceedings more legitimacy and important alternative knowledge, because the participation of states brings only a limited level of interests.

Organizations representing business, civil society, or various expert groups are not the central players; they are formally included in certain parts of the policy process, yet they are at the same time engaged in informal politics. Relations are cultivated in many ways between representatives of states as well as representatives of private organizations. By bringing conflicting interests together, there is a chance that these parties will come up with solutions that can be tabled when states meet, or that can form the basis for private accords.

To some extent this strategy has been successful, especially where business interests are linked to an ecological agenda and where civil society groups are willing to enter into pragmatic cooperation with business. However, the landscape of civil society organizations is characterized by much rivalry, and civic groups do not constitute any uniform bloc directed against business. This uncertainty complicates concerted action and reduces the power of countervailing forces.

The two media attracting events of Davos and Porto Alegre, hosting the World Economic Forum and the World Social Summit respectively, have been seen as genuine platforms of business and the countervailing powers of civil society. In her chapter, Beyeler sets out to investigate how these two private arenas operate and to what degree they address issues of common concern to business and civil society. Given the two very different categories of participants, there are grounds to believe that they have different agendas and priorities and offer different solutions to global problems. Although these arenas concentrate on different issues, flexibility and pragmatism are also observable in these two epicenters of business and civil society.

It is first and foremost at the World Economic Forum that issues raised by civil society are seriously considered by business and where attempts are made to integrate these into corporate strategy. In some cases, business does not merely respond to the demands and expectations of countervailing forces, but rather seeks to build a dialog and enter into formal cooperation wherever appropriate. At the World Social Summit certain forces also take an interest in finding a compromise with those parts of business that are attentive to economic and political values and interests typically expressed by civil society organizations. However, the protest option is generally preferred to participation, a serious cleavage running through many countervailing groups.

As shown in Chapters 6 and 7, public and private forums can play a significant role in policy-making. In the process leading up to the Kyoto protocol, private players also had access to certain areas of policy-making, but they were standing in the background and were far from having the same influence as states – although their diplomatic leverage is hard to assess. There are clearly conflicts between business and the countervailing powers of civil society, but both chapters show that the two sets of actors are not always lined up against each other like belligerent armies. Sometimes there is a wide gap in ideology between profit-greedy capitalists and protesting street activists, but there are also indications of a more complex pattern.

The lack of success in formulating a climate policy for the next generation is not only attributable to antagonized societal interests but also hinges on serious conflicts between states. Of course, various interests have backed governments in the process of negotiating the Kyoto protocol, and states have chosen between different inputs provided by firms and citizens. However, governments have also independently formulated different environmental strategies, which are not the mechanical outcome of interest group activity. Furthermore, neither business nor civil society is acting coherently, nor guided by a unified perspective. Business is divided along many lines and, as seen in the two chapters on labor and consumers and in the two analyses of specific industries, different strategies vis-à-vis public authority and civil society are applied. Also, the life of the arenas discussed in the book demonstrates that a variety of strategies are considered and pursued in business. Although these arenas have not furnished a major breakthrough in cooperation between business and civil society, they contribute to a greater awareness of the problems associated with public and private regulation because they provide an excellent opportunity to discuss these principal challenges. At the same time, conferences with mixed participation from business and civil society can bring these strategies a step further and help business find relevant partners.

Civil society breathes life into many initiatives, networks, and associations, only some of whom pay serious attention to business. Those that do so have also different views about the possibilities and fruitfulness of cooperation and its many organizational manifestations. Because global problems are often complex and cross several policy fields, they challenge many different civil society organizations simultaneously and necessitate the building of new alliances. Indeed, the arenas contribute to the testing and formation of alliances, and in these processes of deliberation, the pros and cons of public and private driven policy arrangements are debated.

The end

Some areas of global politics are today without the direct participation of private organizations from business and civil society, but it is increasingly recognized that these actors can make important contributions to public policy. Thus, new policy arrangements are formed at the behest of intergovernmental agencies that invite conflicting parties into more or less formalized cooperation, or where private actors themselves enter into arrangements to formulate and implement policy. Indeed, the development of public driven and private driven policy arrangements form part of an integrated development in which states and their organizations are not the only vehicles of public policy. This development is not brand new in the sense that such arrangements were unknown until very recently; but they flourish more than ever and, among both public and private sector actors, foster much regulatory experimenting and institutional innovation.

Public driven arrangements are undoubtedly the least controversial of the two because key authority still lies with public bodies. At the public level, the character and degree of participation from external players are decided, and policy is officially the output of public organizations. There is, however, a qualitative difference between policy-making with and without affected interests, and today this issue is drawing a dividing line between intergovernmental organizations including and excluding business and civil society participation. Although significant institutional reforms have taken place during the past few decades, many private organizations are still struggling for access.

Private driven arrangements are far more controversial than public ones, but they can offer a valid regulatory alternative to traditional public regulation. There is no guarantee that they produce a genuine public good – a quality not necessarily found in traditional public regulation either; but by including several parties with diverse interests, agreements can be reached and new rules can be adopted and monitored.

However, private arrangements are not always endorsed by business and civil society; in fact, business often prefers private regulation without outside participation. Although the concerns of civil society can still be accounted for in numerous ways, this form of regulation usually suffers from a lack of transparency, and in the public eye, the regulations tend to be seen as conspiracies merely catering to narrow corporate interests.

Wherever business seeks dialog and is actively involved in establishing private arrangements with relevant civil society organizations, these new institutions can more easily claim legitimacy, while they flavor public policy in interesting ways. There is a risk, however, that these new arrangements undermine existing forms of public regulation, or that they are established with a view to forestall regulation through intergovernmental bodies. Some countervailing forces have seen an imminent danger in these institutions and prefer traditional public regulation to avoid privatization, which they fear will be damaging to civil society in the long run.

In cases where private arrangements are welcomed – or even initiated – by participating civil society organizations, there is still a risk that the regulations will not fulfil any true public function. If there is a significant degree of free riding and not sufficient compliance in a given industry, private regulation cannot play the same role as the public regulation familiar to us from intergovernmental organizations. If only small elites of civic groups enjoy the fruits of these arrangements and if the benefits are not extended to civil society more generally, then it is problematic to ascribe to them a public policy function. Nevertheless, some of the fragile and immature agreements and project-orientated partnerships can serve as an inspiration, gain more strength, and eventually achieve the status of private driven policy arrangements. Indeed, their evolutionary character urges us to closely follow these emerging institutions of global public policy.

Index